IT STARTED WITH
DRACULA

The Count, My Mother, and Me

Jane Congdon

BETTIE YOUNGS BOOKS

www.BettieYoungsBooks.com

Disclaimer:
This is a true story, and the characters and events are real. In some cases, the names, descriptions, and locations have been changed, and some events have been altered, combined, or condensed for storytelling purposes, but the overall chronology is an accurate depiction of the author's experience.

About the Cover:
It Started with Dracula began in a movie theater in the 1950s, when the author fell in love with the vampire in a classic film. This cover replicates the now-extinct Gauley Theater in West Virginia, where *Horror of Dracula* ignited the author's lifelong dream to see the craggy landscapes of Transylvania. Fifty years later, vampires are still fascinating, and movie theaters are still places of magic.

Cover design by Tatomir A. Pitariu and Jane Hagaman
Photo of Jane Congdon by Glamour Shots® portrait studio, Cincinnati

Bettie Youngs Books are distributed worldwide. If you are unable to order this book from your local bookseller or online or Espresso, you may order directly from the publisher.

BETTIE YOUNGS BOOK PUBLISHERS
www.BettieYoungsBooks.com

Library of Congress Control Number: 2011922965

ISBN: 978-1-936332-10-6

10 9 8 7 6 5 4 3 2 1
Printed on acid-free paper in the United States of America

What Others Are Saying about This Book . . .

"Stunning! An elegant memoir of discovery, of dark secrets dragged into the light."

—**Catherine Watson, Lowell Thomas**
Award–winning travel editor and author

"Unfinished business can surface when we least expect it. *It Started with Dracula* is the inspiring story of two parallel journeys: one a carefully planned vacation and the other an astonishing and unexpected detour in healing a wounded heart."

—**Charles Whitfield, MD, bestselling author of *Healing the***
Child Within* and *Not Crazy: You May Not Be Mentally Ill

"Thrilling! Dracula fans will love the movie references and devour the adventures of one of their own in Romania."

—**C. Dean Andersson, author of *I Am Dracula***

"An elegantly written and cleverly told real-life adventure story proving that the struggle for self-love is universal. An electrifying read."

—**Diane Bruno, CISION Media**

"I love this book for many reasons, but as an editor I especially appreciate the structure—the brilliant interweaving of stories and locations. I tend to notice the writing, of course, the way the words are used. This is a beautiful book."

—**Mary C. Noschang, editor-in-chief, Peter Li Education Group**

"Compelling and inspirational! I never tire of the message that hope and forgiveness are possible—even after many years."

—**Sharrie Williams, author of *The Maybelline Story***
and the Spirited Family Dynasty Behind It

"As a Romanian who grew up in Transylvania, I was fascinated by this story and the idea that someone wanted so badly to see my country when I only wanted to leave it. We weren't so different after all; both of us had to escape our own nightmares, and both of us followed our dreams. I loved the story and especially appreciated the intricate description of the beautiful Romanian countryside."

—**Aura Imbarus, author of** *Out of the Transylvania Night*

"This is a perfect book club selection! Our group had some great discussions about travel, relationships, and even the supernatural."

—**Karen Caldwell, Fabulous Book Babes, Mason, Ohio**

"*It Started with Dracula* saved my life. Stuck yet again in O'Hare because of weather, I pulled out the manuscript and plunged in. I was transported to my home in the West Virginia hills, then to the mountains of Transylvania, and by the time my flight was called, O'Hare was a distant memory. Jane Congdon's fluid prose, quirky sense of humor, and narrator trapped between dread and desire gave me one of my most enjoyable trips—on the page or in the air."

—**Professor Anita Skeen, director,**
Center for Poetry, Michigan State University

"*It Started With Dracula* embodies many of the literary techniques that make fiction such great reading: intriguing subject matter, universal themes, and intimacy with the reader. A fantastic read that chronicles author Jane Congdon's journey through her past as her distant memories converge in real time, changing her life forever."

—**Patty Hansen, co-author of** *Out of the Blue:*
Delight Comes into Our Lives, **and eight books**
in the *Chicken Soup for the Soul* **series,**
including *Divorce and Recovery*

"Dracula is a brilliant metaphor for the author's past as she confronts the dark forces that have shaped her life."

—**June Sarpong, MTV**

This book is dedicated to all the kids

who have come home to monsters.

We escape one thing with another.

Contents

Part 3. Myth and Reality

Slovakia

Uzhhorod

Miskolc

Nyiregyhaza

Satu Mare

Satu Mare

Maramures

Baia Mare

Bistrita-
Nasaud

Debrecen

Zalau

Bis

H u n g a r y

Szolnok

Salaj

Oradea

Cluj

Kecskemet

Bihor

Cluj-Napoca

Tirgu Mures

R o m a n i a

Arad

Arad

Alba

Szeged

Alba Iulia

Sibiu

Deva

Timisoara

Sibiu

Timis

Hunedoara

Resita

Rimnicu
Vilcea

Caras-Severin

Tirgu Jiu

Valcea

Belgrade

Gorj

Drobeta-
Turnu Severin

Slatina

Mehedinti

Dolj

Craiova

Olt

S e r b i a

Acknowledgments

Thanks to the following individuals who read manuscript. Talented editors all, they saw what I didn't see and pushed me to tell the whole story.

Publisher

I have been most fortunate to work with a team of consummate professionals at Bettie Youngs Books: Bettie Youngs herself, a first-rate publisher, a wise and generous mentor, and the perfect advocate; her outstanding staff, in particular Designers Jane Hagaman and Adrian-Tatomir Pitariu, whose beautiful work you see on the dynamic cover of this book; Mark Clements, who guided me in shaping the final manuscript; and copyeditor Tania Seymour, who went above and beyond. Many thanks to Randee Feldman of Get Noticed PR, who worked her magic and made it easy to connect with my readers. Amy Cole, Assistant on Call, Cincinnati, formatted and proofread the manuscript early on. The honor is mine. Thank you all.

Mentor

Award-winning travel writer Catherine Watson is an instructor with the Split Rock Arts Program at the University of Minnesota. Catherine's thirty years at the *Minneapolis Star-Tribune* produced stories from all over the world. She has won national and regional awards, including the two most important in her field: Lowell Thomas Travel Journalist of the Year and the Society of American Travel Writers' Photographer of the Year. Catherine's travel stories have been anthologized by Travelers' Tales in their series showcasing the best travel writing in the world. This novice thanks you, Catherine, for your patience and expertise during an extraordinary mentorship.

Readers/Reviewers

Special thanks to my brother, Joe Barnett, who shared his memories and cheered me on as I wrote about our childhood; the Fabulous Book Babes (FBB) of Mason, Ohio—Martha Conway, Michelle Kunkler, Tippy McIntosh, Stacy Shirley—and especially Karen Caldwell, who reviewed the manuscript twice; Mary Noschang; Anne Noschang; Anita Skeen; Greg Brown; Karl Barksdale; Jane Dunshie; Susan Lake; Jennifer Jones Manzanilla; Virginia Wilson; Rachel Shatney; C. Dean Andersson—first eyes on chapter 1; Jessica Page Morrell, author of *Thanks, but This Isn't for Us* (© 2009)—chapter 1; and for helping me find word, after word, after word: the folks behind www.dictionary.com.

For Information about Romania

"Lucian": I hope he will forgive me for some of my thoughts along the way, thoughts he will know between *these* covers for the first time. Also, Monica and Catalin Negrila, Cincinnati.

For Encouragement

Anita and Lisa Phillips; participants in the October Writing Festival at Ghost Ranch, Abiquiu, NM; everyone at Michigan State University who attended my readings; my writing teachers; and everyone who asked, "How's your book coming along?" Your interest helped to keep me going. In particular, chapter 36, "The Symptoms," is dedicated to my physician, Dr. Anthony Brown of Montgomery Family Practice, Cincinnati.

For Inspiration

Bram Stoker for the best novel ever; everyone else who ever cared enough to build on that original story; and especially Christopher Lee—it really started with you.

Prologue

Welcome to My Country

Without a word, the Romanian guide I had known for just three days pulled our Skoda sedan onto the gravel beside a lonely two-lane road. Why had we stopped in the middle of nowhere with a view of flat yellow fields? It was warm out, and still. Few cars passed as we regarded each other for a second across the front seat. Then Lucian slowly and deliberately leaned toward me with both hands out. *Uh-oh.*

It was afternoon. We were returning from a lake resort near Sibiu where I'd been looking for the Scholomance from *Dracula*. It wasn't on the program, but how could I pass through this region of Transylvania without trying to find the fictitious Lake Hermanstadt and the witches' school where Dracula learned the secrets of the devil?

We had walked around Sibiu that morning, stopping to buy a map after I'd talked Lucian into driving me out here. We'd had an outdoor lunch of pizza and pasta near the Liar's Bridge, a lacy-looking wrought-iron affair built to deliver pedestrians across a narrow canyon of traffic through the old part of town. Beggars moved among the bright umbrella-covered tables while we ate, taking advantage of the midday bustle. Ancient pastel-colored German row houses three and four stories high peeked at us across a carpet of construction rubble. One already had a new identity as a night club: Chill Out. In an odd turn, I was trying to do just that, sitting on the side of a country road three hours later with the engine turned off and Lucian's hands mere inches from my head.

I didn't think he was a serial killer, but could this have anything to do with romance? Lucian was cute: tall, lean, muscular, and tan. He was about my age and had close-cropped graying hair, a neat beard, and a deep voice. And I couldn't say that no such notion about my guide had crossed my mind.

This was the man who would be my companion for the next two weeks, driving me through the cities, villages, and mountains of Romania; carrying my bags; explaining the sights. He was my protector, my translator, and even my dinner partner. But what did I really know about him?

Since our initial meeting in Bucharest, he had been prompt and polite. He seemed to know his way around. He dressed well; so far, his casual wardrobe was neat and stylish. His English was good, but he was not a talker, which suited me. He lived in the city, but had a preference for nature: natural foods, the woods, and the land. I'd seen him walk a distance to throw a tiny scrap into a container. It wasn't much information. Lucian was my connection to the country of my childhood dream—the dream that would not die: the dream of Dracula—and I didn't even know his last name!

He was startlingly close to me now in the front seat, his eyes boring into mine. Suddenly I knew I'd seen too many Dracula movies. Nobody had to tell me what usually happened next in Transylvania!

There are places in our minds, vistas of the imagination where fantasy and reality come together. The landscapes of Romania were like that for me. I had imagined them so many times from the movies that there was a magic about the land. I'd never seen this country before, and yet I had. Layers of memory tied the Carpathians to the hills of West Virginia, my childhood, and the little movie theater where I first sat mesmerized by one Christopher Lee playing the most enduring character ever created: Count Dracula.

This story began on a moonlit night nearly fifty years ago, on the silver screen in a town nobody'd ever heard of. A swish of the cape, a bite to the neck, a full moon rising in the sky: Who knows the reasons for what we choose, or what chooses us?

Part 1

Roots of Passion

Chapter 1

At the Movies

Transylvania, May 1885: The Land Beyond the Forest. The Englishman, Jonathan Harker, having presented himself the previous evening as a librarian, has spent his first night at Castle Dracula, sleeping off the effects of a vampire's bloodlust. Next day, confirming the fresh bites on his neck with a shaving mirror, Harker realizes time is running out for his real mission, ending the evil reign of Dracula.

In the dark night of the Gauley Theater, two young girls take in Hammer Films' *Horror of Dracula*. It is the late 1950s. My best friend Billie and I are consumed by the movie, our hearts beating like birds' wings. We are right beside Jonathan Harker as he pulls himself together and walks outside.

No one seems to be about; not even a bird's chirp breaks the afternoon silence. Harker spots a cellar door and goes in. The light is dim; in mere moments the sun's last rays will play on the stained-glass windows, freeing the vampire community from its prison of sleep. As he descends the steps, Harker's host, Count Dracula, lies in a coffin nearby, his long form cloaked in black, his face pale except for a bright drip of blood at the corner of the mouth.

Harker bravely begins, locating the female whose bite has doomed him to a half-life of evil. He readies a wooden stake and hammers it home through her heart.

Billie and I have seen nothing like this in our lives.

As the stake pierces her middle, the vampire's scream could wake the undead, and it does. Dracula's eyes snap open, bloodshot and evil. Darkness has fallen, and now the vampire is free to move about. Harker will discover too late that Dracula's coffin is empty. He will turn toward the door at the top of the stairs just in time to watch it close behind the shape of the Count.

The British movie *Horror of Dracula*, released in 1958, was based on the famous and terrifying story told by Bram Stoker in the novel *Dracula*, first published in 1897. Although the movie didn't follow the novel exactly, both tell the story of a vampire, Count Dracula of Transylvania, and the brave band of friends who sought to find and destroy him.

Dracula was at once a suave count who lived in a castle and a foul, blood-sucking beast that had escaped the grave to walk the earth undead. He was known to slaughter his victims for their warm blood and to turn them into vampires like himself. Possessed of superhuman strength and extraordinary mental powers, Dracula could control animals, shift his shape, fly, and survive means of assault that would destroy ordinary men. In addition, he was seductive, playing upon the warring emotions of his victims.

The themes in *Dracula* include romance, sexuality, seduction, and rape; religion, Heaven and Hell, Good versus Evil; life, death, immortality, and the difficulty of straddling two worlds. The story speaks to dreams and nightmares, safety and vulnerability, violence, the dark. *Dracula* is a tale of addiction, power, survival, control, and the supernatural.

Events, characters, and their relationships are shuffled in the movie—and to tell it in detail is to invite confusion—but the basic story is this: After attacking Jonathan Harker, Count Dracula leaves his homeland for England, where he has bought property, and proceeds to wreak havoc. The Count takes a fancy to Harker's fiancée.

London, "about midnight": Lucy Holmwood has been diagnosed with anemia and put to bed. This night, she locks the bedroom door and unlocks a set of French windows leading to the terrace. After removing a silver crucifix from around her neck, she returns to her bed, loosens the collar of her blue gown, and lies down to wait.

In the morning, the ailing Lucy is hiding fresh neck bites. Though weak, she has a sneaky look, the way she shifts her eyes. By this time, Dr. Abraham Van Helsing has been called in. He alone understands the situation: "If you love Miss Lucy, be guided by me, I beg you." Van Helsing directs the family in the use of garlic for the coming night. What he knows is that garlic will protect a victim and repel a vampire. But which is Lucy? The plants are brought in, and the others wish her a good night's sleep. Around midnight, Lucy's hysterics persuade the housemaid to remove the offending plants, and she again awaits her visitor.

Our shoes stick lightly to the floor of the movie house. Our eyes are wide with anticipation.

Outside Lucy's bedroom, leaves stir and swirl; a few blow in. The night crackles with tension. In a moment, Count Dracula is standing on the threshold in a long, dark cloak, his expression probing and hypnotic. He is the visitor Lucy has been waiting for, and she invites him in with her eyes. Dracula enters the room, rounds the bedpost, leans down toward Lucy, and raises his cape.

The Gauley Theater was our ticket to a larger world than the one we knew in the mountains of West Virginia. As kids, we were spirited away week after week by serials, westerns, cartoons, Elvis movies, and—my favorite—horror shows.

In the 1950s, horror was John Agar fighting giant spiders in *Tarantula* or rising from the Black Lagoon in *Revenge of the Creature;* Michael Landon starring in *I Was a Teenage Werewolf;* and Steve McQueen battling living goo in *The Blob.* Locally, a Saturday night TV show called *Shockwatch* featured older movies about Frankenstein, Dracula, the Mummy, the Wolf Man, characters from Edgar Allan Poe, and Count Alucard, which is Dracula spelled backwards. The movies became classics and the actors, legends: Boris Karloff, Bela Lugosi, Lon Chaney Jr., and Vincent Price.

I found the old horror movies entertaining but seldom scary. Frankenstein's monster had a sympathetic streak, having been put together as a lab experiment. Actor Boris Karloff had the perfect square head to play the title role: Add a couple of bolts through the neck, and there you go. Bela Lugosi's Dracula was a caricature. The Wolf Man, aka Larry Talbot, was a pitiable character trapped in a body that betrayed him. And, heck, my grandmother had a dressmaker's dummy that was scarier than Vincent Price. It stood behind her bedroom door, as headless as the horseman that screamed through the cornfields in Sleepy Hollow, and armless, too.

It wasn't until the British began releasing horror films in the United States that my perception of horror changed. Hammer Films' Dracula movies were filmed in color, and they came alive; suddenly there was scenery and vivid characters and bright-red blood. In particular, the tall, gaunt Christopher Lee playing Count Dracula was fascinating beyond all reason.

The night we watched *Horror of Dracula,* I had left my own world behind. I was transported across the ocean to places I'd never imagined.

"I heard you call me, Aunt Lucy." Little Tania, far too young for a walk in the English woods at night, is looking for her auntie, who invited her out to play at this awful hour and then ran ahead. By now the Count has done his work; Lucy is changed, a predator. It's chilly, and Tania has no coat. Clouds race across the black sky, taking turns at hiding the full moon.

The scene in the woods was scarier to me than Dracula himself, and Tania's words would haunt my dreams, yet I was drawn to the drama of an eight-year-old child who didn't realize that someone she loved had turned into a monster.

Tania starts out alone across the moonlit landscape.

I wanted to cry out from my seat, "Don't!"

Innocent of the danger, she picks her way through the woods. When she stops, Aunt Lucy is waiting on the other side of the leaves. Tania looks through the foliage and sees her aunt's blood-less face. Lucy's gown ripples in the night breeze as she bares her vampire fangs in an evil grin.

That night I was bitten as surely as if Dracula or Aunt Lucy had sprung from the screen and chosen me. I felt *alive,* and it was a prickly feeling:

I was not just living and breathing, but aware of my skin and blood and organs—and *him,* as the Transylvanian peasants would say.

After the movie, Billie and I walked outside and looked up at the sky. A full moon shone down on us straight from *Horror of Dracula*—the way it had shone on the forests of Transylvania, as round and cold as a mirror, with clouds scudding swiftly and silently across its face. I would never think of a full moon the same way again.

I didn't know then that Transylvania was a real place among the Carpathian Mountains of Romania. I didn't understand why it called to me, but from that moment I wanted to see it for myself: the mountains; the villages with their peasants, garlic, and superstitions; the wolves, the bats, the Borgo Pass; the country graveyards and pine forests, the steep cliffs and rugged countryside. The delicious shiver of fear present in the air . . . and *him.*

When I learned the truth—that Dracula's land was real—I knew I had to go to Romania. It might have to wait a while; I was only in the ninth grade.

Chapter 2

Preconceived Notions

"No one is interested in Romania," my mother said from her headquarters on the living room couch. Mom's couch, with its rectangular coffee table in front, was where she sat to pay bills, keep up her calendar, sort mail, play solitaire, smoke, read the paper, and entertain the occasional visitor. She was happiest there, safe and warm, with every object she might use within an arm's reach: Kleenex, a wastebasket, a lamp table, her book, an alarm clock, the TV remote, a few peanut-butter crackers in a pie tin, a candy dish, a notepad, and her car keys. It was the seat from which she saw the world—largely through the Weather Channel on TV.

Mom rarely went out—a combination of physical limitations and the station's constant warnings to stay inside—but she could have told me the weather in Bucharest, the rainfall in Sighişoara, the temperature in Braşov, or the presence of storms over the Black Sea.

It had been forty-five years since I'd sat in the Gauley Theater mesmerized by *Horror of Dracula*. Measured in Dracula nights, that came to about five hundred times I might have looked up at the full moon and thought of Christopher Lee in his black cloak, staring that evil vampire stare. How many Dracula moons had I seen by then, from how many different locations? I was fifty-nine, and Lee was almost as old as Mom, both of them in their eighties with birthdays in May.

Mom couldn't fathom why I'd chosen such an unpopular spot for my vacation. I realized she knew nothing of my lifelong fascination with Dracula, the pivotal role of the movies, or my desire to see Romania. Had it ever come up? Plenty of mothers and daughters have secrets. We'd had a whole houseful back in Glen Ferris. Now, after many years of living apart, my mother and I had reunited—but we still knew little about one another.

She'd sold her home in West Virginia fifteen years earlier and moved to Cincinnati to be near my brother Joe and me. She hadn't seen much of him, but those years had allowed a bonding of sorts between Mom and me. I say "of sorts" because our time together was defined by shopping, eating, movies, and casino gambling—excursions both superficial and late in the game. We may have seemed like mothers and daughters every-where, trying on clothes or sitting in restaurants; but for us, ordinary activities were milestones.

I was glad for the opportunity to spend time with Mom as an adult, but I'd be lying if I didn't acknowledge that there were issues—not to mention the subtle shift as she aged and began to slow down. I'd moved into the lead, and now I often did the planning, always drove, and occa-sionally pushed her in a wheelchair when we went out. Though I'd never seen myself as the nurturing type—or a leader—I understood my role. Any tiredness or resentment I felt was pushed aside as I focused on Mom's company and enjoyed the fact that she now looked up to me as though I knew all and could do anything.

My trip was a surprise to Mom because we didn't talk about hopes and dreams or life or the past. The friendship we'd achieved was more like two people standing on either side of a river with no bridge, or maybe one of those swinging bridges like you see in the movies, swaying above a deep and deadly gorge in the jungle.

The idea of going to Romania, though deliciously exciting when I'd first conceived it as a young girl, had become improbable, impos-sible, and far-flung as I went about my life. The lure of Dracula was always there, but the time was never right. I couldn't leave, or I had no money or no one to go with me. Sometimes the idea seemed ridiculous. Maybe I was just plain afraid to do it. "One day" turned into many days and then years. I grew up, went off to school, built a career, mar-ried and divorced, raised a child, and became a grandmother. Then I began thinking about retirement and a second career: writing. What did I want to write about? Romania.

I'd taken a travel writing course the previous year and had been reading how-to books on becoming a travel writer. There was just one thing that worried me, and that was the universal expectation that travel should transform us; further, that travel *writing* should reflect that transformation. This mystified me. I didn't know how I would compensate in my writing for that obvious gap because I already knew that going to visit Dracula sites wasn't a transformational trip—unless the Count was planning to fly in and teach me how to shape-shift.

Mom had a point about the level of interest about Romania. It wasn't France, Spain, or Italy—the three most visited European destinations for Americans—but Romanian tourism had been increasing. According to statistics from the country's National Tourist Office, 110,618 Americans visited Romania in 2004, compared to 24,800 in 1989.

After waiting so many years, I had much of my history behind me, yet I was as excited as a child. I hoped Transylvania would be a conglomeration of all the Dracula movies I had seen, images from Stoker's novel, and a mixture of Romanian folklore and twenty-first-century reality. The character Jonathan Harker wrote in his diary two pages into *Dracula*: "Every known superstition in the world is gathered into the horseshoe of the Carpathians." I wanted it to be true.

I'd never let go of the images from the movies; for instance, the taverns that were safe havens as evening drew near and innkeepers locked the doors against evil: "Some things are better left alone." And what would a tavern be without a buxom barmaid? Inga defies the barkeep in *Horror of Dracula* to slip Jonathan Harker's diary—and its clues to his disappearance—under a table napkin for Dr. Van Helsing. In *Dracula Has Risen from the Grave*, Zena sets out for home alone after her shift, walking into the night with wolves howling in the distance. In *Scars of Dracula*, the Count summons his humble servant, Klove: "I have work for you." Klove sets out in Dracula's black coach to find the barmaid, Julie, who's walking home through the woods. He stops the coach, shoves her inside, and drops her at the castle door.

I also loved the stories of innocent travelers boarding a horse-drawn coach and being dropped off abruptly when the driver realized the route would take them too close to the castle. I liked the inevitable moment in the woods when the driver refused to go on, leaving his puzzled passengers at a lonely intersection, his horses impatient to bolt and run. I remembered the little woodcutter's hut where one group sought shelter, and the way the sunlit fields of flowers and butterflies gave way to a dark and sinister forest as the sun descended behind the mountains.

I could picture the forest turning dark and eerie, intermittently lit by the full moon; the tasseled black steeds pulling Dracula's coach into the clearing. *Clop, clop, clop,* and here it comes: the horses with flaring nostrils, flying hooves, shaking tassels, twisting necks, blowing manes, and shiny flanks. The coach is driverless, or else has a masked driver dressed in black.

It was a fictitious world more compelling than reality. Bram Stoker and the people at Hammer Films had put Romania on the map for me. It was from them that I'd first learned about Transylvania and its cities—Sighişoara, Sibiu, Cluj, and Braşov—with their old German names: Schassberg, Hermannstadt, Klausenburgh, Krondstadt.

Would I find a completely different Romania from the one I'd dreamed of? Certainly I was prepared for a Romania without Christopher Lee, who had given up the role of Dracula thirty years before. By the time I got there, I'd be ten years older than Lee had been in his last Dracula movie. Never mind that a real prince named Dracula had lived in Transylvania six centuries earlier, and "Dracula" meant something different to the Romanians than it did to me.

Whether I followed the footsteps of the fictional vampire, the Romanian prince, or the actor who played Dracula, I'd be chasing a myth or the past: a puff of smoke. It wasn't surprising. In cases of myth vs. reality, I had always run from reality and chased the myth.

Back in the 1930s, Sir Sacheverell (Sasha) Sitwell wrote in *Roumanian Journey* that he had made up his mind not to read about the country before going there, in order to let it come as a surprise. How could I do the same after waiting forty-five years to go? By the time I started reading Sitwell's travelogue, it was way too late. My whole trip was built on a preconceived notion.

I'd decided to go alone. I couldn't look after someone else or compromise what I wanted to see. My long-awaited journey had one focus: I was going to find out what the land of Dracula was really like.

Unlike Sitwell, I read everything I could—fiction and nonfiction—including my third go-round of *Dracula*. Christopher Lee had read it twice to prepare for his role.

Books on Romanian travel were few; most of the available literature covered the country's turbulent political history and economy. I read the travel guides. I looked up statistics, studied trip journals posted on the Internet, and even found meeting notes from the Transylvanian Society of Dracula, a scholarly group.

Articles on Romania will often urge the reader to get past the notion of Dracula. "Beyond Dracula" is a common theme, and everybody wants to tout the "other" features of the country. Even *Lonely Planet* said, in the beginning paragraphs of its narrative on Transylvania, "Move on!" But moving on wasn't in my plan.

According to the brochures I'd ordered, the Romanian hillsides are covered with wildflowers in spring; torrential rains come suddenly in the summer; and the winters are cold and difficult. Fall is a popular time for Dracula traffic because of those special Halloween tours. I didn't want to get caught up in the Halloween hype and didn't want to freeze, but did want to give myself enough time to get ready for the trip. I chose August.

I'd be gone for nearly three weeks. And now I'd told my mother.

"They always stand in front of Ohio," Mom was saying.

"Who?"

"Those girls on the Weather Channel. How can we see what's going to happen in Ohio when they stand in front of it to show California and New York?"

"Remember," I said, "Anne and Nancy will be calling you while I'm gone." Mom had one of those life-alert squawk boxes sitting on her living room floor, but she'd never had to use it. I'd asked my friends to check in with her; at least they'd know how to reach me if something happened. They were glad to do it. Everybody loved my mother. My friends especially liked her sense of humor and were always asking me, "What did your mother say about that?"

Mom was funny, but her sense of humor was an acquired taste. Once when I was in high school, an older boy from up the river started calling me. Squirrel was tall and bumpy looking with thick, brown hair combed back on the sides in what we called a D. A. (duck's ass). His school uniform was blue jeans with the cuffs rolled up, a white T-shirt, and a brown leather jacket. He didn't seem like much of a student, and maybe he wasn't a student at all. As I remember it, his main activity was to sit on a wall outside the school building and smoke.

I was only fourteen and inexperienced at dating. When Squirrel took an interest in me, I knew I needed to run the other way. I didn't know how, so I dreaded the ringing of the phone. "If a boy named Squirrel calls," I said to Mom and Dad, "I don't want to talk to him. Just tell him I'm not home."

A few days later, Mom called me to the phone. I made my way to the corner of the dining room, where our black telephone sat on a little table with a chair next to it. In those days we had land lines only, and we didn't call them land lines.

As I picked up the receiver, Mom started to hop up and down. Then, still hopping, she turned around in a circle, silently flapping both hands forward at the sides of her head. If I'd been a contestant on *The $64,000 Question,* I wouldn't have been able to connect it to anything.

The second I heard his low voice on the phone, I knew it was Squirrel. Didn't anybody listen to me? How hard was it to say, "She's busy"?

Afterward I went into the kitchen and said, "Mom, why did you call me to the phone? I told you I didn't want to talk to him."

"I tried to warn you," she said.

"What do you mean?"

Mom again acted out her bouncy pantomime. "I was trying to tell you it was Rabbit."

"Squirrel, Mom! His name is Squirrel!"

I pulled a copy of my Romania itinerary from my purse, unfolded it, and handed it to Mom. After giving it a glance, she tucked it into her calendar—a place of honor on the crowded coffee table. Mom had never heard of most of the cities I'd be visiting. She'd have trouble with the names. She'd never try to contact me in Romania, so the itinerary would be useless except as a comfort.

I knew how much she would miss me. Eighteen days was a long time, and Mom would spend most of it waiting on the couch. The days and nights would run together for her, and she'd probably sleep there, with the TV on. The carpeted area around her feet was worn and dirty from her constant presence; she'd already laid a scatter rug over the darkest part.

"I'll leave you some surprises," I said as I made a mental note to buy books, candy, and snacks. It seemed I was always trying to placate her, that I was always leaving and she was staying. It reminded me of a sci-fi story I'd once read about a bedridden patient who regained mobility by forcibly changing bodies with her nurse. So far, body swaps have been confined to fiction, and the process is actually a swapping of minds said to be helped along by such catalysts as magic and fervent wishes. If only.

Mom couldn't keep up with me anymore. It had been a while since we'd even been shopping together. She had a hard time walking and tended to perceive great distances where others would not. She was fragile and unsteady on her feet, so every outing was a risk; a trip was out of the question. Mom didn't care to travel, anyway. Besides her lack of physical stamina, she now became discombobulated trying to organize herself. I couldn't take her with me, and I couldn't stay home.

I couldn't stay home because in the grand hierarchy of life and generations and getting old, I was next. I wasn't ready to sit on the end of the couch and watch television—not yet. Who knew if my body—or mind—would become a prison as Mom's had?

When she looked at me across the room, her face was an open book, exposed after four decades of cosmetics. It seemed bleak, the way a model's face looks before she's been in the makeup chair. Mom could still handle powder and lipstick, maybe a bit of blush, but she no longer bothered with eye makeup. Now and then her expression seemed wild-eyed as a result. Hers had been a good face—the skin smooth, the eyes light, the brows beautifully arched, and the smile wide—when Mom was chosen Apple Blossom Princess at her college.

When I was young, before all the trouble, I liked to stand next to her when she sat at her dressing table to get ready for an evening out. I could smell the loose powder that had spilled in the open drawer where she kept a jumble of hairnets and foundation, bobby pins and lipstick, Evening in Paris perfume. I remember her reflection in the glow of the lamps on the dresser. Now time had turned my mother's face into her mother's face. Soon, I was sure, that face would become mine as well.

"I'm going to make up three bags of treats for you—one for each week

I'm gone," I said, ready to head home. Mom and I didn't kiss or hug; it was too awkward. I couldn't remember her ever kissing me. When I was young, her standard greeting was to stick out her cheek for the other person to kiss. I liked things better now that we were past that, but if I were to hug her, she would go limp and still, her arms down at her sides. It would be like hugging a skeleton.

Mom smiled as I told her about the bags of goodies. Just before I went out the door, I heard her say, "I might cheat."

Chapter 3

Nature of the Beast

It was June, two months before my trip, when my granddaughter Annie and I got onto the merry-go-round at Kings Island. The ride is large, with horses frozen in motion, bits in their mouths and hooves off the ground, rising and falling in rhythm. There was something manic about the excitement of the calliope and the horses' expressions. Annie was just two and a half, so we rode together. I sat behind her, half on the saddle and half on the horse's rump, enclosing Annie with my arms.

The music started and then we were going faster, up and down, up and down. It was glorious. White lights lined the underside of the merry-go-round canopy, and mirrors hung next to each other around the inside of the turning carousel. The mirrors were about three feet high, irregularly shaped, and framed in gold-painted scrollwork.

Annie paid no attention to the mirrors as we rode. She was busy looking for her dad on the sidelines or watching the other stallions rise and fall around us.

I looked for our reflection, but couldn't see it. The way the mirrors were positioned and the speed at which the merry-go-round kept turning, somehow we were already past ourselves, a glimmer in the glass and that was all. Any flash of our reflection flickered quickly and was gone, as though imagined. It was an odd sensation, looking at mirror after mirror and seeing no reflection but a split-second shape already somewhere else. It was as though we were vampires, casting no reflections, thus invisible in a world of fancy scrollwork and glass.

The absence of a reflection is one way to identify a vampire, one of a laundry list of characteristics familiar to those who pay attention to such things—as I do. Although recent stories, such as the Twilight series of novels by Stephenie Meyer, have gone in new directions with vampire traits, legend maintains that vampires:

- Are of an old, aristocratic foreign family
- Are tall, dark, spectral, and dressed in black
- Possess sharp fangs that leave two marks on the neck
- Have unusual physical strength
- Have a seductive power over women
- Cast no shadow
- Fear crosses and religious symbols
- Are repelled by garlic
- Must consume human blood and will become younger and more vital as a result
- Are always hungry (thirsty) but can go for long periods between feedings
- Must sleep in unhallowed earth or the soil of their birthplace
- Cannot die due to the passing of time
- Will disintegrate if they come into contact with daylight or water
- Can control the weather
- Can be killed by a wooden stake driven through their heart or by cremation ("killed" in reference to a vampire means turned from undead to just plain dead)
- Can transform themselves into bats and wolves
- Can pass through a crack as a mist, but cannot enter a home unless invited
- Do not have a reflection when they look into mirrors

I knew about vampires from a young age, thanks to the movies. I knew they were evil shells of former humans who had been thrust between this life and the next by a fateful bite on the neck. They were monsters, doomed to feed on the blood of others, killing their victims or turning them into vampires like themselves. I knew that sunrise and sunset were critical points of the day for vampires, who were our opposites, moving about at night when we were vulnerable in sleep. They could fly and change into animals. They could find us anywhere.

The characteristics, which vary along with their sources, include both powers and weaknesses. For all their powers, say the legends, vampires can't help what they are: monsters. I thought that vampires also led a double life, sometimes appearing human and trying to fit into society. In one story I'd read, a vampire went to the opera.

It's said that Bram Stoker modeled Dracula on a real person. Stoker worked as a personal assistant to the actor Henry Irving, who was described as tyrannical and overbearing and was said to be Stoker's inspiration for the blood-sucking Count. People can be monsters, too.

About the time I became enamored of Dracula—when I was thirteen—I began to notice some disturbing changes in my mother. No, I'm not going to say that Mom was bitten by Dracula and became a vampire; hardly. But she did begin behaving strangely.

One warm summer evening, I was standing on a sidewalk three doors down from ours. A group of kids were cutting up in the back yard. It was the kind of moment you want to hold onto, when lightning bugs start to blink and neighbors linger outside, milking the last few minutes of daylight. There were boys, and it was so much fun. I laughed out loud, and suddenly our back door opened, and Mom called me home.

"I think you're acting a little bit too prissy," she said, her words smacking the fun out of me. Had Mom been watching me? What had I done? I didn't understand why she was so angry, but I didn't ask. Something was off, I couldn't say what, and there was no point in my going anywhere then but inside.

Mom's odd behavior continued, but the incidents hadn't formed a pattern. Not for me.

One night I sat cross-legged on the living room floor, wanting my hair curled like the other girls'. I'd watched it done but didn't know how, so

Mom was elected. From behind me in the brown chair, she reached for the bobby pins. Pins dropped from her hands and landed on the carpet. Her fingers slipped forming the curls, letting the slippery hair escape. Now and then she nailed a curl, but I knew they were going the wrong way, and I should stop this. Tomorrow at school I'd pay. She couldn't even talk right. "Minutes" came out "mints," as in, "It's ten mints to nine."

My stomach always acted up when Mom wasn't herself, and I felt a terrible sinking sensation. I hated it. When she started changing, it was like a puzzle dumped out onto a card table. The beginning was the part I'd never liked, when it was too soon to identify the right pieces.

Chapter 4

Glen Ferris

We lived in a wavy ribbon of a town that followed the course of the Kanawha River as it ran through a section of the Appalachian Mountains—whose name we pronounced with a short *a* in the middle, not "Appa-lay-shun" as outsiders said it. Glen Ferris was stretched long and narrow; most of the town lay on the wider side of the only road going through it, along the base of the mountain that rose behind our house. The other side of the road was too close to the river bank for anything but streetlights and the occasional addition of flower beds, courtesy of the Glen Falls Garden Club. If you stood on the sidewalk in front of our house and looked across the width of the valley, this is what you saw: mountains, railroad tracks, houses, Route 60, the Kanawha River and Falls, more railroad tracks on the other side, and more mountains.

No traveler passing through it would have suspected that a shadow had been cast over our town, and especially that the shadow came from the house next door to the church; for it was a shadow of evil. That was the way I saw things when I was thirteen, and our lives went out of control. All the beauty and innocence of Glen Ferris couldn't sweep that shadow away.

My parents had pulled strings to get our house, a roomy two-story in a section my dad loved to call by its nickname, Superintendent's Row. The houses, which still stand, were built of wood in 1930. Mom, Dad, Joe, and I lived in a duplex that looked gigantic to me. A curved lane separated our property from the churchyard and wound around the back of the row to emerge onto Route 60 again at the other end.

Green hedges separated our front yards from the sidewalk. The houses had large living-room windows and front porches made for sitting. All the superintendents and their families could relax on swings or metal porch chairs and gaze at the falls. They could watch traffic, perhaps rolling their eyes as old Mr. Ritter from down the row tapped his horn as a turn signal and made the hard right into our alley, barely avoiding an accident as he freed the string of cars behind him. They could watch the river flow over the dam or down toward the power plant and the island at the lower end of town. One summer morning, Dad and I were sitting out on the front steps. A big CMX semi went roaring by and the driver threw a bag of powdered donuts to us out the window. That was life in a small town.

We had three places of business in Glen Ferris then: a gasoline station, a company store and post office, and a historic inn on the water. For everything else, we drove to the next village, located a mile upstream. Gauley Bridge was where the Gauley and New Rivers merged to form the Kanawha. It was where my high school was located; where the movie theater and a scattering of businesses one-upped Glen Ferris in the retail sector. We could see the lower end of Gauley from home, its buildings low and small in a vista so stunning that travelers regularly pulled off the road to take pictures. Sun sparkled on the river and the distant water pouring over the dam. The mountains, converging in every view, appeared to encircle us as they cut patterns in the sky like pinking shears.

Glen Ferris had its origins as a company town. Built at the turn of the twentieth century, it became a boom town because of the industrial potential recognized in the convergence of the falls—called the only great water power in the coal fields of America—and the Chesapeake and Ohio Railroad. An aluminum company from North Carolina bought land and erected a power plant and later a dam to span the river at the lower end of town and tap Kanawha Falls as a source of hydroelectric power for the production of ferroalloys—elements used as raw materials in the production of steel. Glen Ferris had its own railroad depot, just outside what would later be my grandparents' front yard.

The town began to grow around its new-found industry, providing jobs for local people and attracting an influx of construction crews and businessmen. In 1907, the aluminum company sold its interest to the Electro Metallurgical Company (EMCO), which would go on to thrive and employ many of our parents and neighbors and friends.

EMCO was good to the residents of Glen Ferris. Our little boom town gained a school and a church, as well as new homes. In 1920, a three-story post office building rose above Route 60. A large private residence located on the river just above the plant site became a stagecoach stop. With its entrance facing the road—also known as the Midland Trail—and the business traffic coming through, it was an instant success.

My grandfather ran the combination company store and post office. His claim to fame was that he had named the town of Notomine, West Virginia, after the number two mine, but being the postmaster in Glen Ferris was what kept him busy. Grandpop wasn't exactly in the middle of the action at home, rising every day at five to fix his own breakfast, read the paper, and smoke before going to work; but I loved going into the store to find him clerking in a white butcher's apron or sitting behind the post-master's cage, where he would conduct business such as selling stamps.

Lincolnesque of build and face, except for being clean shaven, Grand-pop had some Indian blood, giving him a perpetual tan. His brown hair was thin on top. He wore long-sleeved shirts, always with the sleeves rolled up to just below his elbows, and eyeglasses with thin metal frames. Grandpop was constantly worried that one of us kids would accidentally touch the fragile things and break the lenses or bend the frames, causing him a headache. "Watch my glasses!" was his predictable response when we wanted to play, but Grandpop was kind to us in his way. He didn't fuss when I dug into the ice cream freezer in the store to search for broken Popsicles, which I thought I could eat because no one would buy them, and he let Joe "rob" the post office safe with his toy guns. My brother would come in wearing a cowboy hat, boots, and holsters. "Hands up!" he'd say, and Grandpop would surrender and open the safe.

Grandpop always wore dress pants and often carried bags of candy in his deep trouser pockets. He loved horehound candy, a bittersweet hard candy with supposed medicinal benefits. It was nasty. Grandpop couldn't give it away to us, so he kept the horehound candy in one pocket and a bag of chocolate drops in the other.

We had no rural mail delivery, so the store was busy with people stopping to get their mail, pick up a few groceries, and visit. It also served as our school bus stop and later as a classroom for local women interested in learning how to weave using a loom. My mother took the weaving classes in the back of the store, proudly bringing home placemats she'd made herself.

Across from the store, abutting the sidewalk, was the mossy stone wall of the inn, and beyond that a flat, green yard where playground equipment once stood and where Mom was shot in the leg with a BB as a girl. On past the inn was the river, ever flowing by our little town, and a concrete boathouse that jutted out into the water. You could feel daring sitting on its thick half-walls on a summer afternoon, your legs dangling toward the rushing Kanawha while dragonflies buzzed among the weeds.

My grandparents lived in view of the river, in a cinderblock house whose yard was already rising toward the mountain behind it. Their door was always open, Grandmama being the gregarious one. She interacted with the neighbors, cooked for church suppers, and went to the ladies' monthly Circle meetings. Grandmama loved the Lord, and everybody loved Grandmama. She did all the domestic work you'd attribute to a grandma: cooking, cleaning, baking, and sewing. I had original, one-of-a-kind outfits made from material I'd chosen, and even my dolls wore Grandmama's beautiful creations. She could pass a woman on the street in Charleston and go home and copy her outfit without a pattern.

Grandmama kept us in homemade rolls, banana bread, and once even a gingerbread house I'd seen in a magazine. She sang while she worked. She put chocolate ornaments on her Christmas tree and let us pick them off to eat. When I spent the night, we'd sit next to the little gas stove in her bedroom, and she'd read me Bible stories, hoping they'd take just like the domestic talents that already had skipped a generation. And then Grandmama would take down her hair and we'd sleep in twin beds. By then I would have forgotten about Grandpop; with a day that started out before first light, he rarely made it past seven thirty in the evening. I'd crawl between the clean, cool sheets and listen to the sounds of the neighborhood, the mountain, an occasional train whistle, and Grandmama's sweet, even breathing.

Besides the store and the houses we lived in, EMCO built recreational facilities. When I was growing up in the 1950s, we had tennis courts, a bowling alley, a recreation hall, a ball field, and a playground. Parties were held; ball teams and bowling leagues were formed.

Billie and I were inseparable. We roamed Glen Ferris from one end to the other, never lacking things to do. We played sports, hiked in the mountains, swam in the river, and learned to water-ski behind her family's boat.

Billie and I loved to explore the dam. We could swim to it or cross the river in a boat, but usually we climbed down the back of the old concrete pier opposite Grandmama's house, got around the chain-link fence with the "DANGER" sign, and went the rest of the way on a floating walkway.

One day after we'd seen *The Blob,* we discovered Glen Ferris's own version festering over on the dam. It lay in puddles where the rocks dipped and had a reddish-greenish shiny surface like you sometimes see on ham. Little did the residents of Glen Ferris realize what we alone knew—that in fifty years the Blob would come oozing up over the dam, cross the Kanawha River, and take over the town. While we played or went to church or sat at the dinner table at home, the Blob was gathering its strength in the summer sun.

Billie and I sneaked out at night, especially in the summer, occasionally tagging along with an older crowd thanks to her sister, who always had a boyfriend—with wheels. Once we rode in a backseat to the beginning of the four-lane where the river curves on the way to Gauley and watched souped-up cars drag race in the moonlight.

If we stayed home and had the house to ourselves, we might play the music from *My Fair Lady* at the loudest setting just to hear Rex Harrison sing, "Damn, damn, damn, damn" at the beginning of "I've Grown Accustomed to Her Face." It boomed through the house, sending us running and giggling at the audacity of the cursing. Once as a joke, Billie and I got on the phone with another friend, and Billie said, "My dad is really mad. Listen." Then we'd play it again.

Things had continued to deteriorate at home, and my mother was at the center of the trouble. What was the matter with her? At Thanksgiving, our house was too quiet and the smells were all wrong. Mom hadn't put the turkey in the oven. She was supposed to get up at five, but she didn't, and now there was no way we were getting a turkey dinner by afternoon. I remember the stale feeling in the house; the quiet; and Mom still in her long, red robe late in the morning, after the crying: another lost day.

Mom and Dad began to shut themselves away in their bedroom on weekends. It might start with Mom pretending to suppress a yawn. That could happen at any time of the day. "Oh, I'm so sleepy!" she would say, fooling no one, and off she'd go. At first Dad would go to the store and get magazines for the two of them. They'd stay in bed all afternoon, coming out only to use the bathroom. They were just upstairs, but they were as unavailable to Joe and me as the stars in the sky.

In bed or out, Mom and Dad generated a lot of physical noise. There was bumping and dropping and rattling. The floors would creak. There was awkwardness with doors: doors crashing into the wall; doors being repeatedly shut. I didn't think it had anything to do with sex, which I was just beginning to understand from a book called *Sane Sex Life* that I'd discovered in Mom's nightgown drawer. It was a how-to manual, and it *wasn't* about how to stay sane, which, in my humble opinion, was what they really needed.

Occasionally I'd get a peep into my parents' inner sanctum. The magazines would be open face-down on the floor. Glasses of orange juice would be sitting on top of the old record cabinet they used as a nightstand. And a lump might be visible under the blankets, whichever one hadn't gone to the bathroom.

After a while, the magazine idea dropped away, and Dad would make no secret of going to what he called the package store. He'd come down the back walk with a grocery bag in each arm, the bottles clinking inside. Then he and Mom would head for the bedroom, soon to be sealed away like vampires in broad daylight. It could be morning, afternoon, we never knew; but once that door closed, Joe and I were on our own. Sometime later Dad would come downstairs and we would all watch TV, but we wouldn't see Mom again until the next morning. By then I was glad.

Even though the evidence was mounting, I wanted to think it was something else that had Mom in its grip—something resembling drunkenness, but surely not the real thing. Surely our mom had not become an actual, sickening drunk, slurring and bumbling through the day, able to turn on us in an instant like a snake. It had to be something else, something less dangerous, more temporary. And in that time of denial came the birth of the D.M.

"My mom's in a D.M.," I'd say to Billie, who knew it stood for "drunk mood." "She's acting like she's drunk, but she isn't." Billie adopted the term for her mom, too. In her case, it was a general term to describe anything Billie perceived as bad. Those were the times we stayed outside, climbing the telephone pole behind her garage and stepping over onto the roof where we were out of sight.

One day after school, I came home and couldn't get in. Why were both doors locked? My mother should have been home; she'd planned to paint that day. I looked through the glass panes of the front door and saw her pale legs sticking out from behind a chair. There were the two-toned saddle shoes; the white ankle socks she wore around the house; her rolled-up, baggy blue jeans. She was lying on the floor, so still that I could have been looking at a dead body.

I pounded and yelled to get Mom's attention. She tried to get up, twisting around and pushing up with her hands, only to fall back onto the hardwood floor. I was sick inside, scared and angry and let down. When Dad came home hours later, he put Mom to bed and told us she was dizzy from the paint fumes. But I'd seen her, watched him struggle to get her up the stairs, and heard the noises she made when she tried to talk.

I could call it what I wanted, but this was no D.M. Mom was changing steadily for the worse, and I now knew she must be drinking. But why it had such horrible results, I didn't know. Adults drank—Dad drank whiskey for his heart, and he didn't turn into a repulsive version of himself—so why was this different? I couldn't solve the mystery of what was taking my mother away from us. Worst of all, Mom seemed to be pulling our whole family down that wild, dark path with her.

Sometimes things were normal. Mom would do what moms do— cook or clean or get groceries, have a friend over, go somewhere. After school we were likely to find her busy—out in the yard, in the kitchen, or now and then in the basement doing laundry. It didn't matter where she was; as soon as I saw her, I was flooded with relief. Those were the good days. Mostly I thought ahead to the other kind, wondering when the next episode would knock us for a loop.

I began to recognize the signs. Even if she had control of her body—

which she hadn't during the paint episode—Mom's face would change when she drank. It was the facial equivalent of a landslide or an avalanche that would bury my mother and leave in her place a cold-blooded stranger. Her facial muscles would go slack. Her mouth would lose its usual shape, and the skin under her eyes would puff out. Her eyes would take on a different expression, as though the stranger inside was looking out at us and didn't like us much.

As my mother's affliction progressed, our house became a world turned upside-down, a world of secrets where a monster came and went and defined our lives. Unlike Dracula, it didn't wait to be invited in, but was carried into the house in grocery bags that clinked their warning all the way from the car to the kitchen table. Our monster was worse than a vampire; it sucked us dry of safety, security, and self-esteem and filled us with fear.

Increasingly, it was not my mother but that darker being—her other self—that greeted me after school. When I came up the sidewalk, I didn't know who I would get.

I looked to Dad for help. Joe and I came to depend on the sight of him coming home from work, walking up the sidewalk in his hat and overcoat or pulling into the parking spot next to the garage if he'd driven the carpool that day. When Dad came home from work, I felt like I could breathe, that we were saved.

I also knew that we were all right as long as Mom thought she was fooling us, *all right* being a relative term. If she thought we didn't suspect she was drinking, Mom would try to go about business as usual. The choice we had was to play along or call her bluff. For Joe it wasn't even a question; he was too young. Joe was better off staying under the radar. I was the one who did it, stared her right in the face, defied her without saying a word. I couldn't ignore what was happening, even though I knew the moment of recognition was irreversible, that at the end of it I would become the enemy.

My defiance didn't change Mom's behavior, but it made me the target of endless verbal fallout. All the negativity in my mother's heart would be directed at me. It helped to remember that it was not Mom at all, but a monster I was facing down—a monster every bit as frightening as a blood-sucking count from Transylvania. And this was no vampire on a movie screen. This was real.

Chapter 5

The Letter

"Have you tried to interview Christopher Lee?" the editor asked, as though it were the most logical question in the world. I was rendered mute. Was he crazy? Clearly, he didn't know the obstacles involved in interviewing Sir Christopher Lee, the absurd odds against it. He didn't know the fear his question struck in my heart. And that was right out of the gate.

I was in a six-minute meeting with a "real editor" at a writing conference in Columbus, Ohio. In contrast to the way I'd expected to feel in the meeting—calm, brilliant, ready to bowl him over with my book idea—I felt like a grain of sand, intimidated, out of place. My tiny, cheap hotel room was looking pretty good.

This editor didn't know what I knew. He didn't know that Christopher Lee had left Dracula behind when he was fifty. He didn't get that Lee refused to discuss his former screen persona; that he'd even had it written into his 1978 *Saturday Night Live* contract that he wouldn't do Dracula in a skit. How would the editor know, unless he'd dug out the information as I had? He didn't know these things any more than he knew he was sitting across the table from Chicken Little. I was not the type to go charging in.

Travel writer Bill Bryson once said of himself, "The only thing I can do is spy on the world . . . I cannot interact with people. It's against my nature, and so what I do is spy." That pretty well summed up my style, too. I observed; then I put words together.

How could I explain that I wasn't the type to chase celebrities at all costs? This was a man who'd ticked off somebody famous to get a story. He'd been relentless; everything for art. And now he was bragging that he'd been banned or sued—some such thing. He was smiling, conspiratorial: *You, too, can piss off the famous.* But he and I weren't anything alike.

Did I want to interview Christopher Lee? *Could* I intrude on the world-famous actor, a giant who easily dwarfed the giants convening in Columbus, Ohio? I could barely imagine conducting the interview. If I felt like a grain of sand in Columbus, talking with Lee would magnify that humbling experience a thousand, million times.

I didn't want to be humiliated by a withering comment from the actor I loved and respected. As usual, it was a truth from all of my life: I wanted him to like me.

After the conference; after long, intermittent periods of thought and reflection, I realized that editor had done me a favor. I also knew that I did have questions to ask Christopher Lee. The easy one would be, "Where did you go in Romania?" But that was a mere warm-up to the big question: "Have you made peace with playing Dracula?" Had Lee come to terms with being known his whole adult life for playing Dracula? I didn't think so. Had he worked through his indignation at having people remember that role best, no matter how many others he played? Even if he had, would he tell me? There was one way to find out.

I started with an e-mail to Jonathan Rigby, Lee's official biographer, via his publisher. That was roundabout, but I figured Rigby had an in with Lee, and maybe he would help me.

Nothing happened. Except for Rigby's publisher, who kindly let me know he'd forwarded my message, I haven't had much luck with the British. Janina Faye, who played little Tania in *Horror of Dracula,* didn't respond to my e-mail requesting an on-line interview. To be fair, maybe she didn't receive the message. In the case of Rigby, what did I even ask him for?

I then wrote a letter to Sir Christopher Lee in care of his agent in London; but instead of printing it out on good paper and mailing it, I let the file sit on my computer for months. Then one day when I was contemplating my sorry state of gutlessness, I opened the electronic file and re-read the letter.

I'd thanked Lee for his performances past, present, and future. I'd told him how an editor had challenged me to interview him, and I added four words: "I have to try." It was good enough to send.

Mailing the letter wasn't complicated. It cost ninety-eight cents to send a first-class letter to England. When I saw my envelope stamped "First Class INTERNATIONAL," I felt a surge of joy. For most of my life I'd been loath to bother anyone, especially people I'd put on pedestals. That day, as I walked out of the post office, the hand of fear lost its grip on me. I was no longer afraid—even of "Dracula."

I didn't hear back from Mr. Lee or his agent, but you never know. Maybe that letter is sitting somewhere in London right now, waiting for just the right moment for the post. After all, I'd waited a very long time to write it.

Chapter 6

Secrets

Glen Ferris, the late 1950s, afternoon: I'm coming home from school, walking up the sidewalk. Cars and trucks pass within three or four feet of me, whipping my skirt and blowing my hair. The noise level would make it hard to talk if I needed to, but I don't. I'm alone. If there were two of us, the one on the outside would have to watch in order not to stumble off the sidewalk into the traffic.

I climb the cement steps to our front walk, take a few steps toward the matched set of globe arborvitae that flank our front porch, and check the door: closed. Instead of taking the porch steps, I swing around the side of the house. Our house has only one side yard; the other side belongs to the neighbors.

It's quiet. No one is around; even the cars whizzing by are now background noise. I pass the shady corner where I once planted watermelon seeds that didn't grow and where my pet Easter turtle landed after it fell off the porch. How had my tiny turtle crawled outside by itself? I'd found it by searching through the ground cover, reaching into the green-and-white leaves. Its blue-painted shell had gone soft. Soon after, the turtle died, and I had to wonder if I'd doomed it with my rescue.

I can see into the dining room window: nothing. Above me, on the second story, is a window to my parents' bedroom. I used to lie on their bed on Saturday mornings when everyone else was downstairs. I'd look out that window and wish that Superman would come and give me a cape.

The car isn't in its parking space, but maybe it's in the garage, if Dad didn't take it to work. Our back door is standing open, and the kitchen is dark inside. I climb the steps of our little back porch and go in, my stomach starting to be the center of my universe. A stale smell explains the open door: cigarettes and something else. Not good. It is deadly silent in the house, and that makes my senses come alive.

There is no snack waiting on a shiny plate. Once I thought I saw a slice of chocolate cake on the kitchen floor. When I bent down, it was alive—a moving tapestry of tiny brown ants.

On the best days, my mother is in the yard, kneeling over her border garden of marigolds and zinnias, or even seated on her red stool with the chrome legs, ironing our dampened clothes in front of the TV. All that's missing is the perky question, "How was your day?" and I can live with that.

On the worst days, I was in the same boat as Jonathan Harker when he started rattling around Dracula's castle to find the sleeping Count. I, too, made my way room by room through a house as silent as a tomb in broad daylight, holding my breath at every corner and doorway, hoping against hope that I wouldn't find the monster; or if I did, that the monster would be asleep.

Our monster was worse than Dracula because it was personal. That kind scares you in a different way. It makes your heart sink in your chest because it changes someone you love—and not for the better. Our monster was the disease of alcoholism, and it was claiming my mother.

At thirteen, I knew nothing of alcoholism or its treatment; what I knew was the shame of having a mother who drank. That was the secret that ruled our lives. And back then, on certain afternoons when the monster was in residence, I had to find out where it was. I had to know what I was dealing with or running from. I dreaded it to the marrow of my bones.

My search didn't end in the basement like Harker's did; it started there. The basement stairs were just off the pantry in our kitchen. I walked past aprons and brooms on my right and shelves of food on my left. Dad kept his cans of sardines in mustard dressing on the top shelf, as if one of us would try to eat them first. We had a giant plastic tomato full of catsup that Mom stored on the middle shelf alongside the peanut butter and jelly.

Our basement was unfinished. There was no family room; it was concrete, dark and gloomy, lit by a couple hanging bulbs. It wasn't a place you'd go unless you were washing clothes behind the big, round monster furnace, taking something off a shelf, or steering the occasional field mouse into a paper bag for disposal. If the basement was empty, I was happy to hightail it back up the stairs.

Our kitchen had never been remodeled ("Be the last on your block...!"). My mother did dishes in a red plastic tub she put in the middle of the old porcelain sink. The area under the sink was open. Dried dishcloths hung stiffly over the curved pipes leading into the wall. We had a yellow wastebasket with a pedal. The top looked like it had been hit with a shower of golf balls.

Mom liked to hang a calendar in the kitchen. The page I remember showed a boy holding his bad report card in one hand while using the other hand to put a school book in the seat of his pants. The caption read, "Hope for the best and get ready for the worst."

I went on through the dining room and living room. Nothing was out of order. The copper-colored upright freezer hummed in its corner next to the dining room table; the phone was silent on its little stand. Straight ahead, through the archway that served as my dancing partner on better days, was the living room. Under the triple window, our couch turned its back indifferently on the Kanawha River pouring over the dam. The TV was off, and in the opposite corner the easy chair my parents loved was empty. It had been reupholstered often, usually for the same reason: A dropped cigarette would burn a hole through the cover, forcing Mom or Dad to jump up and toss the cushion out the front door like a Frisbee, where it would smoke and smolder on our porch. Luckily we lived on the end; only the people in the passing cars would note what quaint objects some people used for porch furniture.

Upstairs we had the typical three bedrooms and a bath. There was an attic that never saw the light of day. Joe and I used to climb up the linen closet shelves and pop the little door in the ceiling, but nothing exciting ever came of it.

The upstairs was the scariest part of the house in my after-school searches because it was all that was left. The odds of finding everything normal were by then very low. Sometimes I lucked out and no one was home; at other times, I found what I dreaded lying on the bed or—much worse—bumping around in the bathroom. Then it was like that moment in *Horror of Dracula* when Jonathan Harker, trapped in the cellar of Dracula's castle with all the sleeping vampires, realizes that one is awake.

The worst possible outcome of my hunt was to find Mom in front of the bathroom mirror, giving herself a facial.

Mom only gave herself facials when she was drunk. The bathroom door would be open, and she'd be standing in front of the sink in her red robe, her face shiny with cream. Then, with her fingers held so straight they bent backwards, she'd slowly pat her cheeks. To me, those fingers were tapping out a disaster signal like Morse code. Mom would turn to me and say, "I'm gim' myself a facial." And in that moment, hers was the most frightening face I'd ever seen. Give me Dracula any day!

In the scariest moments of *Horror of Dracula,* the hero could appear. Dr. Van Helsing, with his quiet sense of purpose, would pit himself against the Count. Where was my Van Helsing?

On many an afternoon, I slid my dresser into place across my bedroom door and settled in by the window, where the hum of traffic shut out the present, and I could dream of things far away. Sometimes I drew pictures. Sometimes I sang, pretending to be on *American Bandstand.* I watched the cars. The way the river curves at the upper end of Glen Ferris, you can follow a vehicle clear to the next town.

How many kids came home and had to face a monster? How many had to worry about whether their mom or her nightmare half would be the one to greet them? How many families led double lives like ours?

Across the road, the Great Kanawha rolled along, untouched by all our troubles; but anyone who watched knew that even the river had a split personality. When it rained, a line would appear in the water, cutting the flow into two distinct halves that followed the current together. One side was normal and the other was dark and muddy.

I didn't see it then, the similarity to Transylvania, as I looked out at the winding river from my upstairs window under the high peaked roof of our house, surrounded by mountains and forests. Even Dracula's castle didn't come to mind, though I was a prisoner in my room just like Jonathan Harker, dreading the beast.

I'd just started high school—the period Dick Clark called our happiest years—and everything was falling apart. I was growing up, and where was my mother when I needed her? I got my period one afternoon in eighth grade, just prior to a schoolwide assembly. I had no clue what it was. My one wild, heart-pounding thought as I walked past my schoolmates in the gym was whether the toilet paper I'd put into my panties would stay there until I got to my seat.

"Your happiest years" didn't mean a lot to me. I couldn't even invite my friends over. In our family, a knock on the door was a reason to panic. What had happened to our home? I was angry, sad, afraid, and sick of keeping secrets; but I barely knew it. My emotions were already becoming locked down, and my mind was always somewhere else—either behind or far ahead of the present moment.

Chapter 7

Flights of Fancy

The day of my Romania trip, I woke up to thunder and lightning. The radio report promised another day of August thunderstorms. I had my first two cups of coffee reading *The Historian,* trying to finish it before I left home, but the need for a shower nagged at me. I wanted to be clean if the power went out. I'd aggressively begun *The Historian* a few days before, thinking I'd take it with me if I had to; but at 642 pages, the first major Dracula novel in years was too thick and heavy in hardcover to tote around Transylvania.

In the shower I ran my soaped hands up and down my legs to wash, feeling the loose flesh: *Yes, these fifty-nine-year-old legs are about to carry me through Romania.*

And later, standing in front of the bathroom mirror: *This is the way my hair will look. This is what I will put on.* It was like getting ready for a date or a special party, the way you try to fix moments in your mind. My date wasn't with a person, but a place—a little section of Central Europe known as the Land Beyond the Forest, the land of Dracula. If you can fall in love with a country, I had—from across the world.

I unpacked my rain jacket to wear instead of my black sweater and then took my travel outfit from its hanger on the bedroom door. I'd selected the blue blouse and gray skirt days before and set them out for this moment. I dressed and added the silver cross I planned to wear around my neck—especially at night. Was I dressed appropriately to follow the footsteps of Dracula? Who knew? I am five feet seven and slender, with conservative looks. In my long skirt, heavy walking shoes, black socks, and crucifix, I looked more like someone from a religious order. That was a laugh.

Crosses weren't something I had lying around. I bought my first crucifix in Athens, Greece, five years before my trip. I found the chain much later in the gift shop of the Crystal Cathedral in Garden Grove, California, the huge church made famous by TV evangelist Rev. Robert Schuller. Silver chains were a stock item there. I figured it couldn't hurt to have the extra protection of the Crystal Cathedral. I hoped to get a glimpse of Schuller, but the handsome, white-haired minister was retired by then and rarely made an appearance.

It was time to pack the toilet kit. I'd bought mineral-based makeup for the trip after reading that rural areas of Romania had no running water. The makeup was expensive, but I was past worrying about my spending. I was already the financial version of *Girls Gone Wild*.

I'd practiced applying the products with their special brushes. Once or twice the powder clung too heavily, and I looked like the Phantom of the Opera—or possibly Countess Báthory, sometimes called the female Dracula. Elizabeth Báthory of Transylvania was a real person who had lovely pale skin. According to legend, she brutally murdered hundreds of young women in the seventeenth century in order to bathe in her victims' blood as a means of maintaining her youth and beauty.

I zipped the toilet kit, slid it into my suitcase, and pulled my bags to the front door. Soon I'd be traveling the fifty miles to the Greater Cincinnati/Northern Kentucky International Airport, about to suspend life as I knew it for eighteen days. It was the longest I'd ever been away and the farthest I'd ever traveled.

I was an editor for a publishing company. Luckily, I'd taken enough business trips to know how to get organized and get the physical things out of the way. I moved the black suitcase, my camera bag, and my tripod bag out onto the front porch, along with the bright blue rain jacket. The other spots of color on that gray morning came from the luggage tags I'd ordered from the Journeywoman travel website. They were bright orange with the message "What a journey!" on the front. On the back was a place to write my name with a Sharpie. The idea was that when we saw these tags on other women's luggage, we Journeywomen would recognize one another the world over. I thought I might need a few friends.

The tags had been a devil to get on the suitcases. Each one came with a sturdy chain, the type you see on key rings, but these were stronger. In fact, I couldn't get the little ball to snap into place. After a few deep grooves in the ends of my fingers, I decided Steve could do it.

My friends Steve and Anne had offered to drive me to the airport. I wouldn't have thought of it after so many years of hoisting my own bags into my car, driving myself to long-term parking, and going through ticketing and security alone. I didn't expect anything different, living by myself and occasionally even talking out loud to the four walls of my condominium.

Standing on the porch with the rain dripping down, I was filled with elation and anxiety. In twenty-four hours I'd be in Bucharest. *If things run true to form*, I thought, *my mind will take flight before I do. Maybe it already has.* Finally I was going to see the places I'd dreamed about, read about, and watched in the movies; but first I had to get there.

My flying worries always came in stages: Would I get to the airport on time? Did my suitcase weigh too much? Had I forgotten something? Would I really get on the plane, or had there been some mistake, and would I have to return to work on Monday with everyone else? I loved my job, but I still knew the answer to that last one: No, I wouldn't be going to work on Monday. I was going to Romania if I had to flap my arms to fly there. It was the same surge of righteousness that causes drivers to run red lights: I've waited long enough, it's my turn, and by God, I'm *going*.

For this journey, there were three flights. I was to leave Cincinnati for Chicago O'Hare, then board an Air France jet for Paris, where I'd change planes at Charles DeGaulle and continue on to Bucharest. The whole process would take a day. I would cross many time zones.

We left for the airport on schedule. "Maybe you'll have a cute guide," Anne said from the front seat of the car. I didn't answer, but let my mind go there for a few seconds before I jerked it back. It was fun to speculate but dangerous to expect. And I was on a different mission.

We got to the airport around noon. I checked my suitcase and tripod, so had only my camera/computer bag to carry. It was my own little Brinks truck without wheels, a combination purse and grab-bag of journalistic tools. Most of the contents were now irreplaceable. During lunch, I kept eyeing it on the floor next to me, afraid I'd forget it and blow the whole trip.

In spite of the warnings now broadcast in airports—"In the interest of air safety . . ."—it didn't seem that the people rushing around the terminal were going to slip drugs into my pockets, steal my wallet, or pick up my carry-on bag and run. An airport is no place for that; everyone has too much to manage to worry about taking on other people's possessions. Sometimes a flight takes all your attention just to get on it.

I reached my gate an hour early and sat down to wait. I could say I had a feeling of swooping glory in the pit of my stomach—excitement at how, very shortly, I would be flying off above the clouds on the way to Chicago. Only that isn't what I think about when I fly. More like: Will the plane fall out of the sky with me in it, and can the pilot find the airport?

My hands get slimy during takeoff, and I pit out my clothes by the time we reach ten thousand feet. I get red grooves in my fingers from holding so tight to the armrests. The only good flights are perfectly smooth. A little bit of turbulence, and I start seeing crash scenarios, or maybe that scene from *Goldfinger* in which the villain is sucked out of the aircraft through a tiny hole. And if we crashed, would it begin like the time over San Francisco when my plane hit an air pocket and seemed about to drop to Earth? Would there be loud noises and the quick tipping of wings?

If I could have snapped my fingers or clicked the heels of a pair of ruby slippers to arrive in Romania, I would have. Even if I could put my fear aside, a transatlantic flight would wear me out. I knew I wouldn't be able to sleep on the plane, and my muscles would be tired from helping the pilot keep it in the sky. The sun streamed down outside as I made three trips to the restroom, peeing off my nerves.

I had dreams of flying as a child. I would soar over Glen Ferris, my friends and neighbors watching, their heads tipped back and their mouths open in astonishment. They would be like the TV people on *Superman* who shouted at the beginning of every show, "Look, up in the sky. It's a bird. It's a plane . . ." I would look down on them all as I flew over the houses, the little four-room schoolhouse, the red-brick church, the ball field—farther and farther away from the life I knew, escaping the bounds of earth and destiny and what passed for home.

In my best flight dream, I was running on a blacktop driveway near my grandmother's house. I began flapping my arms. When I lifted my feet, I could feel the air beneath me, holding me up. I was three feet off the ground. I was flying! It was the best feeling in the world.

Those flight dreams took an ironic turn when I began to travel on actual planes; they were replaced with a fear of flying. Dreams of flying work, but being in an airplane seven miles up with absolutely no control over the next moment, let alone your fate, doesn't work so well. Even before the aircraft starts down the runway, I'm thinking the worst.

Flying distills my thoughts down to one fine funnel of fear in which I can contemplate death with no distractions. It sets priorities. I no longer have to worry about whether I have a terminal disease, whether I should quit my job and write, whether I will ever fall in love again or want to— just whether or not my feet will ever touch the ground again.

Once when I was on a turbulent flight, the woman one seat over was reading a book on romance languages. She was by the window but rarely looked as the plane bumped through layers of thick, white clouds like a skipped rock. It was like hurtling through the Bermuda Triangle, visibility zero. By then I even wondered about the orientation of the plane in the sky. My seatmate seemed unaffected by the drama; if we crashed, she would go out thinking about five romance languages and would never know what hit her. Maybe that was a better attitude than mine.

Back at the gate, I stared out the window at nothing. At least the rain had stopped; the sun was even shining. It was time to buck up, put my negative thoughts away, and focus on my destination. I had five thousand miles of flying ahead of me.

At last my dream of being in Dracula's land was about to come true. I'd prepared myself for Romania every way I could and imagined the country of my dreams as scary, beautiful, like the movies, and totally different. In other words, I still didn't know what to expect.

Chapter 8

Waves

As the plane shot into the sky over northern Kentucky, I tried to settle in for the short flight to Chicago. Between my trip excitement and the panic of being airborne, I was anything but settled. Maybe it was a good sign that I was sitting next to a minister.

The last time I'd been on a plane, I'd glimpsed the captain's face just before he entered the flight deck. His bright blue eyes had a reckless expression, and his hair hung over the top of his forehead in a straight row, separated into little points. I remember thinking, *Oh, my God, he looks like Frankenstein.*

Dad was the only one who ever flew in our family, and that was when he made his periodic visits to the Cleveland Clinic. In those days, the airlines were trying to convince people that flying wasn't much different from sitting in their living room at home. Yeah.

Dad had been ill with hypertension for years. Mom regularly took his blood pressure. He took medication and watched his diet, but his personality wasn't suited to a life of accommodation. Dad was excitable and blustery. His dieting was only moderately successful; he smoked unfiltered cigarettes; and then there was the stress of just living in our house, having the role of rescuer every day at five o'clock. To top it off, Dad's heart specialist had advised him to drink liquor on a regular basis. That may have been why Mom was as sick as Dad, but with a different disease.

As for vacations, we were not the kind of family to pile into the car and go cross-country every summer, hitting educational landmarks to enrich our lives. Though I've made up for some of it since, I wouldn't have held my classmates spellbound by telling how I spent my summer vacation. Well, I might have if I'd told the truth.

Maybe Joe and I didn't see Plymouth Rock, the Liberty Bell, the Grand Canyon, or Our Nation's Capital, but our parents did take us on trips. We usually headed south, to sun and sand. Our favorite destination was Myrtle Beach, South Carolina. Myrtle Beach was—and is—the hub of the Grand Strand, an uninterrupted sandy beach stretching for more than sixty miles along the Atlantic.

Before the interstate highway system changed car travel, we took two-lane roads through little towns that looked like movie sets from old Westerns, with their flat-fronted buildings lining the main street. It gave us a glimpse of life in another place. After a few stoplights, we might bump across a railroad track and make turn or two. Mom—the navigator—would have to watch closely to find signs for the meandering road.

Dad got angry if he made a wrong turn, and a heated exchange would ensue in the front seat. It was Mom's job—not his—to figure out where they were going. She held the map upside-down—her trick when going south—and told Dad when to turn and what road to take.

When it was time to stop for the night, we chose our motel by spotting one we liked from the road. Thus began a contest between the rest of us and Dad, who always considered price first. Joe and I wanted a place with a pool. To advertise their swimming pools, motels located them close to the road, so that when you drove by, you could see families gathered around the rectangle of water for an evening swim. Joe and I pointed and yelled, begging Dad to stop, and sometimes it worked. We couldn't wait to change into our bathing suits and walk out to the pool just like the other people, like we were in a magazine ad.

In reality, the motel stop was usually preceded by another one—the local package store. After a day of fighting their way through the South, Mom and Dad would "relax" in the evenings with a bottle of whiskey. It didn't matter where we were; another night was on course to be marred by drinking.

After dark, we all sat together on the bed to watch TV. Pretty soon, one or the other of my parents would reach for the bottle. Dad was never visibly changed by drinking, or even interested in it the way Mom was. She was the problem. I dreaded feeling her arm snake around to grab that bottle, hearing the rattle of that damn paper bag.

My parents' drinking was always furtive. At home, we had beer in our refrigerator, but I rarely saw them drink it. Sometimes they'd leave a whiskey bottle on one of the pantry shelves, but they didn't sit around sipping mixed drinks as though it were a normal thing to do. Even Dad's hypertension hadn't brought that out.

I hated the uncertainty of never knowing when things were going to go to hell. I hated that Dad let Mom get so drunk that her children were afraid of her. Mom's venom was mostly verbal—I guess that was good—but her abusiveness had escalated. It was nothing at all to hear her say she wanted to snatch one of us bald-headed or choke us, but at least she didn't do it. Joe says that one time he woke up to find her standing over him with a knife, but usually Mom's messages were spoken, hurled out of the darkest place inside her to sink into us like vampires' teeth.

She was always accusing me of trying to run everything; I was "Your Royal Highness" and "Miss Priss." My failure to snag a boyfriend was a real sticking point. Mom wanted me to be the blond in the convertible, but with my brown hair and glasses, I was plain and bookish—to her obvious disappointment. Still am.

Once long ago, she looked up from her ironing, two sheets to the wind, and asked, "Who's taking you to the prom?" When I didn't answer, she growled, "Get a date!" It's not that you believe everything when someone berates you, but the net effect is that you think they don't like you, which in the long run is worse.

I attracted predators—grown men who knew better, like the fellow who flashed the goods with his own wife in the room. Why me? I wasn't some flirtatious Lolita; just the opposite, but I seemed to draw invasive people. When that happened, I shrank to become the invisible girl. With the flasher, I hadn't known how to react, so I'd just ignored it, pretended it wasn't happening. We soldier on with terrifying secrets.

I wasn't one to make waves, but with the drinking, I fought back. I began to look for bottles and empty the contents into the kitchen sink. This was easiest to do when Mom and Dad had gone to their bedroom for a stint in suspended animation. With vodka or gin, I'd pour the clear liquid down the sink and fill the whole bottle with tap water. With whiskey, I'd empty the bottle and then refill it with a mix of Coke and water to simulate the color. I'd replace each bottle where I'd found it—under a chair, in the buffet, on a shelf in the pantry. If my life was like a vampire movie, in this instance *I* was Van Helsing, doing my bit to try to put an end to evil. The crazy thing was that Mom didn't react. She must have known I was tampering with her drinks. She had to be furious, but speaking up would have been admitting she'd hidden all those bottles in the first place. And what was life without a secret?

The drinking didn't stop on vacation, but my interference did. It was too hard in a tiny motel room. Luckily, it wasn't long before both my brother and I fell asleep, dreaming of the beach.

Joe and I played a game in the ocean. We would walk out to where the waves were breaking and the water was about chest high. We would stand face to face, one of us looking at the horizon and the other looking toward the beach. The game was one of trust. The person looking out toward the horizon was to warn the other when a big wave came along. In the meantime, the one facing the beach could not turn to look.

I liked being the one with my back to the waves. I wasn't a very trusting soul, and maybe that's why the game was so exciting. I remember standing in the sun for long moments, watching my brother's face while low waves slapped playfully against my back and broke closer to shore. The suspense would build, and then the sucking around our legs and feet as the tide pulled at the water and sand. When I sensed a big wave rolling in behind me, the question was whether Joe would warn me in time so that I could turn and jump it. Usually he didn't have to: I couldn't bear the suspense, delicious as it was, and I had to look. When a big one did come, both of us would jump high and let the wave roll past us just before it broke. I remember the feeling of lightness at being suspended in the swelling water. Once in a great while, we got surprised and ended up tumbling end over end until we surfaced again. I would remember that game later, when I was trying to figure out my life.

As we descended into O'Hare, I passed up the temptation to grab the minister's hand and thought instead of Christopher Lee hissing and glowering as Count Dracula. Lee had a fear of flying, too. It wouldn't bring us one moment closer to meeting, but it was a connection.

Chapter 9

My One and Only Dracula

Before he was Saruman in *Lord of the Rings* or Count Dooku in *Star Wars*, Christopher Lee was Dracula. Lee followed popular Hungarian actor Bela Lugosi into the role in the 1950s and portrayed the Count on the silver screen until 1972.

Lee has said of his predecessor that for many people, Lugosi would always be the "one and only Dracula." For me, the one and only Dracula is Lee. Say what you want about Lugosi, Gary Oldman, Frank Langella, and others who have played the Count. To a girl growing up in the 1950s and '60s, Christopher Lee was it—*him*—Count Dracula of Transylvania.

Between ages thirty-five and fifty, Lee spent much of his onscreen time lying in coffins; striding to, through, or from castles; biting necks; and whipping horses through dark forests. He was given only a few lines of dialogue, depending instead on his physical presence, expressions, and movements to capture the essence of Dracula.

Echoing the central character's role in Stoker's novel, the movie Count was absent from most of the scenes. Lee's onscreen appearances were rationed to build tension. He had just six minutes in *Horror of Dracula*—his debut in the role—to convince audiences that he was the suave, bloodsucking Count. In those six minutes, he became unforgettable.

Lee's Count Dracula was handsome, elegant, and full of contrasts: He was charming but aloof; menacing, yet attractive; powerful and brooding; reserved and over the top. He was frightening even when asleep in his coffin, his lean frame as still as the witching hour. Awake, he was hypnotic. Sitting in the movies, I was so completely sold on Lee as a vampire that I held my breath, stared into his eyes, and waited for the inevitable just like one of his onscreen victims—even though I had to watch through my fingers.

The actor has said of his interpretation that he tried to convey the loneliness of evil. No doubt he did, but nobody told the victims—men wearing expressions of terror and women in low-cut dresses, their bosoms heaving.

Lee campaigned for scripts that faithfully followed Stoker's novel, but most of the Dracula movies he made did not. When he was filming *Dracula, Prince of Darkness,* he refused to say any of his lines because they were so far off the mark. For the same reason—a poor story line—Lee repeatedly refused to continue making Dracula films for Hammer. But, because he'd already become famous for the role, he was convinced time after time to continue or put the movie people out of work.

I had it bad for this movie Dracula. One day after I'd begun to plan my trip, I was browsing the horror titles in Half Price Books. I felt suckerpunched when I opened a copy of Chelsea Quinn Yarbro's novel *Hôtel Transylvania* and read the dedication at the front: "For Christopher Lee: a nous les amours et les roses." I couldn't translate it exactly, but the words were basic high-school French. No one had to tell me what "amours" and "roses" were. There was an intimacy to the words, and a flame of jealousy shot through me, right there in the Horror aisle of the bookstore. My face turned hot the way it does when I've eaten too much chocolate.

How did Ms. Yarbro know Christopher Lee? *And why wouldn't she?* Both of them were famous, both linked to vampires. She was at least an admirer; we had that in common. But what kind of relationship would prompt such a dedication for all to see? And what did it really say? The French were famous for idioms, and I didn't trust myself to translate it.

I Googled Ms. Yarbro and found her website, but it had no "Contact me" link. Obsessed by then, I wrote to the book publisher of *Hôtel Transylvania* asking for a translation, and someone there forwarded my request to the author. Weeks later the publisher sent me her reply:

"The translation is 'Let us have love and roses,'" the e-mail said. "It is from the Massenet opera *Manon,* from Act IV, which takes place at Hotel Transylvania; it's a kind of joke, since Lee, like me, is very fond of opera. I'm pleased to say he got it." I was pleased, too—pleased that Chelsea Quinn Yarbro had answered my question and doubly pleased that the dedication to Lee was only about opera. I could go back to being enamored of him as though I had a monopoly on it.

I wondered what he would be like in person. Before I began buying books about Lee, I was sure he'd be as intimidating as the Count. In the movies, he was an expert at taking on the dark countenance of Dracula, and he had no trouble displaying aristocratic reserve, which could have been because a real count—Italian—figured into Lee's ancestry.

At the other end of the spectrum, this was the man who watched Sylvester the Cat cartoons with Peter Cushing—the actor who played Dracula's nemesis, Van Helsing—and sang opera to Cushing while they were in their horror costumes. In my research, I came across many photos in which he was smiling.

I believe you should see your heroes, and in 1999 I had an opportunity to see Christopher Lee. It is one of the regrets of my life that I didn't take it.

Lee appeared in person at Midnight Marquee's Monster Rally in Crystal City, Virginia. What were the chances that the seventy-seven-year-old actor would attend a horror convention in the United States twenty-seven years after he had given up the role of Dracula? But he did, and attending that convention would have given me a rare chance to see and possibly meet my favorite actor. I talked myself out of it, for many of the same reasons I'd postponed my trip to Romania. What did he have to do, ring my doorbell?

Lee held an interview during the Monster Rally. I ordered the videotape, "An Afternoon with Christopher Lee." When it came in the mail, I played it immediately, leaning in toward the TV screen to take in every word. The interview tape is a constant close-up, nothing creative in the way of camera work but a treasure because someone thought to capture Christopher Lee answering questions for ninety-two minutes. I strained to hear it while watching his face.

The disappointing aspect of the tape was the positioning of the camera, the microphone, and Lee's mouth: They all aligned. As a result, for most of the video the microphone blocked his mouth when he spoke, preventing the viewer from seeing him form the words. This is significant: Lee's British accent, coupled with the speed at which he talked, made it impossible to catch the entire interview—a tragedy.

On the up side, the video was full of sweet moments in which we saw Lee unmasked, speaking without costume or makeup of his life and career; his cherished friendship with Peter Cushing; and the Dracula film that might never be, the one that would incorporate Bram Stoker's words and follow the novel faithfully. Lee has often said that such a film would be the only thing to entice him back into the role of Dracula one more time.

Nobody did Dracula like Christopher Lee. I loved the hisses, the bared fangs, the bloodshot eyes. I loved the thrill of him on the castle stairs: his long legs taking the steps two at a time; and, coming down, the way his feet lightly tapped each stair as his full, black cloak billowed out behind him. I loved the way he bounded into a room, full of fury and purpose, as though time was running out for him, and it was.

Lee refused to be defined by his defining role. "At the age of fifty," he said in the Monster Rally interview, "I took the firm decision to Draculate no more. . . . I declared that I'd never get back on board unless the story faithfully followed the book."

Though he has always expressed gratitude for the part that made him a star, Lee also has made great efforts to move on. Even as he continued to make Dracula films, he sought to escape his most famous role. He went on to make more than 250 movies after *Dracula* and was made a Commander of the British Empire by Queen Elizabeth II. He became a beloved film legend, and like his most famous character, immortal.

Lee had been to Romania in the 1970s. Now I was on my way there to follow the footsteps of a fictitious character—Dracula; but it was this man, this movie Dracula, that I wanted to find—or at least his essence. I already knew in my bones that Lee would not be at the other end of my journey. The villagers were not afraid of him. They were not sitting around the tavern afraid to go outside for fear of an actor. But I was thrilled to think that I would see the same sights—same castles, same clouds, same moon—that he had seen when he visited the country to film a documentary; that I might actually step where his shoes had been. It was pure hero worship.

I recently became the proud owner of a Hammer Deluxe Collector Edition action figure of Christopher Lee as Count Dracula. I'd had a picture of it on my bulletin board for months, trying to decide if a grown woman ought to spend $49 on a doll. What would I do with it, really? Would I look at it? Play with it? Act out murder scenes with my little granddaughter's Dora the Explorer? Then my birthday came, and there was a package from Annie and her mom and dad containing the cloaked figure in its own black box with blood-red lettering. Along the side is the word *Dracula* in Old English Text, and on the front a big, black *h*, surrounded in red like a raised seal, the official logo of Hammer Films. The top of the box closes with Velcro over a clear piece of plastic that protects the figure inside, the little souvenirs that came with it, and the stand on which the figure would rest if I took it out of the package.

I call my new friend Chris, a nickname I'd never use if I were introduced to the man; but this is harmless enough, and it gives me a feeling of connectedness—as though he were close by. We can form relationships with inanimate objects, and sometimes they're more cooperative than people. Tom Hanks's character discovered this in *Cast Away*. Marooned on a deserted island, he spent much of the movie talking to a volleyball.

Chris is twelve inches high. He's dressed in "real fabric clothes": black pants, a black cape, and a white shirt sporting little gold cufflinks with red centers. His hair is gray. The color of his eyes is difficult to determine, but they are bloodshot. His fangs are bared, though not bloody. His hands open to hold the three Authentic Accessories that came with the figure: a tiny version of Jonathan Harker's diary bound in red, a flaming candlestick, and a cross on a chain. The little hands have veins and fingernails, and on the left pinky is a Dracula ring, not removable. The fingers are curled slightly, so that you can pose the figure as menacing, with its hands reaching out toward a victim.

Children zero to three years old are warned away from this action figure, which is not billed as a toy. All the same, I ordered one for Annie, who was precocious at three. She knew who Dracula was, and she was already making do in play scenarios with her collection of Disney Princesses. In spite of its lack of a physical resemblance to the Count, Annie had already drafted her little figure of Pocahontas into service as Dracula.

Christopher Lee died many times in the role of Dracula: slowly turning to dust in the sunlight, falling through the ice in a frozen moat, impaled on a cross, falling onto a church altar, burning, and descending toward the Argeş River in a screaming flame. He always came back.

I wanted Lee to stay alive forever. As of this writing he was still acting, though in less strenuous parts. I still wanted to see him play Dracula again. Was it possible that someone in the next few years would create a screenplay that followed the novel faithfully and was so smart, fine, and thrilling that Lee would not be able to resist the leading role?

I hoped to see the actor I loved don the white shirt, red-centered cuff-links, and long, black cape again; but I didn't hold much sway over Hollywood legends. If it didn't happen, at least I'd have my action figure, Chris. I was willing to bet he'd wear his little Dracula cloak forever.

In the meantime, I had a trip to take. I was about to look for my one and only Dracula where the legend had trod.

Part 2

Magic Places

Chapter 10

First Impressions

My first glimpse of Romania was from the window of an Air France jet. We had left Paris three and a half hours before, and now the plane was in its initial descent into Central Europe. We entered Romanian air space from the west and crossed two-thirds of the country to reach Bucharest, in the southeast. As we flew lower, I tried to put my usual paralyzing terror aside and concentrate on the view rather than the nuances of the plane going through its changes.

Spread out below us was a patchwork of farmland: sunny, green and brown, with roads snaking through the landscape and dense woods breaking up the flatness. As we approached Bucharest, the cloud cover increased. *Nuts!* I strained to see the ground, but the clouds were so thick it was hard to get a sense of the land. A mist followed us most of the way down. At least that seemed in sync with all my fantasies.

I was looking for magic, fully aware I might not find it. In his novel, Bram Stoker described a whole country he had never visited. I'd been like Stoker in the months before my trip, trying to picture a place I'd never been. What really was the difference between life and a movie set? I didn't know, but I was about to find out.

I got off the plane in a drizzle. Once inside Otopeni International Airport, I stopped at the first window I saw and took out my camera. I took a picture of the jet sitting at the gate, capturing my own reflection in the process—a ghost image, overlaid on the wet pavement.

On the way to baggage claim, I passed a money-changing counter. Had I read that I shouldn't change my American cash at the airport? I couldn't remember why, and it was so easy to swerve a few steps to my left and take care of that little order of business. Having Romanian cash the minute I entered the country would give me one less thing to worry about later.

The Romanian monetary system was based on the leu ("loo"); plural, lei ("lay"). A dollar was worth about thirty-two lei at the time, so I walked away with a healthy handful of money. I immediately liked the multicolored Romanian bills with their little transparent windows. Carrying so many of them away from the cash counter, I felt like Herman Munster of the slot-machine Munsters. Since the old TV series ended, Frankenstein-faced Herman and the other characters have shown up in gambling casinos on "Munster"-themed slot machines. When you hit a jackpot, Herman's voice cries from the machine, "I'm rich! I'm rich!"

The baggage claim area was dim and almost deserted by the time I arrived. Only a few people milled around, found their luggage, and left. It was easy to find my suitcase and tripod bag on the carousel. Now, with my carry-on, I had three bags to manage. I needed to find my guide from the Romanian travel agency.

When a young man with several suitcases on a cart passed me by, I knew I had not yet found my guide. Deflated, I sat down on a bench and watched people for a while, but foot traffic had really slowed down. I looked around for someone who might also be looking for me. I knew my guide was a man, and I pictured him wearing a black jacket of rough wool, rumpled khaki pants or cheap polyester trousers, simple black tie shoes, and a hat covering strands of dark, greasy hair. He might have a few facial moles. No one that I saw matched the description, and no one gave me a glance.

Now what? I tried my new cell phone, but it didn't work. So much for the international calling service my travel agent had secured for my Cincinnati Bell flip phone. I thought I'd be able to use the phone easily in Romania, but it was useless—at least on that first day.

I felt deserted and frustrated. Was my guide a no-show already? I'd hardly landed! And why couldn't I get a signal on my phone? More to the point, what would I do if I could? Did I know how to reach the Romanian travel agency, now my only hope? Frankly, I didn't even know how to dial a Bucharest number.

I felt stupid and helpless. After all the planning, the anticipation, and the long flight, I hadn't even made it out of the airport yet. My sense of high adventure faded, and in its place were fatigue and abandonment. I couldn't have been any lonelier if I were the last person on earth.

Loneliness gave way to panic as the minutes ticked by. What should I do? I couldn't sit in the airport all day. Most of the other travelers had left. I looked down at the bright orange luggage tags I'd bought, the ones intended to identify me as part of a worldwide network of women travelers. *I could use a Journeywoman or two about now,* I thought, but I wasn't going to find them here. I got up and walked over to a woman who was standing alone near the baggage carousel. "Do you speak English?" I asked. She did. "A guide was to meet me," I said. "Now I'm not sure what to do."

"They are not allowed inside," she said in a heavy accent. "You must go through customs." *Oh.* I'd forgotten all about customs. "Go through that door. Someone will check your passport. Your guide should be waiting outside." And that quickly, I had a new lease on life.

I burst out into the light, and there was the crowd I'd been looking for. A throng of people stood on the other side of a fence. There in the center of the group was a man watching me. Well, they were all watching me because I was the only person who'd come out the door. But this man's arms poked over the top of the fence, and he was holding a sign with my name on it, like in the movies. He didn't look like the guide I'd imagined, but I knew who he was when our eyes met in instant recognition. I don't know what initial impression I made on him. No doubt he'd been waiting a while, probably wondering where in the world I was, but his face bore no particular expression.

Lucian introduced himself—first name only—and swept my luggage off its cart. Relief spread through me like a drug in my veins. First impressions: He was good looking, well dressed, and professional. He spoke to me in English with a nice accent. All of it was gravy on that wet and gloomy Bucharest afternoon.

Right off the bat I could have made something of the fact that his name was Lucian, which was close enough to *Lucifer* to shift my imagination from Neutral into Drive and floor it. But this isn't fiction, and I don't want to overpromise. I will say that I was so glad to see him that he could have been the Prince of Darkness and I would have followed him to his car.

The car was a blue sedan. A light rain was falling. Our first business together was getting my bags loaded into the car and getting me to my hotel. We did all of that around the barest of verbal exchanges, yet I was comfortable with this man sitting a few feet from me in the front seat.

I knew one thing before we ever left the parking lot: Anne was right. I had a cute guide, and he had to be near my age. What were the chances?

Lucian was tall—about six feet—and lean but not skinny. The Romanian summers were warm like those in the States, and his face and arms were tan from the sun. He had a sleek look, the way his head was shaped and his hair cut short, most of it on the sides rather than on the top. His eyes were dark, alert, and gentle at the same time. He had a bushy mustache and a graying beard. I could also see some gray chest hair curling above the open top button of his shirt. Of course my eyes slid to his ring finger. He didn't wear a wedding band, and there was no tan line to indicate where one might have been.

I'd noticed his clothes right away. Clothes were a preoccupation of mine, an awareness that had been drilled into me in childhood when my mother commented on my outfits. *What you wear is important. What others think is important. And what you wear is tied to what other people think.* Lucian wore my favorite type of clothing: outdoor adventure wear. Were we in for an adventure? I hoped so.

Lucian maneuvered the car out of the airport and headed for downtown Bucharest. If you believe the literature—with the exception of Romanian travel brochures—Bucharest is a dump, full of stray dogs, pickpockets, begging children, and women throwing fake babies at the tourists so we'll take our hands off our valuables to catch the infants. Bucharest had been described as a city of mismatched buildings with broken-down cars on the streets and garbage-strewn empty lots, not to mention shady characters and crooked politicians. It sounded about as appealing as a bat bite.

Living near Cincinnati, I'd grown used to cities and their headlines; corruption and crime had lost their shock value. So why was I nervous about Bucharest? Maybe it was the dogs. In Glen Ferris, Joe and I weren't allowed to have a dog. The reason was our location—too close to the road, a rule I understood when Billie's new black puppy, Midnight, was hit by a car. The only dogs I'd known, I'd known briefly. The first, my grandparents' beloved Irish setter, bit me and was put to sleep. The second, a stray we took in when my son was in grade school, resisted all training and finally wound up in a pet shelter. All the other dogs in my life had belonged to other people. Because of all that, I was uneasy around strange dogs.

When I pictured Romanian women, I pictured roundness; pale, bare faces; wide smiles revealing missing teeth; and hair hidden under a black scarf. In one of the few stories I'd heard back in America, someone's grandmother lived in rural Romania. When the family visited and took her riding in a car, she was so frightened that all she did was scream. They bought her a refrigerator, and she used it to store her winter clothes.

As we rode into Bucharest, my impression was that the capital of Romania was tan. Tan buildings, one after another, defined the downtown and looked boring against the gray sky. The first and only one I recognized was the InterContinental Hotel, hard to miss with its twenty-five stories dominating a city block and rising above all the neighboring buildings. A few blocks ahead, my home for the next two nights was tan, too.

Grandmama would have called it bone. Bone was her favorite color because it went with everything. When I was young and Grandmama would take me shopping for clothes in Charleston, West Virginia, I could count on at least one suggestion along those neutral color lines: bone shoes, a bone coat, or a bone purse for sure. If I'd listened to all of them, I'd have looked like a walking billboard for bone.

My hotel faced a street several lanes wide, but there was no parking spot in front of it. A bellman in uniform stood outside as we pulled up onto the edge of the sidewalk. I could tell that he knew Lucian, had seen him before—maybe many times. I liked that now he knew I was with Lucian, as though it would give me an "in." Lucian got out, removed my bags from the trunk, and accompanied me inside.

The registration desk was straight ahead, the lobby off to the right. Just inside the big windows were a few couches and tables, empty. A step at the far side of the lobby led up to a bar and restaurant, also empty. Lucian stood at the desk with me through the short registration process. I got my room key—not the plastic card I'd expected, but a regular key on a metal holder that weighed about two tons.

After confirming our dinner plans for the evening, Lucian left, saying he had to work on his apartment. I needed to get settled, but I thought his departure was abrupt.

The elevator was one of those cute European ones with room for only one or two people and their luggage. It had an iron grille for a door, with a turning knob. The door clicked into place on level "P" (for *parter,* the ground floor); then I pushed my floor button the way I would in any elevator. I got out on four and made my way down a hall past brown wooden doors, all closed. I found my room and dragged my three bags into a little hallway with clothing hooks on one wall and the bathroom door on the other.

The room was about the size of the middle bedroom in a middle-class American home, with the bed taking up most of the space. The furnishings were old-fashioned: a dressing table with a mirror, a small TV, and an armoire. All of the furniture was painted white, in some Queen Anne style, curvy and feminine. The bedspread and sheer curtains were white, too, making the room seem princess-y, truly the last thing I cared about; but I did care that everything matched and that the room was tasteful, not just a notch above a flophouse hell-hole as I had feared.

I didn't unpack because we'd be in Bucharest only two nights before moving on. I hung my rain jacket on one of the hooks, extracted my toilet kit from its pouch on the front of the suitcase, and got out the security cable I'd bought after reading that nothing is safe in a hotel room. I'd need the cable in a few hours. Lucian and I were dining at the Count Dracula Club. I had time alone to wind down and get my bearings before he would come with the blue car, pull the right wheels up onto the sidewalk, and pick me up. No doubt he'd leave the car running while he came into the hotel; I already knew he was that quick.

I'd discovered a minibar in the armoire during my initial hotel snoop, the time when I wonder if the previous guests have left anything interesting in the drawers or closets. Once in Lexington, Kentucky, I found a sex manual taped to the underside of a nightstand drawer. I'd been moved from my original room because the lights didn't work, and they'd quickly put me two doors down from Housekeeping. It was obvious that my new location was the trysting place for the hotel staff.

The minibar in my room in Bucharest contained, in addition to various junk food delights, bottled water. Good. I knew that I'd need *plata*, the flat alternative to the carbonated water sold in Romania. I always thought ahead to the coffee. It was the first thing I needed when I woke.

I turned on the TV, another piece of travel advice carried out. Leaving the television on low can be a deterrent to burglars, so say the experts; when I left, the noise would make it seem that the room was still occupied. There might be a few thieves working Bucharest who didn't know that one.

I flipped through the channels and found an American movie. They're shown on Romanian TV with either subtitles or the sound dubbed in. There was a familiar face: Lexi, the teenage anorexic. I'd seen the Lifetime movie twice in America. Now Lexi's mom, played by former Wonder Woman Lynda Carter, was agonizing in Romanian about the girl's shocking weight loss.

Across the street, the word "Mirage" blinked at me from ground level. The entrance was unmistakable with its flashing neon border that beckoned like an old friend. It had to be a casino! Could it be that the Las Vegas Mirage had a Romanian counterpart? I doubted it, but was that important? No. And what did a casino have to do with Dracula? Nothing, but it seemed I had brought my proclivity to gamble across the ocean with me.

It was only mid-afternoon. The sun was finally shining, and I wasn't going to sit in my room until dinner. While I'd been busy taking preventive measures against bandits of the two-armed variety at the hotel, the one-armed kind were waiting for me across the street.

Chapter 11

One-Armed Bandits

To heck with the displaced dogs I thought would be lurking outside the hotel, ready to jump up and take a hunk out of me. I could hop over a few dogs. Heck with the fake babies and pint-sized pickpockets, too. I used my new locking cable to lash my suitcases to the legs of the white armoire in my room, and off I went to negotiate the wide boulevard below.

Gambling is one of my escapes and casinos, my hidey-holes—places where I can slip away and feel right at home; where they'll take me as I am, and I don't ever have to see them again. At home I tell myself that the intense focus on the spinning slots will clear my mind, or that the one-hour drive to the nearest casino will give me a chance to think. A psychologist might come up with some other possibilities.

Here's what I like about gambling. A casino is like a party you're always invited to, 24/7, with music and noise and people. You can arrive when you want, stay as long as you like, and leave when you feel like it. You can bring as many guests as you want, but you can also go alone. And if you do go alone, you won't feel self-conscious. No one will know or care.

It's a party without the responsibilities of a party: You don't have to dress up, bring food, make conversation, or even be polite. You can smoke and drink, or not. You can talk or not, look around or not, sit in one spot all night if that's what you want to do. You have to spend money, but sometimes you get money.

For the socially awkward, the introverted, and the commitment phobic, gambling is ideal. Going to a casino is like having friends, only simpler. They don't know you and you don't know them. To me, a casino is a wonderland, and who would have guessed I'd be standing at the entrance to one shortly after arriving in Romania?

I went in through the door I'd seen from my room, walking past blinking neon palm trees to a hallway where a woman sat behind a desk. As it turned out, I had to get a membership. *That'll come in handy,* I quipped to myself, knowing I wasn't going to spend any significant time in Bucharest.

Oh, good, I thought, peering past the desk—*slot machines!* The day my fascination with slots started I was probably in junior high, swimming away a summer day with my brother at Hawks Nest Country Club in West Virginia. Joe was maybe ten.

Hawks Nest had a nine-hole golf course, a pool, and a two-story clubhouse with dressing rooms, banquet facilities, and a snack bar. The snack bar had a window to the outside. When we were wet, we simply went up to the window and ordered our hot dog or hamburger. Once in a while, we sat inside with the grown-ups, surrounded by chatter and the clicking of the golfers' metal spikes on the concrete floor as they came through on their way to the first tee.

The restrooms had outside entrances at the back of the clubhouse— another nod to wet suits. The women's room included showers and a changing area, and that was where I saw it: the first slot machine of my life, sitting near the doorway to the women's locker room. It cost five cents to play.

No one else was around. I had a nickel with me, so I put it in and pulled the handle. Wow! I won fifteen cents, and it might as well have been a fortune.

I hurried back to the pool as quickly as I could without getting called down for running, my bare feet making slaps on the concrete and the fifteen cents tucked into my right fist. I found Joe and opened my hand to show him the coins. I'd gone in with one nickel, and now I had three. That was big stuff for kids who got a nickel to spend at the movies.

We decided to try again. I went back into the changing area, stopping a few feet from the door. A lady was standing at the slot with her back to me. She wouldn't notice me now. She had hit pay dirt, and nickels were dropping out of the machine. She was leaning in toward the falling money, her knees bent and her hips pushed forward as she tried to block her winnings in with her stomach so they wouldn't scatter all over the floor. She caught as many coins as she could in her open purse. I remember the sound of those nickels falling, not a series of isolated metallic clinks the way my fifteen cents had sounded, but a heavy chorus. The sound of the money dropping out of the machine was mixed with the sound of the coins that missed the woman's purse and hit the silver metal tray, the ones that hit her hands, those that did make it into the purse, and a few that bounced out onto the concrete floor.

It didn't escape me that I'd missed this jackpot by seconds. If I'd returned to the slot machine a little sooner, I'd be chasing those coins and scrambling wildly for a container. The loss was offset by the possibilities. I had never seen so much free money dropping into someone's hands, and all for a nickel. I was hooked. There would be many slot machines between the one at the golf course and the ones in Bucharest.

Bucharest's Mirage was small for a casino, more like the size of a McDonald's. It was well lit and had a couple gaming tables in addition to the limited selection of slot machines lining two of the walls. Some of the machines didn't work—they were out of order or just being set up—and the ones that did were the old-fashioned kind.

In America, the days of pulling a handle on the side of a "one-armed bandit" were over. Gambling was a push-button world. Most of the older slots had been replaced with electronic versions that contained sophisticated computers, displayed digital images, and offered multiple levels of play.

Slots in America had gone to a ticket system, too, meaning that that no money would come pouring out for the winner as it had in the changing room of the golf club. Instead, the new machines would print a ticket good for the amount.

The money was something I would miss: If you hit a winning combination on a one-armed bandit, noisily releasing the coins, everyone would know you'd won. You could scoop the cash into a plastic cup and carry it around, feeling rich from the weight of it. I guessed I could do just that in the Mirage.

The casino had a betting minimum; it sounded like a lot in lei, but the US equivalent was just a few dollars. I got a cup of coins and headed for the slots, but this was no party.

The room was so quiet. No one was playing the machines until I started. The employees were standing around with nothing to do. Was it the hour of the day? Or because it was Saturday? I was the only patron until a family of three—two parents and a grown daughter—came in. They began to feed one of the slots, and the heat was off me. I forgot about everything but playing.

My mother used to like to gamble, too. We had fifteen years of pure casino fun. Even as she got into her eighties and grew frailer, gambling was one of the few pursuits we could do together. I would do the driving to the casino, let her out, and instruct her to claim the first empty wheelchair she saw. I'd wheel her into the playing area and get her situated on a stool in front of a slot machine.

"Have fun, and don't worry about me," she would always say as soon as she was comfortable. Mom could hardly wait to get rid of me, and she didn't want me to check on her. This was because in her fanny pack she had stowed several Pall Mall cigarettes to smoke while she played. I wasn't to see this, because after sixty-five years of smoking, she claimed to be quitting.

I didn't understand at first that Mom's desire to smoke was the reason she wanted me gone. I stuck to her like tape, worried because lately she hadn't a clue what to do. The changes in her were hard to miss. Mom couldn't comprehend the new machines with their digital screens and ticket system. She kept trying to put her ten-dollar bill into the slot where the payout ticket comes out when you're ready to leave the machine. Mostly she sat staring at the strange screen, very still and frail, the little bones of her shoulders shaping her suit jacket. When she'd spent her limit of twenty dollars, she refused to put any more into "those funny machines."

Mom realized she'd been left standing at the station by the times. She knew that she was no fun; that she didn't understand or enjoy the games any more. She felt ignorant, a horrible feeling for any of us. On top of that, she knew she was helpless without me, without the wheelchair. She knew it was a challenge for me to maneuver it around the crowded floor of the casino, and that when we parked the chair she would have a hard time getting in and out of it.

It wasn't fun for me by then, either. By the time we walked out—well, I walked and she rode—my state of mind was dismal with thoughts of death, decay, aging, frailty, devotion, loss, and guilt. You name it, I felt it. The elderly are between two worlds, this one and the next. Do you think they are not the undead? Think again.

American casinos were loaded with people like Mom—the elderly, the infirm. Some were better off than she was, walking on their own with fanny packs at their waists, out for a day of recreation. Others were feeble but got around with walkers, personal wheelchairs, or electric mobility scooters. Some patrons were worse off than Mom, many of them emphysema patients on portable oxygen systems. It didn't keep them from the smoky casinos. In America, gray heads and wheelchairs were common sights. In contrast, I got the feeling that the customer expected in the Mirage might be James Bond in a tuxedo.

I didn't stay long. Gambling there wasn't all that tempting, and I wanted to be ready when Lucian came to pick me up for dinner. I walked back out into the late-afternoon sunshine and headed to the hotel.

Before going down to the lobby to wait for Lucian, I took the cable off the armoire and instead fastened my luggage to the pipes under the bathroom sink so I wouldn't scratch the furniture. The last thing I thought about before going out the door was how smart I'd been to invest in that cable. It would be very unlikely for a burglar to get those bags loose. If he did, he'd cause a flood.

Chapter 12

Jenny Meets Dracula

The outside of the Count Dracula Club drips "blood." Of course it does; what else would you expect? The thick, red substance oozes from joints in the masonry, dots the front of the bone-colored building, and even drips down the panes of the two lampposts outside the restaurant.

Lucian and I set out for our meal at twilight, dressed for the occasion. He had put on a red shirt, and I was dressed all in black with my large silver crucifix decorating my neck. From the hotel, we made a couple of turns and then drove south along the historic Calea Victoriei (Victory Avenue), so named in 1878 after Romania's victory over the Turks in the War of Independence.

Lucian drove, of course, and I looked out the window. I already thought he wasn't the type to give a running narrative. I suppose he would have if I'd asked, but I wasn't the type to need one. I was happy to take in the loveliness of the neighborhood in early evening.

The buildings of central Bucharest took on a charm in the fading light. I could see why the city had been nicknamed "Little Paris" and "Paris of the East" in the 1900s; its residual beauty was evident in the neoclassical buildings we passed while riding along shaded blocks of fashionable shops, museums, galleries, and hotels. The University of Bucharest was nearby. A few people were out walking and traffic was light, as the rush hour had come and gone. I hadn't been to Paris, unless you count changing planes at the airport, but I had the impression of it for a few blocks that night.

Calea Victoriei runs into Splaiul Independenței, another main thoroughfare near the center of the city and home to the Count Dracula Club. Lucian parked across the street not far from the Dâmbovița River and we walked over to a converted row house I could have identified in my sleep. The black metal sign by the door was shaped like a scroll and lettered in red Gothic type:

𝕮𝖔𝖚𝖓𝖙

𝕯𝖗𝖆𝖈𝖚𝖑𝖆

𝕯𝖆𝖎𝖑𝖞 15–01

𝕾𝖚𝖓𝖉𝖆𝖞 17–01

Red dripped at the edges of the sign, and some of the windows had red curtains. A black metal awning shaped like a bat in flight hung above the front door. It must have had a wingspan of five or six feet. The tail end near the building was high and the front tipped down, so that the bat appeared ready to dive-bomb us where we stood.

Light glowed through the top of the very tall front door, which was black with an ordinary round knob and a peephole in one of the panels. When I was young, my dad frequented a place called Al's Club. When Dad mentioned it, I used to wonder why owls would need a club. I later learned it was a restaurant and bar for people, rumored to have an after-hours operation that was infamous for bootlegging, gambling, and prostitution. Dad liked to bet on sports, and I doubted he'd turn down a drink, but I hope his interest ended there.

The entrance to Al's was a door located at the top of a steep set of stairs. The door had a peephole, and patrons were admitted only after being approved from inside. I wondered if, when I looked up at the peephole of the Count Dracula Club, I'd see a flap open and the bloodshot eye of Igor or Lurch looking us over. I guess Igor would have been too bent over for that.

I'd first read about the Count Dracula Club in a magazine. The brief description had been just enough to feed my fantasies of what I would see inside—a room full of diners chatting at tables in the low light. None seemed to notice the lone gentleman suspiciously dressed in a black cape, his food untouched. He was always sitting with his back to me. Was it Dracula? I wanted it to be Christopher Lee dressed as the Count. That's the nice thing about fantasies: Everyone does your bidding.

A male staffer greeted us and gave us a tour of the club, which consisted of the ground floor and a cellar. The stairwell leading down was part brick, part plaster with deliberate damage to the smoother surface, giving it a run-down, spooky appearance. The walls were decorated with plaster statues wearing cloth capes, life-sized hands that seemed to burst through from the other side, and framed photos acknowledging the movie Draculas. To my great joy, there was Christopher Lee in his glossy black-and-white Hammer Films glory. In the first photo he, lay in a narrow coffin with his hands wrapped around a wooden stake so big it extended out of the frame. With the business end of the stake in his middle, Lee's Dracula face was frozen in a horrific, wide-eyed, fang-baring scream. The other photo of Lee in the little wall gallery showed him about to bite the neck of actress Veronica Carlson, who played Maria in *Dracula Has Risen from the Grave*.

Each room of the Count Dracula Club depicted a different part of the Dracula legend. We toured the rooms on the lower floor—the Cellar, the Library, the Chapel, and the Alchemical Bar, which counted the "Transfusion" among its themed drinks, recalling the scene in *Horror of Dracula* when Dr. Van Helsing dramatically rolled up his sleeve and performed a blood transfusion on the vampire victim Lucy. Unfortunately, it was a temporary solution; Lucy couldn't seem to resist further encounters with the Count.

Returning to the main level, Lucian and I walked through the Transylvanian Room, the Hunting Room—where the skin of a wolf hung upon one wall—and finally the Medieval Room. Diners were scattered throughout the restaurant, but the place was not busy and we had our choice of rooms. Lucian deferred to me, so we ate in the Medieval Room. It was the one with the red curtains I'd seen from the street. The room was small, and we had it to ourselves.

The white walls of our dining room dripped red from the point where they met the ceiling. Each table had a red tablecloth with a flat, black bat appliquéd to the center. The wooden chairs were black. On the windows were detailed black sketches of soldiers in suits of armor. Weapons and wrought-iron continued the battle theme inside. Candles burned in metal holders, their drippings forming thickening arcs of wax between flame and base.

This room could easily have been called the Vlad room for its emphasis on the local hero named Vlad Dracula. Vlad (rather than the Count) was Romania's idea of Dracula; well, more accurately, he was Romania's real Dracula.

In all the time I'd spent falling in love with Romania through books and movies, I had given little thought to Vlad, also known as Vlad Tepes and Vlad the Impaler. Vlad was a Romanian prince who ruled the province of Wallachia in the fifteenth century during a time when the Turks were doing their best to take over everything in Europe. He was a warrior in battle who defended his land and people. Vlad was also a fearsome tyrant given to acts of cruelty, such as torture and mass murder, sometimes against his own constituents. He earned his reputation as the "Impaler" by impaling his enemies on long wooden stakes and displaying their bodies as a warning to others. With his name and evil reputation, it was inevitable that Vlad Dracula would be connected to the fictional monster, Count Dracula—especially in Romania. But that's another story.

I really wasn't interested in Vlad. In fact, for a while when I was planning my trip, I called him "Vlad the Impostor" and "Vlad the Interloper." Vlad was someone who got wedged into my vision of Dracula and my idea of what I wanted Romania to be.

As we waited for our server, Lucian smoked in the dim light while I took in more of the décor. One wall of our dining room bore a cloth banner depicting the logo of the Order of the Dragon, a society of monarchs (including Vlad) with a dragon as its symbol. On another wall, beneath a pair of crossed swords, was Vlad's portrait, the very one I'd seen in books and on the Internet. I'd already dubbed it "old faithful": Vlad apparently sat for only the one portrait, and subsequent portraits were painted from it. The man has been described as handsome, but you couldn't prove it from that portrait.

Vlad is posed in a cape and a pearl-encrusted red hat with a jeweled, eight-pointed star at the front. His dark hair cascades past his shoulders in corkscrew curls. His eyes protrude from a thin face. His nose is quite long, his lower lip is large, and his upper lip seems to be missing—but that's only a guess as to what's going on beneath the sinister-looking black mustache that curls at the ends and extends past the width of his face. And have I mentioned that whoever said he was good-looking needed glasses?

The Count Dracula Club, according to what I'd read, had hired a local actor to entertain dinner guests as the Count on weekends; I was expecting a show that night. After all, the itinerary had said, "Count Dracula himself will make a guest appearance. . . . Don't worry, YOU are not on the menu!" But, instead of a show—or even an actor working the tables—Lucian and I dined in relative quiet. I didn't complain about the lack of a performance; I was thrilled to be sitting in the Count Dracula Club at all. Besides that, Lucian and I were new to each other, having our first meal together as guide and guided.

I was already trying to read Lucian from across the table. He wasn't exactly an open book, sitting there with a pair of little reading glasses perched on the end of his nose. I thought he seemed aloof, bored, or maybe just plain tired. I was tired, too, my body clock all screwed up, and I wasn't even sure I liked this man.

At least he was there with me. I'd traveled to Romania alone, but I wouldn't have wanted to eat alone in that dimly lit red-and-black room with its walls screaming "Vlad" and the Romanian menu a complete mystery. I wouldn't have been afraid, in spite of the bloodthirsty theme of the restaurant, but I would have been self-conscious and probably lonely.

It was fun to look at the black-bound menu with its themed entrées, even though I had no clue what most of them really were: Platou Van Helsing; the Evil's Salad; Count's Castle Mixed Grill; Count Dracula's Beefsteak; and Renfield's Dish: "The blood is life." Renfield was a mental patient who answered to the fictional Count Dracula. When he wasn't wearing a straitjacket or trying to escape, Renfield captured and ate flies and other creepy-crawlies. Hmmm, what would his dish be?

I should have been used to foreign food—if we define *foreign* the way my mother did, to include everything that originated outside West Virginia—and I was. Thanks to my publishing job, I'd traveled and eaten in fine restaurants all over America. But Glen Ferris hadn't been the place to develop a sophisticated palate unless you cooked the exotic dishes yourself. It happened occasionally; once Grandmama, the undisputed cook in the family, made baked Alaska just so I could see what it was like. I still remember the wonder of it when she opened the oven door: the high dome of warm meringue, its whipped tips toasted light brown, and the miracle inside—cake layered with ice cream!

As for dining choices, our town had one restaurant. It was part of the Glen Ferris Inn. The dining room had a certain homey elegance, its printed wallpaper and fresh flowers welcoming not only the townspeople, but many visitors to our region. The inn was a place where home-cooked meals were served on white tablecloths to people dressed for business or church or a trip to Charleston.

We didn't frequent the inn, and I can only guess at the reasons. Maybe it was the dressing up, although Dad in particular liked to put on a clean outfit and go somewhere. It could have been the cost, but we weren't so poor—in spite of my parents' complaints about money—that we couldn't have gone to the inn to eat once in a while. Even Grandmama and Grandpop were missing from the inn crowd. In fact, I don't remember them going out to eat at all; but in those days people didn't ask each other, "Where do you want to eat tonight?" They ate at home.

I wish I'd taken a menu from the Count Dracula Club. It did occur to me, but that's not my style. Besides, it was my first night in town, and I had too many other things on my mind. In choosing my meal, I took the path of least resistance and asked Lucian to order for me. The ordering was easier that way, and quicker, but eating was another story.

All of the Dracula books seem to do the same when it comes to the topic of food, which is to tell what everyone ate. I'll do what I can, but I'm a traveler who dreads the dining part of a trip. Being in the Count Dracula Club was one thing, but eating there just raised a host of issues.

Compulsive overeating is officially a disease, like alcoholism, with its own twelve-step recovery program. It's a disease I know well, although as a teenager I was skinny and lacked an appetite. Food issues abounded in our family. My brother ate one thing at a time. He didn't want his foods to touch on his plate. Dad always told us he was running away from bread, bringing to mind a picture of Dad booking down the street in Glen Ferris with a slice of white bread in hot pursuit. The bread had little cartoon arms and legs, and a face—no doubt with an intent expression. Mom, the product of a traditional home, had a mother who made meals from scratch and panned out rolls every Saturday morning. Ironically, Mom wasn't that interested in food or cooking. Maybe her smoking habit had something to do with it. Of course, Dad smoked too, but what I remember most about him at the table was the way he'd stuff food into his cheeks like a squirrel, then chew and swallow it, and start again. Sometimes he'd talk during the process. "See food," anyone?

Sitting in the Count Dracula Club with Lucian, I thought about my history with diets. Since reaching adulthood, I'd been through a boatload of plans, pills, potions, and programs to address my eating compulsion and keep my weight under control: Overeaters Anonymous, Yoga, Slim-Fast, Metabolife, figure salons, the apple diet, the cabbage soup diet, the Hollywood 48-Hour Miracle Diet, fat-burning recipes, and now Jenny Craig. I was currently counting on Jenny to save me from myself.

By the time I arrived in Romania, I had been on the Jenny Craig weight-loss program for more than three years, the last two devoted to maintenance. I'd lost fifteen pounds, but my time with Jenny had grown to resemble a prison sentence in that I was not sure I could make it outside the program. I was facing nearly three weeks off my twelve-hundred-calorie-a-day diet, in a foreign country with all of the anxieties that could stir up, not to mention new experiences with food. I felt like one of the released prisoners from *The Shawshank Redemption,* afraid I wouldn't be able to take my place in the world and operate alongside those who didn't have my problem.

The Jenny Craig organization publishes a little book called the *Dining Out Guide,* a compilation of advice on how to use good sense when eating away from home. One section provides "Visual Cues for Common Foods," so that when we're away from our diet plans, we can eat reasonable portions instead of the ridiculous heaps of food that restaurants generally serve.

Our server at the Count Dracula Club placed a platter of cheese, peppers, pickles, and bread between Lucian and me. When had I last eaten? It must have been on the plane. Everything looked good; just back a dump truck up to my plate.

To accompany the appetizers, we each had a glass of red wine. I didn't bring the *Dining Out Guide* with me, but I can tell you what Jenny says about alcohol: For those interested in consistent weight loss, it's best to limit your intake to two servings a week. "Over-indulging," the advice reads, "can lower your inhibitions and numb hunger cues, leading you to overeat." As for the appetizers, I didn't have a visual cue for bread, and Jenny's cheese advice pertained to shredded, the kind you would put on a salad. I was on my own. Vlad looked down from his portrait as I dug in. No doubt he would have rolled his big, fat eyes if he could.

The main course consisted of meat, meat, and more meat—I think three kinds—as well as carrots, broccoli, and turnips. Jenny recommends three ounces of meat, which on a dinner plate would be equivalent in size to a deck of cards. The recommended half-cup of potatoes would be the size of a small fist. A cup of raw vegetables would be equal in volume to a light bulb, and to estimate a cup of casserole, Jenny advises that we picture a kitchen sponge on our plate. Ugh.

I thought of all the women in books and movies who go to dinner, then sit and push their food around on their plate because they aren't hungry. I had no idea what that was like.

I got through the various Dracula-themed recipes, tasting each one but managing not to finish them. Then I ordered ice cream for dessert. If Jenny Craig had been sitting next to me, she would have suggested two square inches of cake instead. The ice cream was served in a large glass bowl on a stem, three scoops under a drizzle of chocolate syrup. I ate it while Lucian waited.

By the time we left the Count Dracula Club, it was nearly eleven in Bucharest. I couldn't even count the hours I'd been up, and I was full to the brim with food. If one dinner was difficult, what would the rest of the vacation be? A food nightmare, that's what. I needed one of those colorful rubber wristbands people wear to support causes or research. I could look at it and be reminded of how I would feel going home with five or ten extra pounds—not in my suitcase, but on my body. "WWJD," my wristband would say: "What would Jenny do?" I already knew what Dracula would do. All of his meals were the liquid variety.

Back in my white, princesslike hotel room, I took a few precautions. The bed was luxuriously wide and appeared clean, but I got out my DreamSack anyway. The DreamSack is a silk sleeping bag meant to separate one's body from hotel bedding germs. Any time you're in doubt about the accommodations, just whip out the DreamSack, spread it out between the sheets, and curl up. I left the TV on low and shoved a rubber doorstop under the door to keep the burglars out. Finally, I pinched the draperies together with a plastic clip to foil the peepers. Of course, the only one who would have made it up to my fourth-floor window would have been Spiderman—or Dracula.

I wrote my impressions of my first day in Bucharest and then lay down on the wide bed, which defied its fluffy looks by feeling more like a sheet of plywood. Images of my first day in Romania swirled through my brain along with the wine from dinner. I shut my eyes and there was Jenny Craig herself, looking as she did on the cover of her autobiography, which was displayed in every weight-loss centre: young, trim, entrepreneurial, and smiling with confidence as she walked along a beach somewhere, her red hair blowing.

The food in my stomach felt like a lump of lead. The Count Dracula Club had been fun to see, but I was already experiencing a familiar sinking regret at what I'd eaten for dinner. Maybe I'd be all right between Jenny and Lucian; he seemed only mildly interested in food, and he certainly wasn't carrying any extra weight. I bet he couldn't even "pinch an inch" of that lean body.

Chapter 13

A Gaggle of Gadgets

I had to get my act together. On my first morning in Bucharest, I'd overslept! Lucian would be picking me up all too soon for our day of touring the city, and could I even be ready?

I could blame it on jet lag, but I'd set my travel alarm the night before—or, at least I thought I had. The clock was new. Buying it had been a no-brainer as I was planning what to pack in my lone suitcase: The clock was small and flat, weighed almost nothing, and displayed the time of every country in the world. Who could resist? I'd tried to memorize the instructions back home, but I must have forgotten something. The alarm hadn't gone off, and I'd slept an extra fifty minutes.

I'd been exhausted the night before. In fact, when I'd come back from dinner, I'd started to unlock my hotel room door and found it already unlocked. Yikes! I freaked out—anybody would; but there, cabled to the plumbing, were all of my bags with their contents intact. Nothing had been disturbed. The issue, then, wasn't the burglars of Bucharest finding me with such ease, but my own failure to realize I should have inserted the key in the lock and turned it when I'd left. In America, when you shut your hotel room door, it's locked. In Romania, don't count on it, especially if the key system is as old as you are.

After I got myself ready, I set my day bag on the bed and gathered items from around the room. I could tell a difference in the way I was moving, the way my body anticipated obstacles. In less than two days, I'd learned to take up less space. When I'd arrived, my hotel room had seemed very small. Initially, I knocked over two drinking glasses in the bathroom. Why they didn't shatter, I don't know. Then I noticed I was stubbing the polish off my toenails whenever I stood facing the bed. Unused to the absence of furniture legs, I kept bumping the low frame with my feet. I once had a boyfriend who didn't even have a bed frame, just a mattress on the floor. The blankets, having nowhere to be tucked in, trailed out onto the bare boards. I'd gotten used to that, but a mattress is soft and blankets don't knock the polish off your toenails.

My day bag could hold extra clothing, as well as drinks, snacks, my monastery scarf, and even toilet tissue—but it was made for electronics. I'd stocked up on the latest gizmos to help me record my trip: a new digital single-lens reflex (SLR) camera; a portable hard drive; an AlphaSmart portable keyboard for note-taking; and a digital voice recorder that worked with the speech recognition software I'd installed on my computer back home. The main compartment of the bag had padded dividers that could be stuck to the lining with Velcro to divide off the space and protect a camera. A zippered laptop pouch on the back held the AlphaSmart, and pockets of all sizes kept my cords, batteries, and other gear organized.

Contemplating my day there in my room, I was suddenly flummoxed by the prospect of using the gadgets I'd brought with me. How much money had I spent in the months preceding my trip? I'd had a prolonged shopping frenzy, for sure; but then, true to form, I hadn't touched most of my purchases until I packed them.

Gadgets are great, but learning how to use them—especially the electronic ones—is no walk in the park. You never have enough time to become an expert, especially if you're not versed in journalistic technologies. For instance, with the digital recorder I could walk down the street in Romania and speak into it, storing my thoughts. When I got back home, I could hook it up to my computer and—through the magic of speech-to-text technology—my spoken words would type themselves onto the screen. It was a great idea.

I sat on the edge of my bed and looked at the slim, silver digital recorder in my hand with all its little buttons and bars to press for the various menus. The thing had a sixty-six-page manual, full of descriptions of modes, folders, and other "convenient functions." I'd used the recorder once, back home, to capture an interview with a Romanian couple who lived in Cincinnati. Now I was past the test-drive stage, and my mind was blank. I was too nervous to concentrate on the instructions. Maybe it was a delayed reaction from the enormity of the trip, or anticipation of the excitement ahead, but I was overwhelmed. I wanted to figure out how to work the recorder, but I couldn't process the steps. *Oh, well,* I thought, *best-laid plans;* and I put it away.

For a second I felt like Mom. She couldn't work anything. Mom bought the most basic appliances and then returned them if they gave her trouble. When asked where the recent purchase was, she'd reply in her low smoker's growl, "I turned it in." Of course, Mom had missed the age of technology. As a secretary, she'd typed letters on a manual typewriter after jotting them down on a memo pad in shorthand. She'd started at the plant where Dad worked, reporting to a group of executives. Then she'd commuted to the State House in Charleston for a few years before finishing her career at our county Board of Education in Fayetteville. Mom had loved going to work, and she always liked to remind us that she had "political pull" through her various contacts. It was being home that she didn't like so much.

About the time Mom started drinking, my brother started shining shoes. He began with his own, putting the waxy polish on with a sock while he watched TV. Then he'd set the shoes aside to dry. Later, he'd take another sock and shine them up. I guess shining shoes was a chance for Joe to control something, to impose order in a crazy house. He kept at it, branching out to do Dad's shoes. Before long he was asking all of us for our shoes. He became a shoe-shining fanatic, even borrowing an electric polisher from a friend. We had an outlet on the wall next to the TV, and Joe continued to do his work there in the living room, watching TV and lining up in a row all the bright, shiny shoes of our family. A TV and an electric shoe polisher: That was our technology.

Well, I wasn't like Mom; I knew about technology, and I had definitely arrived in Romania well equipped. After all, I couldn't hop down to the corner store and pick up replacements or go home if I'd forgotten something. I had all of my electronic tools at my disposal in Bucharest. And the pressure was on.

Lucian would be driving up in a few minutes. So far he'd been punctual, a trait we shared. If he hadn't been on time I might have panicked, for Lucian was my only contact in Romania—the only live person I knew. Well, *knew* might not be the right word; my trip notes, written just before I'd fallen asleep, said it all: "My guide's name is Lucian. He's probably in his 50s. Don't know what else to say yet."

I finished packing for the day and made it down to the lobby in time, my bag brimming with high- and low-tech equipment. I hadn't carried the bag much before the trip—at least not full—and now I wondered whether it would be handy or just cumbersome. Before I had time to worry about it, Lucian had taken it from me and put it in the car. Problem solved.

Chapter 14

Dracula in Bucharest

As much as I'd looked forward to Romania, I was unenthusiastic about Bucharest. It was a mixed bag on my itinerary—some Dracula-related sites and others that were memorable in ways that had nothing to do with the Count. Even though I had a specific mission, I'd asked to see some well-known sites that presented a broader view of Romania, for the simple reason that I might never be back.

The good thing about touring Bucharest was that Lucian was going to drive me around. I still felt jet-lagged and had already taken a pill for muscle soreness—no doubt the result of occasionally having to manage my own bags on the trip, or possibly from sleeping on that board my hotel called a bed. I loved the prospect of being a passenger and not having to think about directions, traffic, or keeping to the schedule. Lucian could do all of that and I'd enjoy the view.

Dracula still had a presence in the capital of Romania, six hundred years after his death. And when I say *his*, I'm talking about Vlad Dracula, not the vampire. Vlad the Impaler founded and named the city of Bucharest. The Princely Court, or Old Court (Curtea Veche), was built there in the fifteenth century as the official residence of Vlad III, Prince of Wallachia. It was one of the places we'd be visiting. *I'm in Vlad's stomping grounds now,* I thought as Lucian pulled out into traffic, *and I'd better get used to it.*

The history of Vlad the Impaler began coming to light for most of the world in the 1970s, five hundred years after he ruled and many years after he had become a national hero to the Romanians. Dracula researchers Raymond McNally and Radu Florescu published a groundbreaking book in 1972 titled *In Search of Dracula*. In it, the authors claimed to discover in Vlad Tepes the "bloodthirsty prototype" for Bram Stoker's fictitious vampire. They made much of the connection and later wrote volumes about Vlad. Though their claim was not universally accepted, it was their work that illuminated the country of Romania in the Dracula story, opened the controversy about the role of Prince Vlad Dracula, and pumped up the tourist trade once Romania was out from behind the Iron Curtain.

Now I'd followed the two scholars to Romania years after they had gone poking into the world of vampires. I felt bonded to them because, like me, they were grown-ups who hadn't outgrown Dracula. It didn't matter that their theory of the Count's origin was debatable; the Romanian sites existed, the brochures were printed, and the tours were in place. I was fascinated by the topic and the journey and would draw my own conclusions—the first being obvious: It is impossible to tour Romania in search of Dracula without finding Vlad.

Bucharest didn't look like any other city I'd seen. It was a mix of old and new that didn't always work. So far, the sea of tan that was downtown had displayed little of the quaintness that defined other European cities, quaintness I'd glimpsed the previous evening on the way to the Count Dracula Club. Downtown Bucharest was a busy place, with traffic piling up at intersections and plenty of people on the streets. However, instead of oozing old-world charm, many of the buildings were on the plain side. Attempts at modernism in the architecture were painfully dated. And my biggest surprise was that some of the largest buildings had giant, full-color product ads across their facades. The ads, which were several stories high, weren't painted on the buildings but were attached. They hung right over the windows and must have been made of some kind of mesh, because Lucian said they didn't block the views from inside. The ads gave the downtown buildings a hip, lively look, if you could get used to pictures of giant cartons of milk, faces three stories high, or super-sized models in jeans decorating your bank or apartment building. If not, you might consider them visual pollution, as I did.

We started our tour at the Palace of Parliament, the huge complex built by former Communist dictator Nicolae Ceauşescu. In the 1980s, the Palace was a big cause of the city's epidemic of stray dogs: Because many old apartment buildings had been destroyed to make room for it, residents had been moved to places where they couldn't keep pets, and dogs had been turned loose. Now Bucharest was overrun with feral animals. I've seen news articles on the Internet claiming that 200,000 stray dogs roam Bucharest and that some 22,000 tourists have been attacked. Maybe I was distracted or preoccupied in the city that Vlad discovered, but I don't remember seeing a single dog, though they were on my mind.

The Palace of Parliament, at 3.76 million square feet, is the second largest administrative building in the world, behind the Pentagon. It's twelve stories high, with another four stories underground. Maybe Ceauşescu was expecting the main character from *Attack of the 50 Foot Woman* when he built it, or perhaps the self-proclaimed "Genius of the Carpathians" was operating from a subliminal suggestion generated by oversized ads.

As Lucian steered the car into the stark grounds, my thought was, *What happened to the landscaping budget?* Of course, that question assumes plants could be chosen that would even show up next to such a huge, sprawling structure. The Palace of Parliament is bordered by grass, some shrubs, a group of evergreen trees, and low hedges; but there is no rhyme or reason to it. As Lucian parked, I got little sense of curb appeal.

Inside, Lucian carried on in Romanian with the staff at the ticket counter as I waited near a small gift shop, unaware that my guide was arranging to turn me over to strangers. Lucian hooked me up with an English-speaking group and settled in to wait while I toured the palace. I felt abandoned, but I had little time to dwell on it. I was now in the hands of Florentina, the young woman who'd been assigned to guide my new group.

She led us through vast rooms and halls. We took in hand-carved oak and cherry woodwork; a five-ton crystal chandelier; twin staircases—one apiece—for Ceauşescu and his wife, Elena; and a ballroom in which the draperies were threaded with gold. Materials in the Palace were native to Romania, and all of them were grand. The original decorating plan for the ballroom had included two mirrors facing one another from opposite ends of the long room. A bit of marital trouble changed that plan, and the Mister decided to put a mirror at one end and a portrait of himself at the other. However, the mirror and portrait were never hung because history intervened. After the Romanian uprising in late 1989, the dictator and his wife were executed.

At one point during the tour, a woman left our group and went around a corner alone, perhaps to find a restroom. In an instant Florentina was running after her yelling "Interzis!" which means something like "Hey, where do you think you're going?" or "Get back here!" Later, all of us got a bathroom break, and guess what? There was no toilet paper in the ladies' room. It was a sign, a confirmation of my earlier decision to order eight rolls of travel toilet tissue from the *Magellan's* catalog and always keep one with me.

Riding to our next stop, I discovered more of Bucharest's quaintness in wide, tree-lined boulevards with spraying fountains; older buildings with luscious architectural details; churches, monuments, the opera house, and the Dâmbovița River, which runs through town and has its own locks. The Dâmbovița flows from a point north; it's connected to the Argeş—a real river in a made-up story—located near Dracula's castle in Transylvania.

As we rounded a corner, I saw a touch of whimsy: a fiberglass cow "escaping" down the outside of a hospital via a chain of knotted sheets. Bucharest hosted its first CowParade in 2005, in which artists decorated more than one hundred life-sized cows. Of course, I wasn't looking for cows; I was watching for any sign of Dracula. But even I knew that in the twenty-first century I'd have to look pretty hard.

We parked in a decaying section of town that Lucian called the Barrio to see Curtea Veche, the remains of Vlad's palace, which we viewed through a wrought-iron fence. The partial brick building with its distinctive arches was just sitting there in the sun, with sections of once-grand decorative columns lined up on the ground in front of it. Not a soul was around but us—and Vlad, thanks to a bust of the former prince that sits on a pedestal in front of the palace ruins. The bust is recognizable by Vlad's trademark look: long hair, long nose, handlebar mustache, and big eyes. Carved into the pedestal are the lines "Vlad Tepes" and "1456–1462," his longest reign.

Turning off the main streets of the Barrio, we entered the stone-paved courtyard of a large two-story hotel. Manuc's Inn, built in 1808, was the oldest operating hotel building in the city. A restaurant was open in the middle, its tables shaded by white umbrellas advertising Silva beer, but we didn't sit down. Even though it was rundown, the place reminded me of a hotel where Jonathan Harker stayed in one of the Dracula movies. Lucian said this one had been destroyed by the Gypsies.

When we got back to the car, I said to Lucian for the first time, "I need to write." With that announcement made, I sat in the front seat with the passenger door open and my AlphaSmart keyboard on my lap, typing away. I'd told Lucian I was writing a book. He stood a few feet from the car and smoked with his back to me, giving me my space. Praise the Lord! He got it that I needed to write. I'd even felt self-conscious myself at the idea of being a "writer," but this was the most natural thing in the world.

Next we visited the National Village Museum, which has nothing to do with Dracula. Lucian paid 100,000 lei for me to enter and take pictures of the historic Romanian houses, windmills, gates, and gardens open to visitors. Just after we were in, he said he was hungry. I suspected it was a direct response to the table of baked goods we'd just passed. *Lucian* was hungry—I wasn't—yet I ate the biggest pastry I've ever had in my life. I suppose it was fortunate in the long run, since we had no lunch, but somewhere Jenny Craig was breaking out in hives.

We strolled through the park; down lanes of whitewashed houses with deep, thatched roofs; through a log home that looked as though it had been brought in from the American frontier; past a steep-roofed brown wooden church, its towering steeple topped with a cross; through green yards, garden gates, and a house with bright blue shutters. There was even a carousel, and I remembered my ride with Annie the day I'd looked for our reflection.

Next we went to the headquarters of the Romanian Orthodox religion, where a service was in progress in the church. We could hear the singing. A few begging children ran up to the car as soon as we parked, but Lucian kept them away with sharp words in his deep voice. There are many poor people in Romania, and I hoped I wasn't a mean person for not wanting to be pursued by beggars on my vacation.

By afternoon I felt I'd seen the highlights of Bucharest. We hadn't seen everything Dracula—or, more precisely, everything Vlad. Lucian and I didn't go to the National History Museum, which had a room dedicated to fifteenth-century Wallachia during the time of Vlad the Impaler's rule. But we'd covered a lot of territory in a few hours, and I was ready to move on.

Once during a writing retreat in New Mexico, I had an informal opportunity to read a teacher the poem I'd started for my next day's class. "Throat clearing," she said dismissively after I'd read a few lines. I'd never heard that expression used in a writing context, but I understood it. I'd said nothing of substance and had yet to get to the point.

As much as I was determined to enjoy every minute and mile of my Romanian journey, I couldn't help thinking of Bucharest as throat clearing. Our next stop was more important. We were driving to Snagov that very afternoon to see the famous monastery where "Dracula" was supposedly buried. The site had a certain cachet, even though "Dracula" was Vlad.

Lucian and I would return to Bucharest for the night, and the next day we'd be heading out for two weeks on the road—first stop, Târgoviște, where more palace ruins marked the trail of Romania's favorite evil prince. And we'd be that much closer to Transylvania, the beating heart of the Dracula legend. I was in my glory.

I was also starting to relax and get my bearings. With travel, there is always a transition between imagination and reality, when the anxiety of "What will it be like?" melts into "Oh, this is what it's like." I was beginning to feel my feet on the ground in Bucharest, Romania.

When I'd packed my suitcase at home, I'd wondered—as always—what people would wear, and my time in Bucharest had confirmed the tried and true: You see everything—every color, every style, and no style. I'd wondered how I'd lug my bulky day bag with all its necessities, and Lucian had solved that problem by carrying it for me. As we walked along, we kept a good pace with each other. I frequently had to reach over and unzip some compartment of the bag to get what I needed or put something back. For instance, I didn't want to miss a photo opportunity, but the camera would get heavy around my neck and bump against my chest as I walked, so I'd put it away. Lucian would slow down for this little procedure and do the same thing a few minutes later when I needed the camera again. He was patient that way.

I'd discovered that Lucian was intelligent and could take a hint. He walked next to me so that I felt safe, yet he left me alone with my thoughts—involved, yet removed. It was ideal.

I wasn't sure how I felt about him, yet—heck, I barely knew him—but I was definitely glad I'd decided to hire a guide to take care of the details of my trip. Even if I didn't end up liking Lucian, I didn't really need to. I could separate the personal and professional sides of things; I hadn't been in the workplace for most of my adult life for nothing.

Back at the hotel I realized I was starved. The only things I'd eaten all day were breakfast and the giant pastry in the park. The minibar was alive and well, tucked into the white armoire in my room, and I raided it for a bag of peanuts; we wouldn't be eating dinner until much later, probably nine. Sorry, Jenny.

Chapter 15

Islands

Snagov Monastery was not a vampire site, but a chapter in the history of Vlad the Impaler. I hadn't been kind to Vlad so far; but "When in Romania . . ."—to steal a phrase—one must approach all things Dracula with an open mind.

To get to Snagov, we drove north from Bucharest. The ride was forty kilometers, or about twenty-five miles. What I remember is the highway, some gas stations, and leaving the city behind for the country. The sun was out.

Snagov is the name of a lake, an island, a monastery, and a small village. I knew nothing of the village; I was interested in the monastery, which was Vlad's supposed burial site. It was located on an island by the same name in Snagov Lake, and the only way over was by boat. The accounts of how to accomplish this trip were inconsistent. One writer advised that it had to be arranged in advance; another said that a nun ran a shuttle. Still another source claimed we'd have to row ourselves over. We hadn't made any arrangements beforehand, so I expected difficulties—at least a wait or a bribe. I didn't much care, as long as we got to the monastery. I hadn't traveled five thousand miles to miss it.

As we drove, I pulled out my AlphaSmart and laid it on my lap. The disadvantage of typing on it was that I always needed some kind of "desk."

The advantage was privacy. There was nothing for anyone to overhear except the clicking of keys, and the display screen was small—four lines of text. Lucian wouldn't know what I was writing, not that he was panting to. Even if he was curious, he didn't wear his glasses all the time. When I'd asked him how to spell a few Romanian words, he'd had to get out the little tortoiseshell reading glasses and put them on his nose, then bend down toward the screen where I'd typed. This was not done while he was driving.

Neither Lucian nor I attempted to keep a conversation going. That had been true from the get-go. It wasn't animosity or boredom, just the nature of our business. When we passed anything of note, he told me about it. If I had a question, I asked. When his cell phone rang, he talked in Romanian. Otherwise we were silent. While he drove, I was looking out the window at whatever we passed, drinking it in. The scenery itself wasn't extraordinary—at least I didn't break out my camera and take pictures—but this was Romania, and I was here. *I was here.*

Appearance wise, Lucian was so much better than I'd expected. Not only was he attractive, he was always clean and well groomed. His clothes—so far, half-sleeve shirts and blue jeans—were fresh and pressed. I loved it.

We stopped on the way to Snagov so that he could get a coffee. He parked on the side of the road and we went down a little hill to a tiny, old-fashioned version of a convenience store. A few high tables had been placed outside. They were the kind with small round tops and no chairs, meant for standing but not for lingering. Inside I took the opportunity to replenish my supply of flat bottled water.

It was Sunday afternoon, and we were the only customers. Lucian struck up a conversation with the proprietor, a dark-haired woman of middle age. Maybe he was stocking up on the sound of a human voice. Maybe she was doing the same. I noticed that Lucian became more animated and talkative with her than he had with me. Was it because they were speaking Romanian, or did he just find her far more interesting? It probably wasn't a fair question, considering my lack of interest in chatting with him.

Lucian took his coffee out to one of the tables, and she was tempted out from behind the counter. Most of their talk continued in Romanian, but now and then they would address me. In their accented English, they told me how they would like to travel to all sorts of places, too, but they couldn't afford it. Besides, they had to stay there and work. The store lady said she couldn't get away even to visit her Romanian relatives.

I realized they thought I was rich. I tried to make the point that neither could I travel the world at my whim; I had saved my money for a long time to come to Romania. It was lost on them, so I tuned out and let my eyes drift to the scrubby yard beyond the porch. There, pecking at the ground under a blue pickup truck, were the clucking chickens from my mental movie archive. In *Dracula Has Risen from the Grave,* a boy finds a bloody human body stuffed in the belfry of a church. He runs outside screaming for help. Everything is dirt: the yards, the streets, the roads. Chickens peck and cluck in the churchyard as the citizens realize the murder is the work of Count Dracula. "When shall we be free?" they cry. "When shall we be free of his evil?"

The clucking chickens were oblivious to us, but a tom turkey strutted by as though auditioning for a part. I loved seeing the movies come to life in that small way.

When we were back in the car, Lucian explained that the lady at the store was a Gypsy, a group for whom he had little to say that was flattering. From what I'd read, many other Romanians would agree. But she was a "good Gypsy," he said, because she was working, could speak English, and was doing the right thing with her life. "Does she live here?" I asked him—"here" meaning the store—and he nodded: "Da." It was Russian for "Yes." Sections of Romania had been Russian protectorates in the nineteenth century, part of a rich history that contributed to the fifteen languages still spoken there.

A few miles past the store, we left the highway. Lucian took a couple of right turns and soon we were bouncing through the dirt streets of Snagov on the way to the boat dock. The village was a collage of images: fences, animals, a disco club, and bright clothes hanging on lines. Two girls dressed in black walked down the road; men with messy hair sat on porches; a horse-drawn cart full of freshly cut wood bumped along while its passenger, a dark, jeans-clad woman, turned to look at us from the top of the pile.

Lucian knew the way to the dock, and by the time we'd parked, a group of teenage boys were eyeing us. I knew by the way they perked up that we weren't going to have to bribe anybody, or wait for a nun, or row ourselves to get to the island. These boys had a boat. The oarsman we hired was named Mihail, Romanian for Michael. From the moment we were introduced, I thought of the 1961 folk song by the Highwaymen, "Michael (Row the Boat Ashore)." Perfect.

Snagov Lake, surrounded by forest, is called the Green Jewel of Bucharest. The whole area was much bigger than I'd pictured. The area of the lake itself is 2.24 square miles. Glen Ferris, West Virginia, is 1.5 miles long, so Snagov Lake is the size of a small town.

The water was choppy that day. From the village dock we could see large houses across the expanse and boats trolling between us and the opposite shoreline. Certain areas along the shore are home to vacation lodges, resort-style complexes, and government property—including the vacation getaway of former dictator Ceaușescu.

Snagov Island was near enough that we'd be touching ground again in ten or fifteen minutes. The sun was shining as we climbed off the wooden dock into our fiberglass boat. The boat was orchid, not that anyone noticed but me.

I thought about vampires on the way over; how could I help it? But I was certainly the only one in that boat with such a train of thought. Mihail was a local boy interested in doing a good job to earn money. He rowed and Lucian sat patiently behind me, his thoughts probably miles away. In 1975, Anne Sexton published a book of poetry titled *The Awful Rowing Toward God*. I had always liked the title, disturbing as it was, and there we were—heading for a place of God, islands rowing toward an island.

We had an island just below Glen Ferris; at least, that's what we called it. The Glen Ferris Island was actually a low expanse of flat land on the river, accessible by a gravel road. It had woods on one side, and on the other a narrow sandy beach where the Kanawha River lapped up against the shore. A rough road went around the perimeter, enclosing the gardens planted by local weekend farmers and suitable for the pickup trucks they drove. Every so often the river would rise. The current would pick up, the water would take on the color of mud, and the Great Kanawha would thunder over the dam and flood the whole island, making me wonder what really was the point of having a garden there.

The island was a nice place to get away on a date—so I've heard. Couples could count on relative isolation during the evenings. What they didn't count on was my brother and his friend Wade, who used to camp out on the sandy beach, walking there from town. Joe and Wade liked to make hand-lettered signs and quietly attach them to the backs of cars in the dark. They would crawl along the sand like commandoes in war so that the couples wouldn't hear them—couples who'd drive away later, unaware that they were telling the world, "We've been parking at the Glen Ferris Island."

My other musings on the way to Snagov Island swung between vampire folklore and Romanian history. For instance, touching running water will destroy a vampire; but did a lake constitute running water? I wasn't sure. I could attest to the motion of Snagov Lake, thanks to our choppy boat ride. Of course, if a vampire rode in a boat, he could avoid the whole water issue.

Vlad the Impaler, possible inspiration for a vampire, was reportedly buried underneath Snagov Monastery in 1476, but details of his death are a mystery. One theory is that he was killed in war by the Turks, and his head carried back to Constantinople as proof. Dr. Elizabeth Miller says in *A Dracula Handbook* that it could have been a rival, a hired assassin, or even one of Vlad's own men who killed him in battle "in a forest north of Bucharest." If one of his soldiers did the deed, says Miller's source, it was because he mistook Vlad for a Turk.

When Vlad's grave was opened in the 1930s, it was empty. That would fit nicely with the theory that he was the vampire Dracula, except for one thing. Vampire lore holds that cutting off a vampire's head is one way to destroy it. Even if Vlad *were* the Prince of Darkness, how could he have moved about after he was beheaded?

With that thought, we'd arrived. After Mihail secured the boat, we stepped onto a path and walked up a hill past the priest's quarters, a pristine, white two-story house with a red tile roof, lace curtains, and a collection of ducks and chickens chasing each other past groupings of lilies in the front yard.

Snagov Monastery stands among flowers in a grassy area of the island. It's a solid structure, built of bricks ranging in color from white to cream to reddish brown. The three arched towers on top are nearly as tall as the church itself.

When Lucian and I approached the monastery, we saw that a wedding was about to begin. The heavy wooden door, marked with a cross, stood open, and sunlight filled the entry. We were permitted in but asked to step around a strip of red carpet that went up the middle of the tiny nave, which had no seats. Black wrought-iron stands defined the aisle, each with a length of white netting draped over it. The netting, topped with daisies, hung like a series of little bridal veils against a background of painted icons on every wall.

I noticed a sign on our way in, indicating that for twenty Euros visitors could take photos or videos. Romania had not yet adopted the Euro, so the reality was that we paid for everything in lei. I had my camera out, of course. "Seven hundred thousand lei," a young boy in the monastery said slowly when we got inside. "Seven hundred thousand to take photographs," the boy repeated, drawing out the words. It must have been a lot of money to him. It sounded like a lot to me, too. I peeled off the bills as I looked around.

There was Vlad's stone at the altar. It was flat and looked like part of the floor. Sitting on top of it was a framed metal likeness of the prince surrounded by candles and vases of flowers. One of the candles was burning. The sanctuary was full of icons, heavy on the gold. One wall held a selection of framed and unframed documents, some hung and others tacked onto a red velvet background. It had the look of a typical church bulletin board, but how many churches can display the history of Vlad the Impaler, complete with pictures? I photographed some of it, but felt hurried because a few people had already arrived for the wedding. In fact, we were very lucky. We'd just made it inside with five minutes to spare before the service began.

In a corner next to the bulletin board was another portrait of Vlad. There was no word on whether his body was really there; in my opinion it wasn't, but Lucian disagreed. He may have asked one of the two priests who were in the sanctuary, but I understood nothing they said. The larger, more effusive one gesticulated as he spoke. His assistant, as I thought of the quieter priest, just smiled a lot.

Conversation went on around me, in Romanian. Then the effusive priest told me in English that US television crews had come to film there, and that singer Michael Jackson had been one of the many visitors to sign the register. I signed it, too, adding my name to those of Jackson, U.S. presidents, and others who had come to Snagov. Elizabeth Miller's signature must be in that book. Did researchers McNally and Florescu—known as the Professors of Horror—sign it, too? No doubt, and with my hero worship intact I would have loved to gaze upon those signatures, maybe touch them or take a picture; but that day I didn't even look. I was caught up in seeing the little church before the wedding and capturing the story of Vlad with my camera. The opportunity to look through the register didn't register until I was long gone.

The sociable priest gave me a free postcard and a business card I couldn't read. The business card bore a lovely color photo of the monastery behind long-stemmed wildflowers, under a blue sky. "Patriarhia Romana" was written at the top in script, opposite a crest showing a crown and two facing angels. There was more detail toward the center of it, and "Paste Oile Mele" appeared on the scroll at the bottom. It probably didn't say oily pasta. Religious, I figured. The line above the address read, "Manastirea SNAGOV 'Vlad Tepes' Insula." *Snagov Monastery—Vlad Tepes Island.*

We weren't allowed to stay for the wedding, and there wasn't much else on the island to explore, so I walked down to a wooden dock and looked at Snagov Lake. Lucian was nearby smoking. Cigarettes were like a pastime in Romania. Lucian had told me that after smoking received such a boot in America, the cigarette companies targeted Europe. I could believe it by the way people carried their cigarettes everywhere. Lucian was considerate and kept it low key.

After the ceremony, he and I ventured back to peek at the bride, groom, and guests as they exited the monastery. *Another one bites the dust,* I thought—or, in this case, another two. I hadn't had much luck with weddings. The first one had been a formal affair in a small brick church overlooking the Kanawha River. Glen Ferris Methodist Church was larger than Snagov Monastery; the church had pews, a raised pulpit, and seating for a choir. The music for this Romanian wedding was recorded, played through speakers so that we could hear it outside. My second wedding was performed by a justice of the peace. It was a casual affair to be sure. I supposed the weddings had been all right; it was just the marriages that didn't work.

On our return, Mihail rowed, Lucian watched my bag, and I noted the incongruity of a powerboat pulling a water-skier farther out on Snagov Lake. Behind us was the monastery with its brick towers on top, heavy wooden door, and ancient icons; the mystery of Vlad, six centuries old; and the big white house where ducks roamed among the flowers and grass as yet another bride and groom made their way off the island. I remember how it felt after the powerboat had passed, our orchid row-boat slapping down on the waves under us. I nearly fell in twice before my feet were on solid ground again.

Chapter 16

Fences

On the ride from Bucharest to Târgovişte, the third Dracula site on my itinerary, I was one big ball of emotion. It wasn't because I was about to see the Princely Court of Vlad the Impaler, but because memories of home and childhood swept through me all the way.

It was Monday, the third day of our trip. Lucian and I set out from Bucharest on a beautiful summer morning, the kind you dream about in the dead of winter. A day like that will beckon you like a crooking finger when you're young and in school or grown up and sitting at your desk at work with no prayer of being outside. Now we were out in it.

This was my first real trip into the countryside. We were officially on the road and would not see Bucharest again until I was ready to fly home. That would be after we'd made the full circuit of key cities and Dracula sites in Wallachia and Transylvania and I'd caught some rays on the coast of the Black Sea.

It was on this drive that Lucian and I began spending significant time alone together. We rode for hour after hour in the front seat of the blue compact car provided by his travel agency, setting the pattern of our days. Lucian did all the driving, and I looked out the windows, took pictures, or wrote. Sometimes the only stops we made were at gas stations. Some were open and others were shut down—typical Romania. Sometimes we'd be parked at the pump before we noticed no one was there. Then Lucian would simply get back onto the road and drive on.

Our suitcases were stored in the trunk, so the car was usually neat. It had a back seat, but it might as well have been a two-seater: Everything took place up front. There I kept my bag, which—in addition to my camera equipment and portable keyboard—held whatever supplies and snacks I might need on a given day. The bag was on the floor in front of my feet, so I had to sit sideways or put my feet at odd angles, but at least I could reach into it easily when I wanted to capture a view or a thought. I was always doing one or the other.

Lucian and I kept bottles of water in the car, too. I put mine on the floor and tried to block it in with my feet; but every time he turned the steering wheel, the bottle rolled around in its little space, knocking against my shoes or escaping and ending up under the seat. To avoid that whole scene, I usually chugged the water and then traded one annoyance for another: Now how soon would it be before I had to go to the bathroom?

Lucian kept his eyes on the road, and I stole glances at him. Lots of times my eyes would flit to his hands on the steering wheel. They were a golden tan like his arms and face, and small and smooth. I guessed he hadn't cracked his knuckles for years as I had.

Mom used to tell me that before I was born she prayed I would have pretty hands and feet. "I don't care what the baby looks like," she would pray, "as long as its hands and feet are pretty." It was a strange wish and one that had not come true. Now the memory of it came back to me as I studied Lucian's graceful hands.

When Lucian's cell phone rang, I always knew when the caller was a woman by his brief responses and tone of voice. He wasn't secretive, exactly, but you wouldn't mistake him for a chatterbox. I found myself filling in the blanks. *She* would be on the other end asking questions: I imagined "Where are you?" or "Are you in the car?" as the first one. Most likely she wanted to know whether he was alone or had me sitting two feet away to hear his end of the conversation. I wondered how often I was mentioned. And, on an even juicier note, what conversations had they had before he took the assignment? Did he tell her all about it first? Did he ask her opinion? Did she care that he was spending more than two weeks—including days and nights—driving a single woman around

Romania? Did they argue? If I'd been the wife, I wouldn't have been able to handle it. I suppose that partially explains why I was the single one in this scenario.

I said "wife," didn't I? *Was* Lucian married? He hadn't said. In Bucharest, when he'd left me at the hotel that first afternoon, he'd mentioned he had to work on his apartment. *His: singular.* But he could be married even though he didn't wear a ring. Well, I decided, if he didn't have a wife, he at least had a girlfriend. And it was really none of my business.

It was nice to be driven around, and I can say that from both sides of the fence. In Mom's later years, she hated to drive, especially on the interstates, where she would have to maintain a speed of at least forty miles per hour. She'd come from an area where a two-lane road, occasionally expanding to four, could take her where she needed to go.

Mom's style of driving was to accelerate into the turns and slow down on the straightaway. She would gun it and then quickly lose steam. When she and I went anywhere together, I did the driving no matter whose car we took. She was tickled, and if I'd resented the imbalance of responsibility, a couple of turns in the passenger seat cured that. Though I tried to be the easy-going companion, my stomach clenched when Mom let up on the gas and every vehicle within five miles tried to pass us. After a few glances into the side mirror at the line of traffic behind us, I was glad to take over.

Mom may have hated city driving, but she loved her car. In an arrangement understood only by the two of them, she'd traded her dark blue, bare-bones 1998 Pontiac Sunbird to her financial manager for his 1999 Ford Crown Victoria. It was the most luxurious car she ever owned. After Dad died, it had been her habit, when she needed a new car, to ask a man to pick it out. She would select a neighbor or someone she knew from work. Mom didn't even go along to the dealership. Her one instruction regarding the Pontiac had been, "Just don't get blue."

Mom loved the cushiony comfort of her big Ford and the fact that the radio was already set to a station that played swing music; she just didn't want to drive. So she'd limit her trips to Walgreens, which was just up the street; or—better, yet—drive around her apartment complex listening to the radio.

As soon as Lucian and I made our way through the congestion of

Bucharest and emerged onto a two-lane highway, the land changed. Traffic thinned out, little villages took the place of the beige cityscape we had left behind, and the view became greener. According to Lucian, a tree in the yard is a status symbol for Romanians. Beyond that, there is an affinity between the forests and the people that dates back through the country's embattled history: The woods are still seen as protection against enemies. "Codrul efrate u Romanul," Lucian said from the driver's seat. "Be sure to write in your book that Romanians are brothers with the forest." *What about the sisters?* was my automatic thought, unexpressed.

A light-colored dog crossed the road in front of us as I settled in for the ride, my eyes alert and my camera around my neck. How Dracula-esque that the mile markers looked like tombstones, sticking out of the ground with their rounded tops and lettering on the front. The tops were blood red, with white numerals. I snapped away with my Nikon.

We passed a village that was largely blighted. Some of the homes were large tents, while others were constructed of traditional materials and topped with towers. "Gypsies live there," Lucian said, pointing to a dark house with three towers rising above the roofline. "Traditional Gypsies have a caste system. The number of towers on top of a house tells what level Gypsy lives there, how much gold they have. Gypsy women sometimes have in their hair 'coin of gold.'" We passed a young woman walking along the road. Her hair bore only a scarf, but her clothes were colorful the way you would picture.

Houses in Romanian villages stand close to the road. Many times a fence separates the property from the street; so you have the house, a yard, a fence, and then a little strip of land between the fence and the highway just wide enough to park a car or walk to the store and back. Life in these towns takes place by the side of the road. Men sit on benches and watch the cars. Women in headscarves and gathered skirts talk in groups, holding their brooms, or carry groceries home. Couples sit together, not going anywhere.

The sunlight coming in through the windshield was not just warm. It carried memories, sending me back to other places and times, and I was off on my own inner journey on the way to Târgoviște. The little villages we passed were reminiscent of Glen Ferris and its neighboring towns along Route 60, and if I closed my eyes, the driver could be my dad.

When I was young, Dad would take me with him on his Saturday morning errands, which were little more than an excuse to get out of the house. He would get up and dress in a nice shirt and trousers, his shoes shined—by Joe—and him squeaky clean from a bath. I always knew from his attire that Dad was going to Montgomery and that if I went along, we would look at magazines in the corner drugstore and get a sandwich before we started home.

I was quiet with Dad, the way I was with Lucian. With Dad, I didn't need to talk. He used to sing in the car, songs like "Red River Valley" and something that went, "I've got a gal six feet tall; she sleeps in the kitchen with her feet in the hall."

It was odd to be riding through Romania thinking of the past and Glen Ferris, a town I'd left at age sixteen to go to college. I had fled West Virginia entirely after graduation, marrying someone from out of state—which guaranteed an exciting, new life, didn't it?—and I hadn't looked back for a long time.

Romanian fences are a coffee-table book waiting to happen. They line the villages, mismatched, often individually ugly but charming when you see them one after another stretching past your vision, a mélange of clashing hues, divergent styles, sundry materials, and myriad states of repair. Some are metal, tilting and rusty. Others are brightly painted—green, orange, robin's-egg blue—with profusions of flowers peeking through curved sections of wrought-iron, plump balusters, or wooden spindles. Often views that should have been hidden are exposed; for instance, a lumber yard visible between the ornamental rails of a black-and-silver fence.

In the National Village in Bucharest, we had seen handsome wood fences of picket and hand-woven twig. Out here in the real villages, a fence was as likely to be of rotted wood or corrugated metal, its sections leaning in on one another or falling toward the house. These fences went from straight to fancy, solid to see-through. They topped rock walls and sprang out of the ground with their scrollwork, arches, dividing pillars, and balustrades. Some boasted; others begged for attention.

Another piece of my past came to mind, a fence memory. One year for Christmas I got a doll I named K-K-K Katie, after another song Dad used to sing. I took Katie outside after the weather warmed and the leaves came out and Mr. Douglas's garden started to grow. Our backyards were separated by a wire fence, and the Douglases had a gate that latched. It was like something from *Peter Rabbit*: I didn't venture into their yard unless I was invited, which I was once, to see Mr. Douglas's canes. He used to sit out on his back porch and carve wooden canes with fancy handles that he would send as gifts to U.S. presidents and other dignitaries. That day, he had several in progress, one to work on and the rest stripped of their bark and bright with fresh, yellow wood, leaning against the trunk of a shade tree. Sometimes Mr. Douglas made the newspapers, or the president did, walking along with one of Robert Douglas's canes.

The day I lost K-K-K Katie, I'd climbed up onto the concrete gatepost and jumped off into the alley barefoot. I landed on a big piece of glass, the thick kind used to make pop bottles. I screamed as the sole of my foot split open and gushed blood. After the doctor visit, I had to lie in bed all afternoon to keep the bleeding at bay, so I forgot about Katie—who I concluded had fallen over the fence into the Douglases' greenery. Several days later, when I went back outside, there was no sign of my doll. If Katie had been made of wood, I might be sitting here in my declining years wondering if she'd been carved into a cane handle. Though I'm sure she wasn't, her disappearance remains a mystery.

I could tell as Lucian drove us through village after village that the planned community concept hadn't hit rural Romania. Every fence we saw seemed to have been put up without a consultation with the neighbors. Did each family assert its own personality that way? What appeared to be a contest among the residents—or a total lack of regard for the style and color of a street—could just be the Romanians preferring variety. Sometimes a fence even clashed with the house it was put up to frame; for instance, one bright blue house, plain and solid in its construction, stood behind a delicate mint green metal fence.

As we approached Târgoviște I was surprised to see prettier villages, more like suburbs, containing the nicest homes we'd seen so far. "This belong to Târgoviște," Lucian said. "Rich people." A city of 89,000 people, Târgoviște didn't look like a playground of the rich to me. Lots of big apartment buildings lined the streets, but they were old. Târgoviște is modern as opposed to something in a Dracula movie, but the descriptor would have been truer a few decades ago than it is today.

Târgovişte was the first capital of Wallachia. Dracula researchers McNally and Florescu spelled it *Tirgoviste* back in 1972. Even though I like that one better, *Târgovişte* is the spelling used today. It's the spelling the Romanians used when they put up the marble plaque at the entrance to the Princely Court of Vlad the Impaler.

After we'd parked, we realized that the complex was closed on Mondays. We got in, nevertheless—I don't know how, but I'll credit Lucian's charm. I didn't understand a word of his conversation with the woman at the gate—who looked immovable to me—but suddenly we were inside. My relief showed me how poised I had been for disappointment, how important every stop on this trip was to me.

Bracing for disappointment was a response I'd learned years before while coping with my rollercoaster life back in Glen Ferris. It was a good idea in our house not to over-expect. For instance, one Saturday during the wonder years—years when I wondered how I would survive—Dad stepped out of character to ask Joe and me, "How would you like to go on a picnic tomorrow?" *Huh?* "We'll get your mother to make some fried chicken, and we'll drive up to Four-H and go swimming." The place we all called 4-H is officially titled Fayette County Park. At that time it offered acres of woods, ball fields, picnic grounds, and three swimming pools.

Ordinarily Dad hated being inconvenienced and was not the kind of guy to initiate a picnic, but that day the house had been full of a horrible, tippy-toeing silence thanks to Mom being drunk. Dad knew how much we all needed an antidote, and maybe that was why he made a promise that someone else—unfortunately, Mom—would have to keep. I didn't think about it that way. All I knew was that *finally* our family was going to do something that regular people did.

For example, how many years had I asked Mom and Dad to take us to the West Virginia State Fair? Held fifty miles away in the month of August, the fair was a popular destination for families—other families. We never went. "It's nothing," Mom or Dad would say, dismissing the highlight of many people's summer as a collection of cheap sideshows and farm exhibits. I *wanted* cheap sideshows. I longed to see something different; to know something new about the world. I wanted to join in when the other kids talked about the state fair at the start of school. Well, so much for what I wanted.

I did make it to the fair one summer evening after I was grown. The only thing I remember about it is filing into a tent to see Hester-Lester, half man/half woman. The audience couldn't see the arrangement of male/female attributes that would have been the most interesting—Hester-Lester was clothed—but I do remember thinking that she/he was unremarkable—until we in the audience were offered a chance to see, for twenty-five cents more, Hester-Lester "without benefit of costume." You can bet I paid a quarter for that—and got a sealed envelope containing a picture of Hester-Lester posing much as she/he had onstage—and still not naked. Yes, I know: There's a sucker born every minute. Sometimes we just want to take a chance.

Joe and I were excited about the 4-H picnic, but the next morning we didn't find Mom bustling around the kitchen. I remember her back as she stood at the stove in her red robe, head down, frying the chicken; but her movements were spare and slow. She was not in good shape. In fact, she was still drunk—or drunk again.

Dad was in charge that day; it was his show. He drove and tried to keep up some chatter as the four of us made the thirty-minute trip to the park. I don't remember Mom saying a word. Joe and I were in the back seat, and I was getting hungry. I kept picturing our picnic table spread with a paper cloth and laden with a plate of chicken, maybe some macaroni salad or coleslaw, drinks, chips . . . what had they come up with? When we arrived, I offered to help unload the car. "Where's the food?" I asked.

"It's right there in the back seat," Dad said.

Joe and I looked around. There, nesting in the crack of the seat where it met the back, was a small, grease-spotted paper sack, the kind you would use to take your lunch to work or school. The top was twisted shut. It was so tiny we hadn't even noticed it. I peeked into the bag at a few greasy chicken legs. This was a "picnic lunch" for four people? Dad tried to make up for it later by putting on his trunks and swimming with Joe and me—another rare occasion—but the day was doomed, and the person who really ruled it sat on the concrete observation deck and watched us like a dark shadow cast across the water.

In Târgoviște, Lucian and I started at the back of the Princely Court complex. The Chindia Tower has become an emblem of the city. It was built by Vlad the Impaler in the fifteenth century as a watchtower and was restored between 1847 and 1851.

The structure is over one hundred feet tall, its round tower rising from a thick base the size and approximate shape of a two-story house. Lucian sat under a shade tree and smoked while I went inside and climbed a wooden spiral staircase to the top. It was like going up in a bell tower—not that I ever have—around and around. The walls were covered with framed maps, handwritten documents, and line drawings of Vlad, including the famous woodcut in which he's eating outdoors while his countrymen are being hacked apart and impaled a few feet from the table. Other drawings showed men dressed up for war: in armor, on horses, with weapons, and on the attack. And no display would be complete without "old faithful," the portrait of Vlad I seemed to see everywhere. He hadn't gotten any cuter.

But the highlight was this: There in one of the framed groupings was what looked like an old cover from McNally and Florescu's book *In Search of Dracula*—in Romanian. The title was *A la recherché de DRACULA*.

M&F were two of my heroes. Dr. Raymond McNally, a horror fan since his childhood, had begun teaching history at Boston College around the time I was at the movies beginning my love affair with Dracula. McNally was a handsome man with thick, white hair who was known for wearing a black cape around campus. Oh, how I wish I'd seen him, just once, strolling along in that cape.

Radu Florescu was born in Romania in 1925, the son of a diplomat. His ancestors had ties—*blood* ties?—to Vlad the Impaler. By the time Florescu met McNally, he'd come to America to live and was also teaching history at Boston College. Beginning in the late 1960s, the two formed a team to research a topic of mutual interest—the history of Dracula.

At the top of Chindia Tower, I walked out onto a flat roof encircled by battlements. What a view! In one direction I could see the Princely Court complex laid out below me and acres of woods—perhaps a park—with low mountains in the distance. This was where Vlad had stood to observe the surrounding forest. Was he looking at his own impalement victims? Watching for the enemy? Some of the nearby land is still forest, but most of it is Târgoviște, its homes and businesses stretching nearly as far as the eye can see.

Vlad wasn't the only Romanian ruler who struck fear into the hearts of the citizens, and Târgovişte is now known for something else: On December 25, 1989, Nicolae and Elena Ceauşescu were taken outdoors and publicly executed following a closed trial on a military base in Târgovişte. Their shootings were the culmination of a revolution, ending a reign of terror that had defined Romania since 1965.

I went down and walked among the palace ruins while Lucian waited; then we walked together to the church. It had been built by Vlad's grandfather, Mircea the Old, in the fourteenth century, so I guess it had its day. It was dark inside, but we went in. We were rushed through; I was told I could take two pictures. Maybe they were two of the many black rectangles that appeared later in my photo file.

After touring the Princely complex, we had coffee in a restaurant across the road—Lucian's idea. The sign read, "Pensiune Cazare Dracula," leading one to expect something vampire-ish or at least Vlad-ish; but inside it was an ordinary café, one that we had to ourselves.

I didn't see the point of a coffee break in Romania. Romanian coffee is served in small cups like espresso; it's very strong, and ours was lukewarm. But the whole thing was companionable—or would have been if I hadn't been writing. If I didn't keep taking notes, the days would blend into one another in my mind. Lucian was content to sit silently and smoke—no surprise.

Our next Dracula stop would be the Poenari Citadel, a castle ruin on top of a mountain. I'd read about it. Of course it had belonged to Vlad—who else? But I wasn't giving up on the other Dracula yet.

Chapter 17

Say "Brînză"!

By the time we'd left Târgovişte, Lucian and I had seen the city, the country, and the little villages in between. I loved it—a summer day, people out walking, flowers in bloom. In addition to enjoying the scenery I was always scouting for pictures.

We were headed for the Poenari ("Poy-ya-NAR") Citadel, which, according to McNally and Florescu, was the "real" Dracula's castle. But in the meantime, there were all these villages . . . photo ops galore. I hadn't just bought a new camera for the trip; I'd equipped myself as though I were going on assignment for National Geographic. My skill as a photographer lagged just a tad behind my ability to spend money.

For a while, I'd thought my friend Susan would be traveling to Romania with me. When we'd discussed cameras back in America, she'd said, "I think I've solved your problem of what camera to take to Romania. What if I go along and take the pictures?" My heart lit up with hope.

I'd already decided not to invite anyone because my agenda wasn't negotiable, but Susan would have been an easy companion. Having her along would have banished the loneliness and trepidation that occasionally threatened to offset my sense of adventure. However, Susan's plans hadn't worked out, and I was—for better or worse—a photographer in the Romanian countryside.

My guide seemed focused on driving, as he should. While I wiggled around on the passenger side, swapping out my equipment, locating my water bottle, and positioning myself for the next photo, Lucian kept us on course.

Who said I didn't have a traveling companion? I had Lucian, and he was perfect. He didn't talk my ear off; he did all the driving, planning, and paying; and when we left the car, he walked with me and I felt safe. He didn't whine or sulk or get weird because we'd spent too much time together. And I didn't have to take care of him; that was the main thing. I never wanted to take care of another adult again, or even clean up after one. It was probably that idea that prevented me from seriously considering remarriage. Of course, the reverse might have happened and someone would have to take care of me, but that wasn't where my thoughts went.

It didn't take long to discover the difficulty of taking pictures on the move. Lucian didn't slow down when we drove through the villages, so the scenery—which looked fine through the front windshield as we approached it—flew past my window in a blur. I didn't want to leave the window down all the time because of the wind and the noise, so for every shot I had to crank it open manually with a handle. By the time I did that, grabbed the camera, put its black-and-yellow strap around my neck so I wouldn't drop it when I leaned out, took the picture, and checked the digital results, there was no doing it over. We were already down the road. To add further irony, by paying such close attention to the camera, I was missing the essence of Romania as we passed through it.

I ached to get out and stand still, plant my feet and look around; to hold the camera steady and take my time photographing the day-to-day life we glimpsed from the car. I could have asked Lucian to stop, but the truth was that even as I wished to be on the ground, I felt safer there behind the passenger door with the car moving. Even photographing the Romanians on the run made me feel like a criminal.

People in some primitive societies believe that a photograph can steal the subject's soul. Were the Romanian peasants afraid of cameras? Sir James George Frazer called it the "evil eye of the box" in *The Golden Bough,* published in 1922. Maybe we'd progressed since then, but for many societies the phrase "take a picture" had a literal meaning, affording the photographer an opportunity to cast spells or even drain life from the subjects in the photos. Shades of Count Dracula!

I wanted to get out of the car, yet I also didn't. Getting out was fraught with obstacles. For one, I didn't like to ask strangers to pose. Occasionally I did it, but some refused, like the little kid in the Barrio who'd held up both hands, palms out, and had given me a bad-ass look: *Forget it, Lady.*

There wasn't much chance I'd go unnoticed in these villages, even if I stuck to scenery and animals. Besides, I was more likely to be accommodating than to go clumping along village streets with a camera, skirting the flower beds and fences that called to me from the roadside. That shyness, that desire not to bother anyone, was the kiss of death for a journalist—and I'd *been* a journalist! In my twenties I'd worked on both daily and weekly newspapers—walking a beat, conducting interviews, and writing stories. I'd loved it. What had changed?

Now I didn't even like the news. Well, let me amend that: I liked to know what was going on in the world, but I wasn't fanatical. I didn't subscribe to my hometown paper—too much emphasis on sports—and I couldn't stand to watch the TV news with its preponderance of medical commercials.

I kept up with world events by skimming them on the Internet, but I followed Hollywood gossip slavishly and knew how competitive and aggressive photography could be. Movie stars, bands, sports figures, and even criminals had to fight off the paparazzi. The job of the photographer was to persist, insist, and press on until the job was done, the prize photo captured. Of course, shooting the famous is a far cry from photographing Romanian villagers, but let's face it: Taking pictures of people is personal.

No doubt my shyness was another survival trait from my teenage years in West Virginia: Don't stir the pot; you never know what will bubble up. I knew I'd have to get tough if I intended to become a better photographer, but at least I didn't have to find my own way around Romania.

In Piteşti we stopped at a traffic light, and two young men leapt at the windshield to "wash" it, hoping for money. "Gypsies," Lucian said. They actually made the glass more difficult to see though; Lucian had just washed ours at a gas station. He became angry, yelled, and ran his wipers to stop the Gypsies from squirting the glass again. It was all very quick; the light turned green, and we sped on.

Apparently the Poenari Citadel was secluded; we were going to make our base camp in Curtea de Argeş for the night. It was on the way and large enough to have a good hotel. I don't think I ever said *Curtea de Argeş* out loud, but I loved the name before I ever saw the place. The Argeş—pronounced "Ar-jesh,"—was the river that flowed below Dracula's castle. In the novel, Jonathan Harker writes in his diary that the castle is located "on the very edge of a terrible precipice." Maybe we would see the Argeş River far below us that afternoon, as we stood among the ruins of "Dracula's Castle."

The sun was shining as we slowed down on the outskirts of Curtea de Argeş, stuck in traffic. I don't remember what Lucian did sitting there in the car—probably nothing—but I took pictures, knowing that my eyes couldn't memorize everything. Stretching out to our left was a flat, green plain that ended at the foot of a mountain dotted with houses. Rain clouds hovered in the distance. With a little imagination, I could be looking across the Kanawha River at Montgomery, West Virginia.

Curtea de Argeş, once the capital of Wallachia, is a charming place that looks from a distance as though it's nestled in the Swiss Alps. In fact, it is the huge, rugged peaks of the Făgăraş Mountains that define the surrounding landscape. Part of the Southern Carpathians, they're also called the Transylvanian Alps—even though we weren't in Transylvania yet. It was confusing, as was my attempt to imagine one of those peaks topped with a spooky castle full of vampires when I almost expected to see Heidi and her grandfather coming down the road.

As we entered the town proper, we passed under a series of banners stretched across the street. I got excited, thinking they were signs for a festival, until I realized they were only ads; this country had ads in the strangest places.

When Lucian drove toward the center of town, a surprise revealed itself. More than a mere stop, Curtea de Argeş was a tourist town, quaint and beautiful, reminiscent of the excessively hyphenated Carmel-by-the-Sea in California; and just like that, it was calling my name. Roads wound out of view, and I wanted to follow them. The shaded streets were lined with shops, one after another, that called to me; but the castle at Poenari called louder. We were going to climb the 1,480 steps to the citadel after checking in to our hotel. Otherwise, I was afraid we'd run out of time and good weather, as the forecast was for rain.

I went to my room long enough to change into my walking shoes. It was set up a little like my bedroom in Ohio. The large windows to my right—sources of light and noise—were especially similar: like mine, they overlooked a parking lot. Near the bed was a wall shelf that held a coffeepot, the first one I'd seen in a Romanian hotel room. Whoopee! Maybe I could give my little Brisk Brew—another new gadget—a rest the next morning. It was a godsend but made only one cup at a time.

I knew that Lucian was in the room next to mine; I could hear his deep voice through the wall. No doubt he was on the phone, his volume and cadence giving it away. Was it his wife? He still hadn't told me if he was married, and it was still none of my business. But I wondered.

Lucian had been to the Poenari Citadel before, but he hadn't been there often. "I do not take many American tourists there," he'd told me in the car, "but I take Japanese."

"Oh?"

"The Japanese are very interested in Dracula. They say they want to see 'Dura-gul, Dura-gul.'"

The sun was still out and the front seat warm as we set out for the castle. Lucian drove us up, down, and around the hills between Curtea de Argeş and Poenari. I dozed on the way, obviously taking no pictures, and completely missed the little village of Arefu, which Elizabeth Miller lists among the points of interest for a Dracula fan. I doubt it was a blip on Lucian's radar, as he didn't try to wake me up.

Chapter 18

A Tale of Two Castles: Poenari

Every thought I've ever had or hope to have about the Turks could be engraved on the head of a pin. Still, I couldn't help thinking of history's premiere population of medieval land-grabbing warmongers as Lucian and I climbed the steps to the Poenari Citadel.

Poenari is one of two structures in Romania known as "Dracula's Castle." While both have been open to tourists for years, Poenari is definitely the lesser known, less castlelike, and less frequently visited cousin to Bran Castle, which we would see on another day. While Bran is an actual standing castle in a village in Transylvania, the remaining walls of the Poenari fortress sit on top of a mountain in the countryside, in the neighboring province of Wallachia. For Dracula fans, both castles are on the short list of "must-see" sights—and the entire list of Dracula sights isn't very long.

Poenari Citadel became known to Dracula insiders as the "real" castle after McNally and Florescu spread the word in their book *In Search of Dracula*, first published in 1972. Many tourists unaware of the nuances and controversies in the Dracula legend are automatically directed to Bran and go home thinking they've seen Dracula's Castle, end of story. But maybe they haven't.

Did the "real castle" look anything like those in the movies? Would it be perched on a craggy and forbidding mountain with a river far below, the way it was in *Horror of Dracula* and *Dracula: Prince of Darkness*? I pictured Dracula's movie castle with its mullioned windows, moat, and wooden bridge; the stone birds outside with their huge talons wrapped around a gatepost, the flat stoop where Dracula's black carriage pulled up with its visitors, and the big wooden door. And would a real Romanian castle have flocked wallpaper inside, shields and crossed swords decorating the stairwells, a giant fireplace, and a table set for one? Would it have balconies running wall to wall, overlooking the living space and just perfect for Dracula's appearance?

Not this castle.

The Poenari Citadel was built by subjects of Vlad the Impaler in the fifteenth century—not that they planned it. The story goes that Vlad captured his own people after treating them to an Easter banquet at his royal palace in Târgoviște. Following the festivities, he impaled the older citizens and forced the younger ones—men, women, and children still in their Easter clothing—to walk fifty miles to the site far above the Argeş River and labor at rebuilding a castle so that Vlad could take refuge from the Turks. Six centuries later—after time, the Turks, and an earthquake had contributed to its deterioration—I knew to expect a ruin.

To get to Poenari, we followed a winding two-lane road out into the country. Eventually we rounded a bend where we saw the small, white sign for "Cetatea Poenari" on the right side of the road. In hindsight, I should have asked Lucian how to pronounce more of the place names. My mind wasn't on saying the words so much as spelling them correctly when I typed my notes.

The citadel was located a couple of curves this side of the biggest dam in Romania, but it was almost deserted. A parking lot sat on the opposite side of the road from the little sign, at the base of a mountain, and when I looked up I could see the Poenari fortress peeping over the top. Parking was free. It was an unsophisticated operation; in fact, we didn't even pay to see the citadel until we were nearly at the top, where we met the caretaker coming in the opposite direction.

The mountain on which Poenari sat rose above everything, and at the base of it were a souvenir stand, a couple of picnic tables, and a few animals—that day, dogs lying lazily in the grass and a bull swishing its tail. Occasionally a car would go by and one of the dogs would start barking.

There were no lines to see the fortress. After visiting Poenari in the mid-1990s, Dracula expert Elizabeth Miller reported amazement that no other tourists were there, and it hadn't changed much. Even if other visitors were present, it would be hard to get a sense of them because the way up the hill is long, and people could be anywhere between the bottom and the top.

It was a short walk through the grass to where the concrete steps began, and there was no ceremony; we just started up. A restroom sat off to one side among the trees, and I had to use it. The modest shed was repulsive, with air so stinky I had to hold my breath; little bugs flying around; and, of course, no toilet paper—but I carried my own. If Lucian hadn't been waiting for me—that is, if I hadn't worried I'd be visible—I'd have skipped the shelter and used the open woods.

Shortly after Lucian and I had left the sunny meadow below, the woods swallowed us up. I thought about those tourists in the Dracula movies, being left off in the forest below Dracula's castle. In daylight or at their edges, the woods were friendly enough, but they were deep and thick. Day could become like night in an instant. Well, there we were, not in complete darkness but climbing through the dim and dappled hush of the forest.

When you're climbing them, the steps to the citadel tend to disappear out of sight above you. The same is true if you look backward. The sets of steps switch back and forth, with landings along the way. I had practiced for the climb for months back in Ohio, taking the ninety-six stairs to my fifth-floor office instead of the elevator. Even so, I rested at every opportunity and concentrated on getting to the top without complaining; after all, it was at my insistence that we were there. Lucian said not a word, stopping when I did but not even breathing hard. Yet he was the smoker, and, besides that, he carried my bulky bag all the way.

The image of Vlad holed up at the top of the mountain awaiting the Turks was in my thoughts as we climbed. Now that I could see the route in person, I wondered why in the world anyone—even the conquest-obsessed Turkish army—would go to the trouble to climb this mountain and storm Vlad's remote citadel. As the saying goes, they must have wanted him *bad*. Our ascent, aided by concrete steps and a handrail, was a picnic compared to theirs. As Lucian said in a bit of guide dialogue, there were "no steps for them," no railings to hold, no easy path. They presumably couldn't ride horses but had to go on foot at night, without torches, in order to be undetected from above. The mountain is densely wooded, and the attackers—carrying heavy weapons—would have had to climb straight up through dirt, rocks, and thick trees to reach the fortress where the Prince of Wallachia was ensconced with his wife, or girl-friend, or mistress—take your pick; the stories differ.

If the thrill of Poenari was history, it was not just the history of Vlad and the Turks. The same man who collected Elizabeth Miller's money in 1994 took mine that day. Caretaker for the past thirty-five years, he also must have taken McNally's and Florescu's when they climbed to the fortress. And on the subject of "taking money," there was some confusion as I was getting my ticket. With my scanty knowledge of the Romanian monetary system, the fault could have been mine, but Lucian seemed to think the caretaker had short-changed me. They held a brief, spirited discussion, and the only thing I understood was that I got change back at the end of it.

It was a thrill for me that McNally and Florescu had gone this way; Elizabeth Miller had, and who knows how many others—and Vlad. When I'd started out on this trip, I didn't care a hoot about Vlad, but he was, after all, the Romanian hero. I hadn't thought lately about my movie idol, Christopher Lee. Had Lee also made the trek up to the citadel? I wanted to go where he'd gone; the trouble was, I didn't know where he'd gone.

Once we reached the top, I stood among the crumbling red brick walls that were all that remained of the Poenari fortress. Was Poenari ever used as a setting in the movies? It would have been hard to stage anything on that mountaintop, with most of the space taken up by the rambling walls of the former castle. In spite of some restoration, it still had no enclosed rooms.

I loved seeing Poenari, even if it did point locally to Vlad the Impaler rather than Count Dracula. Its mountaintop location was perfect for Vlad's purpose—gaining an edge on his enemies—but with a bit of imag-ination it could have been the Count's castle, too. In the novel, Jonathan Harker wrote this about his arrival at Dracula's castle:

We kept on ascending, with occasional periods of quick descent, but in the main always ascending. Suddenly, I became conscious of the fact that the driver was in the act of pulling up the horses in the courtyard of a vast ruined castle, from whose tall black windows came no ray of light, and whose broken battlements showed a jagged line against the moonlit sky.

Harker later opened his guest-room window in daylight and wrote this in his diary:

The view was magnificent, and from where I stood there was every opportunity of seeing it. The castle is on the very edge of a terrible precipice. A stone falling from the window would fall a thousand feet without touching anything! As far as the eye can reach is a sea of green tree tops, with occasionally a deep rift where there is a chasm. Here and there are silver threads where the rivers wind in deep gorges through the forests.

Except for "vast" and the whole idea of the coach and horses, the description fit what we'd seen. Lucian and I had stood on the flat ground around the castle ruins and looked down at the sparkling thread that was the Argeş River, now with a tiny road running parallel to it. We'd seen the view of green trees and mountains in every direction. We could vouch for the precipice; in fact, one of the castle walls began well below the edge, creating a sheer surface that would have been impossible to climb up or down—unless you were the Count.

I gave Lucian the camera and backed up so that he could take my picture in front of the castle ruins. How far I'd come from the hills of West Virginia! There I was, standing on a mountaintop in Central Europe, looking out over a countryside rich in local history and woven into the legend of Dracula. Lucian was silhouetted against the sky, his back to the surrounding mountains and the sharp drop to the Argeş River.

In Dracula movies, "guests" of the Count contemplating escape would have their hopes dashed by the sobering view out the castle window: the ribbon of water flowing past treacherous rocks far below. In one movie, Count Dracula himself goes out a window, flattening himself face in against the steep outer wall and crawling away, his black silhouette like that of a bat. Even the Count with all his strength and powers wouldn't want to end up in the Argeș, where he couldn't survive its moving waters.

Vlad's lady met an unfortunate end, according to legend. She apparently chose the Argeș River over the Turks, jumping to her death from one of the fortress walls. It would have been a long trip down. I tried to picture it, but my mind wouldn't complete the fall.

I'd looked over the edge from a safe distance. It wasn't a sheer drop; clumps of bushes grew below the mountaintop. Hurling yourself off the precipice would be a little bit like jumping into the Kanawha River from the old tower at the end of the pier back in Glen Ferris: You'd have to aim your body outward.

Maybe for her the experience was like the time my sled flew off a cliff in Glen Ferris with me on it. I blacked out long before I hit the ground, and in my mercifully unconscious state missed the crash entirely. I woke up twenty minutes later stretched out on the back of Teakettle, my old Flexible Flyer with its bent red runners. My friends were pulling me along the sidewalk toward home. "We thought you were dead," one said, as they took me the last few yards to our house. My mother was already standing at the front door, ready to take care of me, and that was a nicer ending than Mrs. Vlad's.

Going back down the concrete steps wasn't so bad when measured against a screaming tumble into the Argeș Valley. Walking down was much faster than walking up had been, but my legs shook like crazy. By the time we crossed the grass to the souvenir stand, my lower extremities were wobbling like tires about to go flat.

Lucian and I ordered cold drinks from the stand at the bottom of the hill and took them to a picnic table. Soon we'd be piling into our little car and heading out to see what was around the next bend; but first, a well-deserved break. It felt good to be still after practically bouncing down the 1,480 steps. I could barely speak for trying to draw a normal breath. Lucian was his usual quiet self, and we sat together in silence in the sun.

Chapter 19

The Runner

A lot of photography is about a moment.

When we'd come down off the mountain at Poenari, the open area was deserted except for the souvenir-stand clerk and two young men with beers sitting at a picnic table. One of them caught my eye as Lucian and I walked by. He motioned me over, and in my single-minded, thirsty state I rudely waved him off. I figured he wanted something, though it was a mystery what he could want with me. Lucian didn't indicate he'd noticed the exchange, and we took our drinks to another table.

After a while—once I'd rested and my brain had re-engaged—I realized I did know the young man. He was a runner I'd photographed earlier in the woods.

All the photography books tell you to be ready. You never know when a great shot will materialize and you'll have only seconds to take it. Well, it's true.

We were two thirds of the way up to the citadel, and I'd been thinking about the Turks. I had my camera around my neck from trying to capture the long climb through the woods—the steep grade, the shadows, and the stairs that tapered to vanishing points in both directions. Suddenly I was startled from my reverie by a runner coming the other way.

A runner! Was I seeing things? I'd been hoping for enough breath and strength to make it to the top of the mountain, and there was a young man dressed in shorts and a tank top running down the steep stairs toward us.

I stopped climbing and grabbed my camera. For a moment it seemed that time had stopped with me. It even seemed like the runner stood still for that moment, stopping just before our paths would have crossed on the steps. No doubt he was as startled as I was.

The part of photography in which you translate what the eye sees into a series of hand movements over the camera is a psychomotor skill, like driving or typing. I'd stocked up on photography books before my trip, but here's a secret: You can't cram and be better at a skill; it takes practice. With enough practice, your hands will know the right buttons to push on a camera, the right amount of twist for the lens. My friend Susan says you have to take a thousand pictures for that to happen. I hadn't.

As I brought the camera up, it felt like slow motion, holding it to my eye and pushing the shutter. And then the moment was over and we all came to life. The runner went on, my voice following him down through the dappled woods: "I can't believe you're running on these steps!"

I didn't expect a reply, but I heard one in English. "It's healthy!" With that, he continued down the hill and was gone. We went on to the top.

As soon as I realized that one of the young men at the other table was the runner, I felt terrible for my earlier snub. I got up, went over, and apologized. His name was Andrei; he wanted to thank me for taking his picture on the steps and to ask me to send him a copy.

Andrei was a second-year student at the police academy in Bucharest. He walked the road from his house in a nearby village every day to run up and down the steps to the Poenari Citadel, building his endurance. "Today," he said, "is the first time I made it all the way up and down." Andrei would make a worthy member of the Politia Bucharesti. He had youth, strength, persistence, and a sense of right. In fact, if I'd been battling for control of the citadel in the fifteenth century, I'd have wanted him on my side. I pulled out one of my homemade permission slips for Andrei to sign, feeling righteous as I tucked it back into my bag.

When I was young, I had an Official Girl Scout 620 Camera. One weekend Mom took Joe and me to the elegant Greenbrier Hotel in White Sulphur Springs, West Virginia, to watch a professional golf tournament.

We were standing in for Dad, who'd gone for a checkup at the Cleveland Clinic.

As we followed the stars—Sam Snead, Arnold Palmer, and Gary Player—around the course, Joe borrowed my camera to take a picture of Snead. Joe didn't know the camera was noisy. He tripped the shutter during a critical putt and broke Snead's concentration. The golfer snapped at Joe in front of everybody. Maybe it was a sign.

The whole weekend was a nightmare. Mom began to drink with her friends the first evening. Partying was one thing, but Mom couldn't stop. She stayed sloshed and sloppy all weekend, turning surly when we were in our cabin. As usual, I was the main target. Nothing I did pleased her, and the tension was terrible. By the time Sunday arrived, I was beyond ready to go home. Dracula couldn't have done a better job on me; I was drained.

Finally we all got in the car. Joe was in front with Mom, and I was in the back seat—the outcast. Mom was still blitzed, of course. We hadn't been on the road long when I noticed a car in the distance coming right at us. It was passing and should have moved back into its own lane, but instead it seemed a certainty that we were going to crash head on.

As the car got closer, Mom kept driving as if the road were clear. Was I the only one who saw the coming disaster? I remember everything slowing down in my mind. I watched the approaching car through our windshield and knew—*knew*—that in a few seconds I was going to die on that road. All of us were.

I didn't even scream; what was the point? It was too late, but that wasn't the only reason. I realized I wasn't scared. It wasn't just a case of being worn down from the drunkenness and drama of the weekend; for the first time in days, I felt calm. Let the car hit us; I didn't care. I was fourteen or fifteen years old, and so sad and miserable at home that I was all right with dying.

At the last second, the oncoming car swerved back into its lane and we continued on. We'd been saved.

Lucian and I left our table for the parking lot at the same time Andrei and his friend were starting to walk along the winding two-lane road toward home. It was obvious that all of us were going in the same direction, and Lucian turned to me: "Do you want to pick them up?" Of course I did.

Andrei and his friend rode with us a few miles before we parted ways. For a change the car was filled with conversation, most of it about cameras. His friend was quiet, but Andrei was animated, telling us about his avocation: photography. "I love taking pictures of nature and pictures of places where I have been," he said; and then, "I wish I had a good camera." But he was young and on a budget.

"It isn't the camera that's important," I said. "It's the photographer. *You* are the one who can make a beautiful photograph." I said it magnanimously. I said it with authority, as if I knew—after all, I was the one with the $1,200 Nikon.

The irony came later, when I found out that my photo of Andrei hadn't turned out. I hadn't learned the camera settings well enough, and it had all happened too quickly. It was too dark in the woods for whatever setting I had used. My skills weren't there for such a sudden opportunity.

If I'd been a proper photographer, I'd have looked for the shot on the camera while we were sitting at the picnic table. Then I would have known it was only a black rectangle, and I could have taken another photo of Andrei in his running clothes at the base of the mountain. But I didn't think of it. I had to e-mail him and tell him that I'd failed to produce the photo he wanted so much. I hoped he'd forgive me.

Forgiveness is a tricky thing. I would never see Andrei again, but at home I now saw my mother several times a week. Had I ever forgiven her?

Chapter 20

Monsters and Monasteries

Poenari took a big chunk out of our day. That was all right with me, but on the way back to Curtea de Argeş we still had to tour Manole's Monastery. I could have said, "Let's skip it"—after all, it was my trip—but skipping it didn't even occur to me: the programmed mind.

Manole's Monastery is legendary; more than 100,000 people visit it every year because of its beauty and the story behind its construction. Details of the legend are inconsistent, but the gist is this: Manole was a master builder in the sixteenth century. The ruler of Wallachia—not Vlad, but still cruel—hired Manole and his crew of nine masons to build the most beautiful monastery ever created. They worked each day, only to find the next morning that the walls they'd built had collapsed. Manole discovered in a dream that the project required a human sacrifice.

The ten men decided to go outside their little group and sacrifice whichever of their wives was the first to come to the construction site. Manole's wife, Ana, brought his breakfast and so it was she whom they buried alive in one of the walls. After the deed was done, construction proceeded and the completed monastery proved to be a work of extraordinary beauty. The ruler, afraid the builders would create another church to rival his, removed the scaffolding and stranded them on the roof. They somehow constructed wings and attempted to fly to the ground, but all ten perished.

We arrived at six fifteen, with barely enough time to see the monastery before it closed. When Lucian and I parked and walked up the front steps, I didn't know anything about the place. I paid 50,000 lei to take pictures, all the while trying to remember the differences between this monastery and others. Lucian told me about the woman buried in the masonry, which certainly distinguished it, but I was focusing on looks: *yellow, twisty posts; yellow, twisty posts.* Many of the internal posts and external towers looked as though a giant had twisted the top of each one, throwing the vertical lines into beautiful diagonals that wrapped around and around.

Touring churches wasn't something I did in America, but once in high school I fell prey to the lure of the Scrabble Creek Church of All Nations, known to nonbelievers as the snake church. I had classmates who attended the controversial church—the preacher used live rattlesnakes in the service—and, though I wasn't interested in membership, I was fascinated enough to slip in the door for a few minutes one Saturday night to watch.

The newspapers had brought it all to light: Members went into trances, spoke in strange tongues, and handled poisonous snakes while trusting their faith to keep them safe. Who wouldn't be fascinated? Except the sobering truth was that people were bitten; then, because of their beliefs, they refused medical help. One man died and a sweet boy in my class nearly lost an arm that way.

By the time Lucian and I sat down for dinner back at the hotel, it was getting dark. We ate outside under a porch roof, where we could watch the traffic along the main street. It was a lively scene: people driving by or walking from one shop to another, crisscrossing the road at angles under the large trees that overhung the street.

Lucian ordered our dinner in Romanian. The dish was chicken with garlic. "Do you like garlic?" he asked. In Romania? Heck, yes, I liked garlic! Bad breath, be damned. No vampires would get near me that night, thanks to that chicken. Even Dura-gul himself couldn't hurt me now. We also had cabbage salad, potatoes, a few cooked onions, and then ice cream for dessert. Well, that was me; Lucian smoked.

We had wine with our meal, which hit the spot, but I felt it afterwards—queasiness with a tinge of regret. After the plates were cleared,

Lucian put on his little reading glasses, spread out a map on the table, and unfolded a copy of my itinerary. He was already planning for the next day. I still longed for my time in town and would have liked to walk along the lighted streets. But the shops closed at eight, and we didn't finish eating until seven fifty. Given that, I was ready to turn in.

Something woke me up. I glanced at the clock—12:15 a.m. I figured I must have been too warm under the wool blanket. And I'd fallen asleep with the light on, something I did occasionally at home.

I heard bursts of dog-barking and noise from the street. Then I thought bugs were biting me, attracted by the light. It was my night for worrying. I lay in bed and wondered how I was going to keep everything straight. It seems so clear when you're there, but in two weeks all of the monasteries and all of the villages would blend together, and I'd have no idea when I got home what was what. The business of journalism is not simple. Lucian probably felt like a pack horse by then, carrying my big bag everywhere; and even without the bag to worry about, I wasn't keeping track between the photos in my digital camera and the descriptions on my keyboard. *Curtea de Argeş. Twisty poles. Dura-gul.*

Night was the only time I could reconcile what I'd seen that day. The keyboard required no maintenance—hooray! But I would have to get out my plug adapter and recharge the camera battery. This was after I'd transferred the images to my portable hard drive. I also had to recharge the hard drive, so that was a lot of management after a day of touring and possibly a drink of wine. Sometimes I forgot or was too tired. One time the plug, heavy with its attached converter, fell out of the wall while I was asleep.

At five, I gave up on sleep. I knew I was going to have to rethink the wine-for-dinner thing: Bottles of wine were expensive, were not on my menu from the travel company, and drinking it left me too fuzzy and my stomach unsettled. Last night's dinner had been good, but I had no appetite now except for water, and I needed to use the only bottle I had left for my morning coffee.

Sometimes I still wondered if I could become an alcoholic. I knew I might have the gene, and weren't alcoholics predestined or something? But not every child of an alcoholic would become one. If I were going to succumb to drink as my mother had, wouldn't I know it by now? It would be nice to have a glass of wine without slipping into the same old inner dialogue, the frightening questions that had become automatic from decades of wondering. I had everything else: a raging food addiction, a fondness for casino gambling, a compulsive personality. I understood cravings: insatiable thirst, hunger, the need for excitement; sports fanaticism, a gambling habit, a caffeine fix, or just an acute desire to watch TV. They were all alike—temporary fixes for something else. I indulged mine with caution, knowing that a true addiction is the highlight of your existence beforehand and the bane of it afterward.

It seemed that five in the morning was a common time for rain in Romania, just as it was at home. I was making my coffee when I heard something and went to look out the window. As in Bucharest, there was a semisheer curtain under the draperies, and it didn't part. *Claustrophobia, anyone?* But it was raining hard for sure. I heard a car go by splashing water, and who can mistake the sound of an early morning rain? We'd had two beautiful days in Bucharest and one in Curtea de Argeş; now we would see Sibiu in the rain unless the weather was different there.

Suddenly I realized that the door to my balcony had been open all night. No wonder I'd slept fitfully and heard so much noise! I wasn't concerned for my safety; intruders couldn't reach me on the second floor, and soon the sky would be getting light.

Lucian and I were about to set out for Transylvania. Largest of nine regions in Romania, it lay near the center of the country, north of us. Our route would take us through the Olt River valley to Sibiu, described in my official itinerary as "once the richest town in Romania." Sibiu was the supposed location of the Scholomance, the mysterious witches' school from *Dracula,* and that was the extent of my expectations: I hoped to look for it. No doubt we would catch a monastery or two on the way.

We were scheduled to leave at nine. I didn't look forward to the drive. Lucian was a good driver; you'd have to be, especially to do it for a living. But driving in Romania is like a sport, only there are no cheering fans— possibly just passengers trying not to cower against the door handle. I was often scared in the car, though I tried not to show it. If I paid any attention at all, it was nerve wracking. Lucian scooted in and out of lanes, swerved, accelerated, and occasionally seemed to be trying to kill us, as when he'd made a quick U-turn in Bucharest while I looked out the passenger side at an oncoming car headed straight for my door.

The cars are small in Romania. You see the occasional Beemer, but there's a wide gap between most people and the rich. Lots of Romanians don't drive at all; we saw people along the road in village after village, waiting for a ride. There's a hand signal a driver can make that means "I'm not going far," so the hitchhiker will know why you aren't stopping. I wish I could remember the movement, because Lucian did it often. The people wanting rides are possibly the only citizens of Romania who pay attention to what's coming on the road. Generally adults and even children walk along as though they're magic and won't be hit.

In the hotel I packed and began getting ready for the day. There was no hot water. The faucet had indicators for hot and cold, but no difference in the temperature. I knew to expect this in Europe, maybe in a remote village in the wilds of Transylvania, but not in a supposedly modern hotel! Luckily I wasn't filthy, but my hair had gotten quite a workout from my tossing and turning. Well, the rain today would have had an effect anyway. A hairdo is like a banana: There are about three seconds in time when either one is just right. I looked in the mirror. It was interesting how good my hair looked to me once I knew I couldn't wash it.

Outside my window, the clouds were being swept away. Could it be a change in weather? We'd see.

When we were in the car, just starting out, I heard a noise and thought it was a flat tire, rhythmic and floppy the way flats sound when they hit the pavement. Once when I was in grade school, my mother took a carload of us to a PTA event. Afterward Mom pulled out of the school parking lot in the dark, turning onto Route 60 toward home. We were quiet in the car, the way you get at night—except that one of the other passengers had a nervous habit of sucking her lips against her teeth. I'd heard it a million times: a squeak like air escaping slowly through the end of a balloon.

Mom pulled off onto the dirt. "I think we've got a flat tire," she said, and got out of the car. We all sat in dead silence while Mom walked around our 1951 Buick, examining the tires. Then the familiar squeak came from the back seat. I knew we didn't have a flat tire, and so did everyone else—everyone but Mom, who was puzzled but relieved as she got back into the driver's seat and continued up the road.

Now Lucian got out in the rain and looked at our tires, which were fine. It was the clopping of horses' hooves down on another street that I'd heard. They seemed to come from another era, perhaps Dracula's time.

I laughed to myself at the memory of my mother's "flat tire," but I didn't mention it. Would Lucian even get the humor in the story? Besides, he and I didn't talk about anything personal.

I'd learned a few things about him by then, mainly his opinions. The strongest ones he offered were comments on the government and the country's law enforcement system, which were boring topics to me. I did ask him one thing over and over so that I could remember it: "Tell me again what the Japanese call Dracula."

We rode in a silence that was more like white noise, with the combined sounds of road traffic, the wind, and my keying. It was a relief not to have to worry about how to behave or what Lucian thought of me. And I had no inkling that would ever change.

Chapter 21

Valley of Memories

The Olt River valley wasn't just an area we passed on our way to Sibiu; it was the location of Cozia Monastery, built in the fourteenth century as a fortress by Vlad Dracula's grandfather, Mircea the Old, who's buried there in a sarcophagus. It was ironic that an ancestor of Dracula would build a church, but this was Romania's real Dracula family. The vampire Dracula, whose skin bubbles and burns at the touch of a crucifix, would have skipped this stop.

According to Lucian, we were traveling the main road through the heart of Romania. Curved like the two-lane on Gauley Mountain and just as full of trucks, it wound past big haystacks, green hills, and many villages, a thousand pictures in each one. In one little town a sign said "DISCO ECSTASY." Just beyond it sat a house with clothes hanging out on the line—clearly not the disco. Between villages, there was nothing but country.

An old peasant woman standing on the road watched us approach the monastery entrance. Except for her face and hands, she was covered head to toe in black: head scarf, jacket, a skirt that hit just below her knees, leggings, and even black high-top tennis shoes, the cloth kind basketball players used to wear. She could have been in mourning or just dressed for the day.

Lucian parked and we headed in. A monastery is not just a place of worship, but also a religious community. It's a fortress built to insulate and protect its residents. Cozia was what I would come to know as typical. The property facing the road was bordered by a stone fence. A wide flagstone walk led to the church itself, which was a work of arches: The three framing the entrance were echoed in the roofline and the crowning dome. A whitewashed wall thick enough to house living quarters surrounded the church on the other three sides.

It was still early and the sky was overcast, but other tourists were already there, going in and out the main door and taking pictures. I did the same, even though it was almost too dark to expect the photos to turn out.

I wasn't patient in monasteries. The ancient churches of Romania were beautiful, but there were too many unfamiliar names and icons; too much history, too much meaning—and most of it had nothing to do with me, or even Count Dracula. At Cozia we saw colorful stained-glass portraits as big as doors depicting Mircea the Old and other voivodes from Romania's history. But even with its connection to Vlad Dracula, the interior of the church failed to keep my attention.

The monastery is located on the banks of the Olt River, but you can't tell from the front. The thick outer walls at the back seem to rise up out of the water, and that to me was the best part of Cozia. After dutifully checking out the inside, I followed Lucian onto a large balcony that hung so low over the Olt that it could have been a boat carrying us over the dark, choppy water.

On another day the view from the balcony might have been tranquil and lovely, with the sun shining on calm water and a little breeze blowing. Maybe over the centuries the monks had brought their lunches outside, sitting at primitive tables and leaning back between bites to turn their pallid faces to the sun. Did they have those straight bangs ending halfway up their foreheads, and if they lingered too long, would the sun line tell the tale? The day Lucian and I stood on the balcony it was dreary out—the sun having yet to make a significant appearance—and white mist lingered between the mountains. No tables awaited us on the damp flagstones.

The scene before us was large, noisy, thrilling, and frightening. The Olt River filled my senses as it raced by. The balcony was enclosed with a black wrought-iron railing, giving us a safe place from which to view the churning water. The current was a visible force, pulling the white-capped water downstream beyond our view. There was nothing welcoming about it unless you were contemplating suicide.

Growing up on a river, I learned to swim in moving water. We had to be able to take care of ourselves. Once Mom followed me across the Kanawha in a rowboat to make sure I had the stamina I'd need not to drown, or be swept downstream to the hard wall of the dam, or end up in the mysterious innards of the hydro plant. I couldn't imagine a group of kids swimming across the churning Olt River. It seemed like a crazy idea.

Once a group of us did swim the Kanawha. We got across all right, and then a storm broke. We stood on the other side in mud, shivering, with little bugs jumping up on our legs. We had nowhere to go but back, and in minutes we were swimming the wide river again, plowing through the chop and current with dark clouds overhead and rain pelting us, Joe in a life jacket trying to keep up. We swam for our lives, with thunder and the threat of lightning driving us toward the dock. On the other side of the road was our house. I could see the lights on and Mom upstairs by the window. That day—before the end of my innocence—I was instantly warmed by the yellow rectangles of light, the image of my mother, and the promise of soon being safe and dry.

The Olt wasn't as wide as the Kanawha, but it was Romania's longest river at 457 miles, and it was water running between green mountains— a sight as familiar as home. There was even a hydroelectric plant in the distance.

The Romanian government built some one hundred hydroelectric plants between 1965 and 1985. The one we saw was one of a chain constructed along the Olt with a total capacity of twelve hundred megawatts—twelve million watts. But never mind all of that that. The water flowing past us was coming from the Carpathians, and *that* gave me a thrill. We weren't close enough to see the details of the plant, but the structure reminded me instantly of our hydro plant in Glen Ferris—the creepiest building in town.

Our plant was located at the lower end, where the river flowed over the dam. It consisted of two connected buildings, each red brick with a concrete foundation. They were two stories high, with only the top story visible from the street. Both levels could be seen from the island, farther downstream.

Between the buildings and connected to both by a walkway was a giant block of concrete topped with transformers and electrical-looking boxes. It was hard to tell just how big the configuration was because it rested on a large rock in the water. Surrounded by metal railings, it looked like something out of *The Terminator;* and even if I could have, I wouldn't have gone near it.

The plant buildings were forbidding, too. The one closer to the road had two big arched openings over the water. You could see a little way in, but then it got dark. What was down there—was it just a place for water to run through, or something else? The other building was solid at the bottom, with the falls running right beside it. Joe and his friend Wade used to take a boat over from the island and look around, but I had no interest in that. The plant looked to me like a bad wall plug times one thousand-thousand, and I preferred not to be turned into a shower of sparks.

Dad and I used to walk past the plant sometimes, on the elevated sidewalk that ran along the front of the building beside the road. We had to pass a cage-like area built in the water to catch logs and leaves and other river debris. We couldn't see to the bottom of the trap, so it too was threatening. If you fell into that, would you die from electrocution, or would you just be imprisoned and slammed up against the sides of the cage? Or maybe you'd come out through one of the arches below, whooshing into the river as though from a giant water-park slide's evil twin.

We could look right into the plant from the walkway and see big machines—six turbines with round tops that tapered into little caps, giving them a shape vaguely like Hershey's Kisses—grunting and groaning in an orange glow. When I was small, I was afraid of their size and the sounds they made. Over the years, I passed the plant a million times in the car, and sometimes I didn't even look over, but it never lost its creepiness for me.

After we'd seen Cozia, Lucian and I hit the road, driving farther into the Olt Valley as the sun rose in the sky. He was dressed all in blue. Sure, I noticed; but then I fell easily into my writing routine, glad for that simple framework around our relationship.

The Olt Valley has a history as a center for spa resorts. Romania is sprinkled with such resort areas, intended more for healing than for beauty treatments. The country's therapeutic mineral springs have been used for cures since the Romans conquered what was then Dacia in the second century.

We drove by once-grand spas that in livelier times had attracted visitors from all over the world. It was easy to picture, even though the buildings now looked empty. The Romanian ministry of tourism still released full-color brochures showing people on exercise bicycles, in spa tubs, and lounging beside blue-green pools. Lucian said that many of the spas and hotels were indeed closed, but the country hasn't given up. The National Organization of Spas, formed in 1993, now has sixty members. The spas are still advertised (www.spas.ro), particularly as destinations for those with digestive afflictions and internal diseases.

A big moment: We entered Transylvania from Wallachia. *Woo hoo*, but I wouldn't have known if Lucian hadn't told me. Nothing appeared to have changed. He said the villages in Transylvania would look different from the ones we'd seen. *How?* Would the villages in Transylvania look more like those in the movies? Would they be more reminiscent of Dracula? I kept my window down and my camera ready, expecting that any minute the scenery might turn grim. The sun did its part, going in and out from behind the clouds.

I looked for sharp, craggy peaks and dark evergreens; a menacing mist; and a gloomy castle looming far above us, casting a long shadow—scenery befitting my image of Romania. But everything I saw reminded me of Glen Ferris. A blue train went by across the river. The sun played on the water and warmed up the hills all around us. Dots of houses appeared on the mountainsides ahead, with larger buildings lower down, all of it just past the place where the river began to curve.

I felt a tug inside. There I was in the ancestral homeland of Count Dracula, yet the scene before me had taken me back to the West Virginia hills.

Chapter 22

The Brukenthal

Oh, my God, I thought from the doorway, *I should be ruling a country to have a hotel room like this!* It was late Tuesday morning, and we had just arrived in Sibiu. Lucian had gone down the hall to his own room.

I pulled my bags inside. The room was royal, not in size but in style, with high white walls and white painted woodwork. The wall-to-wall carpet was a rich navy blue with a pattern of gold flecks and medallions that could have been the official seal of some principality. At the opposite end of the narrow room, street sounds rose like music through a tall casement window framed with flowing drapes of shiny gold.

I don't care if nothing works in this room, I thought, recalling how I'd given up on hot water in the previous hotel. *I'm never leaving here. I'm staying!*

The room even had a partial second story. To the right of the window, an open staircase led to a loft just big enough for a bed and two nightstands. The wooden bed was honey colored, with a carved headboard and footboard. On it was laid a lustrous spread of gold-on-gold brocade. Back downstairs, a glass-topped table for two sat next to a studio couch tucked under the steps. On the furniture a satiny fabric, navy with gold fleur-de-lis, caught the light.

I quickly spread my suitcase open on the floor of my beautiful domain to get ready for the day. Lucian and I had agreed to meet in fifteen minutes for an afternoon of touring, starting with the Brukenthal National Museum.

I'll confess right here that I'd never heard of the Brukenthal Museum in Sibiu, Romania, and hadn't even remembered it was on the tour; it was another bit of Romanian culture the travel agency had inserted among the Dracula sites. I'd made a general request for just that, so it was all right; but I felt a shade ignorant when I realized how little I knew about Romania, aside from the story of Dracula.

The Brukenthal is an art gallery housed in an eighteenth-century palace in the old German section of Sibiu, the city once called Hermannstadt. Samuel von Brukenthal, governor of Transylvania from 1777 to 1787, had lived in the palace with his collection of art. The collection spans the fifteenth to the eighteenth centuries and represents Dutch, Flemish, German, Italian, Austrian, and Romanian artists.

On the short walk from the hotel, we passed torn-up streets and flattened construction sites. Workers wearing hard hats peered down at us from a balcony. It seemed that every city we'd seen was under renovation. It was part of the country's rise from its Communist grave after the end of the brutal Ceaușescu regime.

At the entrance to the Brukenthal, Lucian got my admission ticket and then left me to wander through the exhibits on my own. I was briefly surprised, though I shouldn't have been—not after he'd also waited for me to tour the Palace of Parliament and the Chindia Tower. I figured he'd seen the museum many times before, and I didn't really mind going through it alone. I could choose my own level of detail, and Lucian would return later to pick me up.

Having a male guide was a comfort walking down a strange street or sitting at dinner, but awkward in my secret thoughts. *We could pass for a couple,* I thought, not for the first time. It was inadvertent, the way you picture yourself going down the aisle with someone you just met. In a flash, you've taken a step that is simultaneously natural and disturbing, logical yet out of the question. Maybe you pretend to slap your own face, as I did: *Bad, bad.* Were my years of singlehood going to step out onto the stage of this vacation and do a can-can?

As for the museum, I approached it casually, feeling no pressure to study or memorize anything. It wasn't a lack of interest, exactly, just a freedom to view the exhibits as I wished. In fact, my thoughts wandered wildly from the magnificent displays. All of this is to say, don't hold me to these descriptions; but this is what I remember.

The Brukenthal has three floors. I began in the first-floor rooms, getting a sense of the exhibits: music rooms, ancient furniture, white ceramic stoves in corners; books; manuscripts of plays and operas from other centuries. There were even early printed manuscripts from Shakespeare. The written works were under glass, each with its own little identifying card folded like a place card at dinner. The items were arranged on glass shelves, each title page stamped with a seal of the museum.

The Brukenthal had the air of an elegant residence whose master has departed but whose servants remain. Museum employees, though unobtrusive, were everywhere. Walking through the first floor, I lightly touched the antique painted furniture, my eyes alert and some part of me waiting for a reprimand that didn't come. The furniture and display cases were arranged against the walls for the most part, leaving huge floor spaces as though the rooms had been set up for a dance.

I took in the elaborate moldings, silk wall covering, and chandeliered ceilings. My shoes made little echoes on the wood floors. Though the rooms weren't crowded, there were other tourists, silent but for the occasional swish of clothing. No photos were allowed, so with my camera already around my neck, I made sure to have my hands behind my back or in my pockets. Lucian had taken the bag back to the hotel.

Lucian was no stranger to camera equipment. He told me he'd been a photographer in the past, taking shots for local magazines. In Bucharest he'd shown me how to hold my camera correctly for a vertical shot. Sometimes when we were riding, he would say, "Get your camera ready," and we would round a bend to some jaw-dropping scene I might have missed without his help.

Religious subjects welcomed me to the second floor of the museum, home of the painting gallery. I took in the paintings of Jesus, Mary, and the angels that covered the walls. The painting collection included works by the masters; there was Botticelli among the names. Museum staffers flowed silently from room to room as knots of tourists gazed upon Virgin and child, Christ on the cross, *A Test of Faith*.

I thought again of Lucian. In any movie, we would become lovers; I knew that. As defined by current movie standards, we would have exchanged a significant look at the airport, flirted over dinner in Bucharest, and no doubt had wild . . . I couldn't even finish that sentence, couldn't even say it to myself and then face Lucian in a little while down on the street.

Our professional relationship included keeping a respectful distance from one another, and so far it had worked. Even so, I'd occasionally pictured another scene as we were driving along. It began with a shared hotel room somewhere: whitewashed walls, a window open to the familiar view of red-tiled rooftops with mountains in the distance. . . . What was the harm? I knew I couldn't conduct myself in a way that made me ashamed—except in my mind. And what did Lucian think across the many miles of silence? I had no idea.

The themes of the painting collection progressed in the opposite way of what you might think: from the spirit to the flesh; from the heavens to the earth—and the earthy. I came upon a room of works with a hunting theme. There was nothing polite about the paintings of slain, bleeding game—game splayed on the ground; game with dogs watching over it; game piled around the hunter, who rested against a tree with his eyes half-closed and a contented smile upon his face. They were evocative, sensual, flagrant, haunting. I wanted to look and turn away at the same time, the way people do at a terrible accident, or upon discovering they've been taken to a porn site on the Internet.

Onward.

I turned a corner and found myself facing a giant nude Venus. She was reclining, with one hand placed low in—I supposed—a gesture of modesty. As I continued through the collection I saw Venus again, along with Jupiter, Neptune, Aphrodite, Adonis, and a seeming cast of thousands—all naked, engaged in sensual pleasures or else posed coyly in anticipation. It was a riot of nymphs and satyrs—room after room—the females with their pale skin glowing off the canvas, the males painted as part of the dark. Nymphs and satyrs, breasts and torsos, everywhere I turned. Nymphs and satyrs frolicking in a wood, taking a break, sharing the moment with others in the countryside as you would a picnic.

It was these images that filled my mind when I left to meet Lucian on the bustling street in front of the museum. I forced the provocative pictures back at the sight of him striding toward me in denim with the camera bag over his shoulder, and we went on.

Chapter 23

The Lake

As a good Dracula fan, I couldn't travel through Romania without at least wondering about the Scholomance, the legendary witches' school near Sibiu mentioned in *Dracula*. According to the novel, the Scholomance was where Dracula learned about the occult. In fact, the whole Dracula family of Romania reportedly had direct connections with the Devil, having learned his secrets there.

The Scholomance wasn't on my itinerary, and there was a reason: Very little is known about it. The Scholomance is one of the last Dracula frontiers in that no one has found it—if it ever existed. According to legend, the school once run by the Evil One was located in the mountains over Lake Hermanstadt [*sic*]. Hermannstadt was the old German name for Sibiu.

I did more than wonder about the Scholomance; I wanted to look for it. We had a free afternoon; what the heck?

The reference to the Scholomance in *Dracula* is brief, part of a longer paragraph about the heroic "Voivode Dracula" who fought the Turks and whose family—"a great and noble race"—had dealings with the Devil. Yes, the voivode sounded a lot like Vlad—always Vlad; but at least it came from Bram Stoker.

Stoker took his cue from another author, Emily Gerard, who wrote about Transylvania in the nineteenth century. She described the Scholomance as a school "supposed to exist" in the heart of the mountains, where the Devil taught students "the secrets of nature, the language of the animals, and all imaginable magic spells and charms"—in person. Gerard even described the lake: "A small lake, immeasurably deep, lying high up among the mountains to the south of Hermanstadt [*sic*] is supposed to be the cauldron where is brewed the thunder, and in fair weather the dragon sleeps beneath the water."

Gerard's books covered folklore and superstitions including devils, werewolves, witches, dragons, and vampires. Some of the stories were indigenous to Romania, and others had been brought in with the Germans or Gypsies who settled there. The point was that strange things happen in Transylvania.

The description in *Dracula* says that the Scholomance was a school "where the devil claims the tenth scholar as his due." It was a kind of tithe—a levy of one tenth of something. Only ten scholars were admitted to the school at a time. Nine went home after the instruction, and the tenth stayed on as payment to the Devil. Dracula was the tenth scholar. This meant that after his instruction, he remained as the Devil's right-hand man.

Author C. Dean Andersson created a full and believable setting for the Scholomance in his 1993 novel *I Am Dracula*. The story covers Prince Vlad Dracula's transformation into my favorite vampire under the tutelage of his wife, Tzigane, a Gypsy witch. She prepped and trained Vlad in stages over several years, some of the training taking place in the Scholomance. Andersson expanded on the description of the secret school and wove a fascinating tale of the young prince's transition from mortal to immortal. We see how Vlad acquired his bloodlust, superpowers, and immortality, the last coming at the cost of his soul.

In Andersson's novel, the school was located in a "vale of fog and flowers" in the mountains above Hermannstadt/Sibiu. Andersson had never been to Romania, but there I was with a car and driver at my disposal and the afternoon before us.

Lucian was game to take a side trip. We bought a map, taking our best shot at the location. We didn't have much to go on. When I asked the store clerk about Lake Hermanstadt, we were told that not only did it not exist today; it had never existed. Even so—even though the trip might turn out to be little more than a gesture—I couldn't wait to get started.

I wondered why the Professors of Horror, McNally and Florescu, hadn't gone after this one. They'd been to Romania several times, not to mention locations in the United States and Europe, tracing the legend of Dracula. They had written three books about their findings. One, 1989's *Dracula: Prince of Many Faces,* includes a theory about the Scholomance but gives no indication the researchers visited the site. They do identify a village—Păltiniş—which lies high in the mountains near Sibiu, and a spot near Păltiniş called "Solomon's Rocks," where wandering students traditionally took oaths to uphold their scholarly way of life. The authors say those students were studying alchemy. It fits nicely with the legend, except that in McNally and Florescu's description there is no mention of a lake.

I'd researched the lakes surrounding Sibiu before I came on this trip. There were a lot of them, so which one was it?

A bottomless lake does exist near Sibiu. One lake at Ocna Sibiului contains salt water under fresh water. That one was a good candidate. As for the others, Bâlea Lake is a preserve. So are the Cindrelul Mountain Lakes, where some wild animals are protected by law. In addition to those, there were the glacial lakes Podragu and Avrig. Cibin, Sadu, and Hârtibaciu were listed as dam lakes. Until we narrowed it down, I was beginning to think of them all as damn lakes.

Armed with our map, Lucian and I set out for Ocna Sibiului on a sunny afternoon. Did Vlad Dracula take this route long ago? I could envision the scenery surrounding the Scholomance, at least until we started driving. We went down the highway leading out of the medieval town of Sibiu and turned onto an ordinary-looking two-lane road. This was no vale of fog and flowers. The land was flat: yellow fields under a big, blue sky. We could see mountains in the distance, but the key word was *distance*. Given our time frame of just a few hours, we had to stick to the local area.

I could still picture Vlad and Tzigane picking their way among the foggy hills on horseback. As we drove I was willing the scenery to morph into something reminiscent of a witches' school in the wilderness—hills, caves, rocks, and a mysterious lake or two—but when we reached our destination, what I got was a parking lot. Colorful, yes, but so far this set-ting was anything but mysterious.

Ocna Sibiului is a huge resort dating back to the early nineteenth cen-tury, when research was being conducted on the curative powers of the salt lakes. Its services include "mud packings" and warm bathings (let's hope that "worm bathings" in one of the descriptions I read was a typo-graphical error) intended to cure rheumatism and other diseases. The resort became a town in 1968. We were in a part of the complex desig-nated for swimming.

The area we entered had a tired, has-been look. The lawn was scrubby in spite of bunches of flowers planted in concrete rings. The fences needed painting, the road hadn't been paved in a while, and even the mint green signs looked flat. It didn't matter; there we were, and I was ready for the unveiling of the magic lake—or, in this case, lakes. The resort had four lakes within walking distance of one another. All of them retained a raw, natural feel despite the commercialization of the site with a slew of white pavilions.

The first lake was the largest, with stores and refreshment stands peg-ging it as the main lake. It most resembled the "old swimming hole." If you were alive in the 1950s, picturing this will be easier for you. If, on the other hand, your idea of a resort comes from the top ten beaches on the Travel Channel, you'll need a shift in your vision.

A rickety picket fence defined the irregular shoreline around the bathing area. In places it even crossed dips in the rocky border of the lake, hanging in the air like a stiff little suspension bridge. The ground was covered with a thin coating of sand, rutted and uneven, spread with a few towels and blankets. Sets of wooden steps led into the water at differ-ent points; the rough, weed-choked, rocky bank between the beach area and the lake was not a place to stick your toe in.

The resort was not crowded, but bathers came and went. We saw men in stretchy bikinis, young boys dressed in knee pants, and a naked child with a middle-aged woman whose stomach overlapped her suit bottom. She was one of several women wearing the blue two-piece bathing suits sold on the premises.

The most mysterious element so far was the black mud on the bodies of many bathers. Meant to cure afflictions including skin diseases, this treatment looked like it *was* a skin disease. A far cry from the children of the night mentioned in *Dracula,* these people had covered their bodies with the vitamin-enriched mud for healing purposes, giving them a strange appearance. With a little imagination, they became zombies straight out of the grave. Some chose to spot-cover, for example behind the knees or on the torso only, so that they were half black and half white. It was like being tattooed to the max, but this body covering could be washed off.

If this section of the Ocna Sibiului resort was regarded as a prime vacation spot, I had a much easier time believing in people turning themselves over to the Devil in droves. Lucian and I walked along one side of the lake, and I looked across the water for ways to connect the natural scenery to the scanty information I had about the Scholomance. I was looking for indentations in the sandy bank, curves leading to quiet lagoons, signs of a cave—anything to conjure up an image of the evil ones of long ago.

I mentally cleared the area of sunbathers and souvenir stands, emptied the parking lot, and took down the signs. I tried to picture a wilderness in place of the Tweety Bird beach towels; Coke and Pepsi logos; the now-empty umbrella tables set out for partying; and, on a bluff high above the lake, a campground. In my mind I changed day to evening, dropping in a campfire to replace the blazing sun. It was still hard to imagine a witch-fest there.

We walked away from the center of activity, up a dirt road to where two other lakes lay across from one another. They looked like holes dug by a backhoe and left to fill with rain. One was rectangular and about the size of a soccer field. It didn't look accessible, and no one was in it. The other one was irregularly shaped and about the size of a backyard swimming pool, but with banks of dirt. A few mud-covered bathers took a dip in the murky water. The grounds were left to nature; there was no evidence of landscaping, only patches of dirt and tufts of grass growing at different lengths. I couldn't picture this being the setting for the Scholomance, and we were running out of lakes.

The fourth lake was farther up the hill, and so deep in the ground that we couldn't see the water until we had almost reached the edge. As with the other lakes, there was no concrete; natural banks of dirt rose on all sides. We peered over at the bathers, who'd had to descend a long flight of steps to enter the water. It was like looking down into the crater of a volcano. Was this the "lake without bottom"? Did Dracula ever gaze down at the surface of Lake 4 as I was doing? Did witches once bathe here by firelight, mysteriously floating and bobbing on the surface, their bodies kept buoyant by the high salt content? Perhaps salt was part of the mystery and magic of Lake Hermanstadt.

I thought about what those witches from *Dracula* would find today if they could suddenly emerge from their magic school and fly over Ocna Sibiului or the twenty-first-century world beyond it. Even now Ocna Sibiului is reminiscent of a bygone era, before everything we did became huge—before water parks and wave pools, before megamalls and amusement parks with techno-miracles like roller coasters speeding along on skinny pipes.

As for the location of the Scholomance, did I really think I'd found it? I hadn't gone to the mountains, but we had gone to a lake south of Hermannstadt. I hadn't seen the village of Păltiniș, or Solomon's Rock, but could the bottomless lake at Ocna Sibiului—Lake Number 4 at the top of the hill—be the mysterious Lake Hermanstadt referenced by Emily Gerard and Bram Stoker? "A small lake, immeasurably deep," was what the description said.

Before the Dracula experts stage a revolt, let's call this a fun afternoon and be done with it. But can the question of whether I found the Scholomance really be answered? Because we still don't know the location of Lake Hermanstadt, who is to say?

One thing was obvious that summer day: The Romanians populating the lakes at Ocna Sibiului weren't witches or vampires. I doubt they had magic on their minds, unless you want to count the ones slapping mud on themselves as a cure. It's a safe bet that I was the only one with an agenda out of *Dracula;* the others were getting sun or, in Lucian's case, humoring the tourist.

Except for the whereabouts of Vlad Dracula's body, believed by some to have risen from its burial site in Snagov Monastery, the Scholomance is the last unsolved Dracula mystery. *Or*—as they say in the horror movies—*is it?*

Chapter 24

What Ails You

We were returning to Sibiu from the lake expedition when Lucian abruptly pulled the car over, turned sideways in the seat to face me, and leaned in with his hands out. This was the Romanian countryside, not a busy urban street, and we were alone out there. What was he doing?

I met my guide's hypnotic stare, suddenly thinking of all the vampire movies I'd ever seen. But that was crazy; this was the twenty-first century! As much as I might like to experience some semblance of the movies on my trip, this wasn't it. In the few seconds I had to think about why Lucian might be reaching for me, I knew I had to trust him.

Without making contact, Lucian's hands and fingers began to move around my upper body in something between a spell and a caress. This went on for several minutes, during which I was to be still. That part was not a problem; I was frozen in place, watching the moment unfold. Once or twice there was a light brush as hand passed shoulder or as Lucian reached around to do the back. Finally he started the car. "You feel better?" he asked, and I wondered if he could hear my pounding heart.

"What was that?" I asked when we were back on the road. "What were you doing?"

"I fix people," he said. "My wife can do it, too." And there it was: the crucial tidbit I'd been waiting for finally revealed. It was official, and I was off the flirting train.

"How did you meet her?"

"Patient," was all he said. *Patient?*

"Even doctors come to me for treatment," Lucian continued, lowering his voice; and that quickly, we were back to the original subject. He looked over at me and put his finger up to say "Shhhh," indicating that the doctors had sworn him to silence. When certain expressions crossed Lucian's face, he reminded me of the actor Ben Gazzara with his kind, dark eyes.

I'd awakened with a scratchy throat, and my bottle of Throat Rescue was in my nightstand back in Cincinnati. I'd asked Lucian to take me to a pharmacy and help me pick out medicine. "I will give you something," he'd said, dismissing over-the-counter remedies as "no good."

What did that mean, *no good?* And what did he intend to do instead? At that point, suspicion wasn't much of a leap, and I wondered if Lucian might have a dark connection to the world of street pharmacy. Maybe there was some code word a guide could use. How would he get what I needed, and would it be legal? Safe? It seemed that he had let the whole subject drop as we'd become absorbed in the street life of Sibiu—its churches, museums, shops, people, and the lakes. Now I was relieved to have the mystery solved: Lucian was a healer.

Once back in West Virginia, I'd had a wart removed by my grand-mother's neighbor. All the kids knew her hands were magic. We had a girl in town—a pretty girl—who was cursed with warts. She had clumps of warts, clusters of warts—white warts grouped like mushrooms at her ankles, on her knees, and even on her fingers. I'd seen her cured, so one summer evening I went to see the old woman.

She was sitting alone on the couch in her living room. Even though it was twilight, no lights had been turned on. I stepped close enough to let her rub the place just below my elbow. Her touch was light. She said nothing. Some days later, I looked and the wart was gone.

Now I wanted Lucian's cure to take. All the way back to town I swallowed repeatedly, testing the irritation and wishing it away, curious about how and when it would disappear. I had my doubts, but Lucian expected it: "You came for Dracula," he beamed, "and you got me!"

It seemed fitting that I'd met a healer in Transylvania; medicine, blood, and doctors had profoundly influenced the imagery in *Dracula*. Bram Stoker had been a sickly child, confined to his bed with a mystery ailment for the first seven years of his life. His mother entertained her ailing son with vivid tales from Irish folklore, horror stories, and accounts of the famine and cholera epidemic that had struck Ireland in the 1840s. Those tales, and the many books he read, shaped Stoker's imagination and fed his interest in the dark themes that would later show up in his writing.

Lucian and I arrived back in Sibiu. Instead of driving directly to our hotel, he took a different street, and we wound up on a side street in a residential area. When we came to a dead end, he stopped. *Now what?*

Chapter 25

The Accident

"This is the home of the King of Gypsies of the whole world," Lucian said, indicating a large white house on our left as he tore backward out of the side street. I didn't get the best look in those circumstances, but the house must have been three stories high, adorned with hanging containers of red flowers all across the front. And from that point, Florin Cioabă's esteemed residence was a blur, then out of sight.

Lucian had been doing me a favor. I'd been fascinated with the Romanian Gypsy culture—"Roma," as they called themselves—since I'd arrived. In the last chapter of *Dracula*, it is the Gypsies (called Szgany in the novel) who guard and transport a cart bearing the Count in his coffin. Their destination is Dracula's Castle high in the rugged mountains of Transylvania. Van Helsing and his party, following the way that Jonathan Harker documented on his fateful trip, plan to intercept the Szgany and destroy the Count before the setting sun releases the "Thing" into the night.

The Roma were part of a larger group, the Romani, who traced their roots back to India. The Romani had migrated west in medieval war times, ending up in Europe. With their unfamiliar ways, they were regarded with curiosity and then hostility; many were mistreated. The Eastern (now Central) European Roma who settled in Romania were enslaved for centuries until abolition in 1856—during Bram Stoker's time. Although most now live in homes, as a people they feel that they have no homeland. Some Roma are still mobile, traveling in covered wagons pulled by horses. Many are poor and make their living by selling handmade items or begging.

Lucian told me the King of the Gypsies looked ordinary, not as I might have thought: like some curly-haired pirate in patterned fabrics and gold earrings walking down the street. He drove a Mercedes.

Now we were on this strange street because Lucian had shown me the prize. We'd penetrated the heart of a Gypsy neighborhood. Across from the big white house—where no one appeared to be home—a young, dark-haired woman had watched us pull in. She was standing in a yard on my side of the car. From her stance and expression I got the distinct feeling that we were not welcome. Lucian murmured that she was the king's daughter.

They began a lively dialogue through my open window. I hadn't yet learned to tell if Lucian was angry or just animated; at any rate, I assumed he'd made a wrong turn and was asking for directions, or possibly apologizing. I couldn't understand the quick exchange, but I did understand how uneasy I felt, and why. We didn't belong there.

Now Lucian seemed hell-bent to leave and the whole scene was in motion. In a flash we were down the hill from the Gypsy houses, plowing backward. Lucian whipped the rear of the car around to do a three-point turn, when I felt and heard a huge crash. It surrounded us, swallowed us. Lucian did nothing without vigor, but this one rocked me. Something was so close behind the car that I was surprised to be sitting in the passenger seat in one piece. Had we backed into a building? Had a car or truck rear-ended us? It could have been anything from the impact.

The idea of an accident wasn't a surprise. I figured it was bound to happen; Romanian traffic was wild. We'd already had two close calls. The pattern of living dangerously had begun in Bucharest when a car barely missed us. Then, outside Sibiu, Lucian had been looking off to the left at Bâlea Lake and didn't see the yellow car right in front of us. I don't remember which way it was facing, just how yellow it was and how I thought: *This is it.* "Look out, look out!" I screamed, and somehow Lucian recovered from the accident that, seconds before, had been a sure thing.

This time he had backed the car into a concrete utility pole. In Romania utility poles are gray and open, like cinderblocks stacked high. Against a neutral background, they can be hard to spot—especially when you're in a hurry. Lucian got out and so did I. The Gypsies were starting to line up. They were silent, watching. I hoped it was curiosity and not animosity that had brought them over to investigate.

The two dents in the rear fender of the tour company's car were small; for all of the noise and impact, it wasn't as disastrous as I'd expected—at least not to the car. While Lucian concerned himself with the fender, I got back inside. He could deal with the Gypsies, too, if any dealing were required. I was worried about the banging my head had just taken as it was jerked back against the seat. Did I have a concussion? Was I going to vomit? Worse, what if the collision set off a chain of events leading to a detached retina? I knew the symptoms well, because I had already experienced them twice—once in each eye.

First come the floaters, dark or dark-rimmed shapes in the vision—often showers of them—moving with the eye; or it might be flashing, the name for bright light flashes that take jagged shapes when you blink your eyes. Sometime later the dreaded veil, or curtain, will emerge. A circle the color of blood slowly floats into your vision from some corner of the eye, descending or rising and then crossing to the other side like a ship at sea—or a bat in flight. You can't see through it or around it. That is your retina, detached. "It's off," as my doctor would say.

I worried that all of this would happen to me again, and I would have to cut the trip short and leave Romania. Of course it would be necessary to make arrangements immediately at the first sign.

My retinas had previously been reattached by a surgery called scleral buckling, a delicate process followed by a period of quiet recuperation on the part of the patient and warnings from the doctor not to sustain any head injuries. It had been years since my two surgeries; how vulnerable was I?

I didn't go into it with Lucian, sure that this new worry of mine wouldn't seem so pressing to him. He'd practically accused me of being a scaredy-cat already. While he gave me credit for braving Dracula, he was too perceptive to miss my concerns over Romanian driving, stray dogs, street thieves, pickpockets, scams, and bacteria, to name a few. Was he trying to analyze me now? With all the self-analysis I'd been doing, I could have saved him the trouble.

I knew my fear of detached retinas was legitimate, but it's no wonder a traveler can turn paranoid; aside from well-founded global fears, visitors to foreign countries are warned regarding a range of everyday topics. Carry your own medications; be sure to get your shots; don't drink the water; don't surrender your passport. Keep your papers and money on your person; don't leave your belongings in the hotel. Lucian thought I was fearful, but when I left home to travel alone to Romania, all my friends said I was brave.

My guide said he'd seen plenty of tourists who wouldn't take risks—wouldn't try new foods, didn't want to travel to new places, and complained because things weren't like they were at home. I guess he didn't want me to be another client like that, but I didn't think I'd been complaining. I'd gone into this trip knowing there would be some risks and disappointments. I knew I might not like the food, that it might violate my diet; that Romania might be a letdown; that maybe I was staying too long. I wasn't sure I was taking the right clothes. I knew I could get sick—anyone could. But I counted on prevention to put a big dent in my concerns. I got ready and I came anyway, not to die on some pitted highway far from home, not to leave on a medical airlift I'd purchased with my travel insurance, but to have my Romanian vacation!

It was unsettling to have Lucian see my fears, but let's face facts. He had wrecked his company's car in a quick, stupid move that could not be taken back. That's the trouble with all of this: Some things can't be done over. Our mistakes are often quick, our egos bruised for a longer time. We may not even have time for regret.

After the accident, we left the car near our hotel and walked along the streets of Sibiu for a while, cutting through a park. Neither of us had obvious injuries, but I was still shaken. Lucian noticed I was quiet and asked me, "Are you all right?" It was about time.

"No," I began, "I'm not all right. There *are* some things I am afraid of." And I started to ramble, or maybe the better word is *rant*. I described the crazy traffic, the close calls, and the little mishap below the Gypsy house. Lucian knew what I meant, but this was Romania, and in time I would learn the rhythm of the traffic. It would take two more weeks of hair-raising travel for me to understand that most of the time the system worked.

Lucian said he didn't think I trusted him. I argued, but the truth was, I didn't fully trust Lucian yet. And he was asking for a lot of trust.

I trusted him to show up on time; to follow my itinerary and to honor my occasional special requests, like the lake trip. Obviously, I trusted him to show me Romania. I'd even allowed him to try to heal my sore throat. I knew that he was kind and smart, and I thought he was open to about anything, but the rest would have to be earned.

When we got back to the hotel, Lucian spent a few minutes in my room trying to take the whiplash out of my back and neck. We'd never touched—I, for one, had been careful about that—and now he'd turned me around and was rubbing my shoulders from behind. It was the second time that day that he had offered me something quite personal. I was a bit uneasy—would I be me if I weren't?—but I stood still and let him.

If he was going to turn me back around to face him, it had the makings of a damned-if-you-do, damned-if-you-don't dilemma of the highest order. But he didn't.

I had no lasting ill effects from the accident; but later, on a curved mountain road in the rain, I had a flash of insight. I was looking at the white scratches on the underside of Lucian's dashboard—made by my camera, no doubt, as I was taking it in and out of the bag. I thought again of the accident and the face of the Roma woman in the yard, how she had watched us as though we had crossed some line into forbidden territory.

"Do you think *she* did it?" I asked Lucian, out of the blue. "Could that Gypsy woman have caused the accident in Sibiu because we were on her street?"

"It's possible," Lucian said.

"Do Gypsies have powers?"

"Some of them do," he said. "Some of them claim to be *Wicca*." He used the English word, which I knew meant *witch*.

Of course, we would never know what forces had intersected at just the right moment to cause the accident. What I did know was that my retinas were still intact and that, thanks to Lucian, I had seen the house of the King of the Gypsies and his daughter, too.

That evening we had dinner at a farmhouse in Sibiel, a village a few miles outside Sibiu. Lucian and I ate alone in a little room set up for guests. There were two daybeds head to foot against the wall next to the table. Our hostess brought each course of food, then disappeared. The meal included *tuica* (pronounced "tweeka")—which was plum brandy— served in little glasses. Lucian said, "Drink it all at once," and I did. I don't remember what we ate. Though we'd arrived in daylight, we left in darkness, and I realized how unusual it was for us to be in the car at night.

The images of the day came back to me: the portrait of Venus; the bleeding game; the sated hunter; the naked, frolicking nymphs and satyrs; and Lucian with his healing hands. They followed me home after the museum tour; after the hours spent exploring Sibiu and the lakes; after the accident; after the home-cooked farmhouse dinner and plum brandy; and after the drive back to town. Now the street sounds had faded and I was once again alone. The images came crowding back in the dim light of the hotel room, in the quiet of the loft at the top of the stairs, in the beautiful carved bed where I was queen. It was there that I issued my first and last royal command of the day: *Send them in.*

Chapter 26

We Thirst

Morning in Sibiu: I go downstairs to the glass-topped table and lay out my supplies on a silver tray. I am delicate with each piece—the little spoon, the straw. I go to the bathroom for a towel, in case. Holding everything over a wastebasket, I shake the grains out onto the spoon. I measure carefully, steadying my hands. I find the adaptor plug and stick it in the wall. *Come on, Baby.*

Dracula wasn't the only one with a wicked thirst. I like morning coffee the way he liked blood. Listening to the slurpy breathing of the machine as it broke the five o'clock silence, watching the slow drip until I thought I'd go mad, it was easy to understand the desperation of the vampire: To a vampire, blood brings life, survival, vitality, energy, youth, and power. Without blood, the vampire is doomed. I could claim that most of that is true of coffee, too. Well, I wouldn't suck mine out of somebody's neck, but once in a Boston hotel I drank my morning coffee out of an ice bucket after looking in vain for a mug. Another time, in Chicago, I had to drink it out of a Pringles can. "Hog butcher for the world," indeed. Try putting a coffee cup in a hotel room.

Many Romanian hotels—even the good ones—don't place coffeepots in the rooms, which is just what I expected. I carry my own little coffee maker and don't rely on the caffeine of strangers.

In my little queendom in Sibiu, I'm all thirst as the coffee stream does its dance, the one that says, "I'm about done here." The noise level increases to a series of last gasps; the stream turns to a trickle and then a drip. A little sadness comes and goes. It's a familiar signpost of my addiction, mourning something while I still have it. I stick a straw down into the hot brew—to avoid staining my porcelain veneers—and drink. *Ah!* No vampire diving into the whitest of lily-white necks would feel any more satisfaction.

Now all I needed was a newspaper. That wasn't going to happen, nor did I have a book to read. It was on my to-do list: *Find novel written in English.* No, all I had for company that morning was my dear little buzzing brain.

When I thought about Lucian, the new phrase that came to mind was, *Well, well.* He'd started opening up to me—at least that's the way I saw it. Yesterday he'd not only revealed that he was married and a healer, Mr. Silent had also told me in our travels that he made his living as a psychologist, that his tour-guide work was freelance. That revelation was a surprise, especially considering our usual mundane exchanges, but the information wasn't. Lucian was polished and smart. Of course he fit the profile of an educated professional.

Now I could connect the dots. Yesterday's cryptic reply, "Patient," must have meant that Lucian's wife had been a patient of his before they'd married. And he'd definitely been trying to analyze me.

I'd had short-term psychotherapy from time to time, anything from women's groups run by hospitals to regular appointments in an office. One therapist was a man who worked from his home. He had a family, but during the day they were elsewhere. After a few sessions, he began showing an interest in me, or at least I thought so. He was *quite* empathetic. I developed a crush on him and started paying more attention to what I wore to the sessions. Although we didn't sleep together—far from it—he allowed intimacies to occur. Then one day he invited me to a weekend of group workshop sessions several hours away.

By then I was reading a whole other layer of meaning into the invitation, but my romantic expectations were vague and girlish. I had no idea what would really happen. I remember it snowed, and I was frantic to get to the meeting place in spite of the bad roads. After all the anticipation, I wasn't going to stay home.

We carpooled to a mountain cabin. When we arrived, everyone piled their baggage at the bottom of the steps instead of claiming a bed. I didn't get it—that was the opposite of what I wanted to do—but most of the others knew something from experience that I didn't: There would be opportunities before bedtime to pair up. When I realized it later in the evening, I knew I'd made a mistake in coming. I was in over my head. This wasn't just a weekend of group therapy sessions in which I might have had occasion to flirt with my therapist; it was a touchy-feely, sexual free-for-all!

I didn't want to participate in the sex and made arrangements to bunk with another woman. As I lay on my bed, far from home, I felt like the biggest fool ever born. It was Friday night, and I was in agony—alone and lonely. I didn't have a car and my husband was out of town. I was stuck in a love-in on the side of a snowy mountain until Sunday afternoon, and that wasn't even the worst. My therapist—the only person I knew—chose a partner, and from that moment on I had to watch them make goo-goo eyes at each other. One morning I even heard them showering together through the thin walls of my bathroom. Talk about a slap in the face; but by then all I cared about was getting through the weekend.

Now I was traveling around Romania with a psychologist.

Okay. With my flushed reaction of the previous evening still fresh, I knew to bury any and all romantic notions. There was no way that Lucian—*my hired guide*—could have any other kind of role on this trip.

I was so weird around men. I hadn't had many boyfriends—not in school, not afterward—unless I counted in the oddballs like Squirrel and the quiet, homely boy who'd had a crush on me when I was fifteen. Brent wore glasses and had a squinty expression that unfortunately exposed his uneven teeth. But talk about canines! Had he been better looking, more charming, he might have resembled You-Know-Who; but I'm stretching. I didn't bother to know Brent. He was one of those invisible people who hung with his own crowd but made not a pucker in the social fabric of our high school. He drove up and down the road past our house one summer, playing the radio loud and dangling one arm down the outside of the car door like a tough guy—to no avail.

I'd also attracted my share of men who liked to drink. The experience of spending time with them wasn't terrible the way it was with Mom, but it had the potential to be terrible. And because I didn't know the difference, I was always watching and counting—counting their drinks. I didn't enjoy being drunk, though; who could? Did alcoholics have a better experience than I had the few times I fell into bed with the room spinning?

To add to all of the screening I needed to do, I was never a girlie-girl. I didn't even know how to flirt. The whole idea of it gave me the creeps, I suppose because I'd always tended to attract the wrong types and repel the ones I liked. I didn't know how to act, not a clue. My bones didn't know, my skin didn't know, and my heart was just plain buried somewhere inside my shirt. I sought safety in relationships, but it wasn't the kind of safety that comes from security and consistency and steadfast love. I couldn't even recognize that. I wanted the safety of knowing the other person wasn't really available. In Romania I was more comfortable dreaming of Christopher Lee, the octogenarian ex-Dracula, than facing the reality of Lucian—who was flesh and blood, sitting beside me every day.

New cup of coffee; next subject: Mom. I realized I'd hardly thought about her, except for memories; and that was Glen Ferris Mom. The current version—Cincinnati Mom—was the one who lived ten minutes from me; the one who was in her eighties; the one I'd come to know in recent years.

Mom was like I was about coffee. She had no problem admitting she was hooked on the stuff. I'd given her a mug that said "Starter Fluid," and we both knew it was truth in advertising.

I wondered how many of the goodies Mom had used from the bags of books and snacks I'd left her. I'd asked a couple of my friends to check in on her, too. She'd be glad for that. Cincinnati Mom took every opportunity for companionship—all the better if it came to her. Most days you couldn't blast her off the end of the couch, where she would sit for hours watching reruns of *Matlock* and *Law & Order*. Mom had few visitors besides me, but she'd made friends with the man who delivered her Meals on Wheels, and she usually engaged her part-time housekeeper in conversation to the exclusion of any real cleaning.

Glen Ferris Mom was in and out of the workplace during my adolescence, and housekeepers filled the gap. They came and went, but Mom stuck like a haunting. Even when we were apart, she was a wave of darkness moving across my thoughts. It's a terrible way to have to describe your mother, but that's the way addiction works. The addict is preoccupied with her addiction, and the rest of us are preoccupied with the addict. As with Dracula's rationed appearances in the movies, the monster always lingers just outside the frame, waiting to terrify us. What will it do next? In the worst of times, Mom seemed unbeatable, inescapable, and pure evil.

I held onto one idea: that the passage of time would enable my escape from our house and the hold my mother had on me. Soon I would grow up and my brother would be left behind until he graduated and went on to West Virginia University. Joe later settled in Cincinnati, married, and fathered two children. Now divorced, he was the reason I'd moved to Ohio, but I hadn't seen him in years.

Mom and I hardly knew a thing about Joe, except that he avoided us. He'd become a shadow figure who worked the three to eleven shift in a plant, cleaning the machines that shaped various meats into hot dogs. It was a very different career for the Joe we knew—the clothes horse with perfectly shined shoes, the smooth talker who'd convinced Mom and Dad to buy a red 1966 Mustang back in the day, the guy who got the girl. From our unreturned phone calls and the occasional messages from his two sons, it seemed that all Joe did was work and sleep. Mom wrote him letters that went unanswered. She offered him money. Nothing pulled him out of hiding. I wondered why he was avoiding me, but Mom took it especially hard. She couldn't understand it: "I don't know what I've done," she'd say. *Well, for starters . . .* But I never said it out loud. We really didn't know, not for sure.

I didn't think Joe's issues were about Mom or me or what we might have done to alienate him; I thought they had more to do with his demons—or his heritage. My secret thought was that Joe had become an alcoholic and didn't want us to know. Who could sleep so much? Did he wear himself out at work? Was he trying to escape? Was he even really asleep? It wouldn't have surprised me if the kids had been told to lie; after all, concealment was a reflex in our family.

I often pictured my brother snoring away, sprawled in his clothes on dingy sheets or hanging halfway off the bed with the blankets. He would be passed out or maybe hung over. The sun would rise high in the sky, and so what; he'd sleep on. If that scenario had ever occurred to Mom, she hadn't given it voice, but I thought about it a lot. Had Joe been the one to catch the gene of insatiable thirst? I'd worried about myself, but maybe it wasn't me; maybe it was him. It was possible, but how could I know? He was a stranger.

How could things get so screwed up, and where was my brother? At one time even Grandmama hadn't been able to get Joe's address. She told me that when she'd asked him, he'd said he didn't know it. "If he doesn't know his own address," Grandmama huffed, "he ought to be in the insane asylum!"

I couldn't think about Joe any more—that was a dead end—and I'd done what I could for Mom before I left for Romania. I was glad to realize that for once I could let her go.

My thoughts continued to swirl. This is what happens when you drink coffee and don't have anything to read. So what was left to ponder? It was only Day 5 of my trip. How did I like Romania so far? I loved it, loved it because I was there and ready to accept the country for whatever it proved to be. I would *not* go home disappointed. I would not mourn it before it was over, the way I did my morning coffee. This trip was mine, my life's dream. And all I really had to think about—the only person I had to take care of—for the next two weeks was me.

Chapter 27

Crossroads

This is Klausenburgh, I thought, savoring the old German name from the Dracula movies as we drove into the city of Cluj-Napoca, short version Cluj. *I'm finally here.*

In the novel, Klausenburgh marked the last leg of Jonathan Harker's journey to Dracula's castle. In the movies, Klausenburgh was a stopping point not only for Dracula hunters like Harker, but also for the finely dressed tourists who passed through the city and ended up spending an unplanned night at the castle—often their last.

According to the story in its various versions, travelers unaware of Count Dracula's reputation would stop for a meal at the tavern; then, failing to heed the barkeep's warnings, would insist on continuing their journey in spite of the low position of the sun in the afternoon sky. They didn't understand that the shadows were already too long, that the sun would soon disappear behind the Carpathian Mountains, and that *he* ruled the night. They gaily exited the tavern and climbed into a waiting coach, only to become agitated later when their driver refused to tempt fate.

Knowing the danger that lay ahead, the driver would stop the coach at a crossroads, letting the tourists out and throwing their luggage onto the dirt road. Then he would turn the spooked horses and speed away, leaving his former passengers stranded in the deepening Transylvanian forest. A few hours later, when the travelers were desperate for food and shelter, Dracula's black *caleche* (carriage) would race down the hill from the castle and beckon them in out of the night.

I had never tired of that story. But it wasn't Dracula I feared in Cluj.

Lucian and I checked in to our hotel and then set out on a walking tour, trying to beat the rain. We'd driven toward the storm from Sibiu, a black sky and black clouds looming ahead of us like a wall and casting the landscape in a strange light. "Dark in front of us and light behind us," Lucian said. And I didn't miss the fact that we were headed into the dark, like the travelers in the movies.

Cluj is the second largest city in Romania. *Napoca* was added in 1974 to reflect the city's original name dating from the days of the Roman Empire. In the interim, the city was known by both German and Hungarian names. It was named *Klausenburgh* in the thirteenth century by the Germans who settled there. The city was twice the capital of Transylvania before Transylvania became part of Romania. And there I will stop with the history; you would need a scorecard to capture this city's past, volleyed as it was among the Romans, the Saxons, the Austrians, the Hungarians, and even the Turks over the centuries.

Cluj-Napoca today is a cosmopolitan city of more than 300,000 inhabitants. The streets are full of well-dressed people hurrying in all directions among businesses, retail centers, churches, museums, and universities. Men and women in suits share the sidewalks with colorful Gypsies and peasants who wear clashing patterns or wool in summer.

As in every other town we visited, restoration was going on. The city contains many large, old buildings that house multiple businesses, for instance a plethora of travel agencies and all kinds of stores—some expensive—selling clothes, jewelry, electronics, you name it. Shops reminiscent of those I'd seen along Melrose Avenue in Hollywood catered to the young and had names such as Bad Boy and Fashion Victim.

Dracula was definitely missing in action from this modern city, but that didn't matter to me. I was thrilled to be walking the streets of former Klausenburgh along with its citizens.

I was starving when we arrived, and in Cluj I found the sidewalk cafés of my imagination. Before I left America, I would picture myself sitting at some shaded café table on a busy street, typing away on my AlphaSmart while Europeans hurried by and my guide was somewhere smoking. That vision was not far from the truth the day we toured Cluj. As I wolfed down a sandwich and coleslaw, Lucian sat across from me and smoked cigarettes. He was seldom hungry the way I was.

It began to rain hard. Water poured off the restaurant awning just beyond our table, and suddenly there was no hurry. We had lost our window of opportunity to tour Cluj on foot; I could see it on Lucian's face.

We made the best of it, despite the weather, since we had only the one afternoon to see the city. Even though the rain let up after I had eaten, we went back to the hotel and I put on my rain clothes: the bright blue jacket and a pair of black rain pants that had gone in and out of the suitcase so many times at home that they should have worn out.

We saw the Someş ("So-mesh") River in all its muddy glory. I photographed it rushing past the backs of houses and restaurants, then under the street where we stood. The Someş, probably the width of a two-lane road where it passed through Cluj, eventually flows into the Danube. Television news had been showing floods in Switzerland, Germany, the Netherlands, and Romania. According to CNN, Romania had the most fatalities of all the flooded European countries. The rushing Someş certainly wouldn't have been Count Dracula's cup of tea, and it wasn't mine, either. The roiling water was completely brown. I made sure to stand back from the railing as we watched it slosh its way south.

My experience with floods dated back to my childhood in Glen Ferris, when occasionally the Kanawha River would rise up and flood the basement of anyone who hadn't installed a sump pump. It was not uncommon for three feet of water to surge up through the floor drain, so we kept everything on shelves.

Once when we lived in the lower end of town, the overflow came up through the sewer grate in the alley, creating a miniriver a foot deep. I ran home and put on my bathing suit to squat with my friends in the rushing brown water of our sudden swimming pool. I suppose, looking back, that we should have been afraid—if not of the water itself, of the germs and vermin it might carry. But why would we? We were young, and this was our alley in Glen Ferris, our home.

I could make the alley sound better if I called it a lane, the way my grandmother always did as we walked to the post office on summer days.

She also called our town a village, deliberately implying quaintness. I think Grandmama liked to go to the post office—which she pronounced "Goat the post office"—because Grandpop worked there.

The alley we walked was unpaved and rutted like the streets of Snagov, and just wide enough for one vehicle at a time. People rarely drove down it, and when they did, you could see the car or truck leaning and bumping its way over the thin veil of gravel, sinking into puddle holes and grinding back out at five miles an hour.

In spite of the occasional high water from the Kanawha, I'd never been in a serious flood. I'd only seen them on TV, where the disaster remained in the abstract. Even as an adult I'd thought of flooding as an inconvenience. *Wrong.* Standing on the street with Lucian, watching the water churning below us, made me uneasy. The Someş even had whitecaps. I didn't want to be near water that was out of control.

Lucian and I wandered through a few stores, and in one I bought a wooden plate hand-painted with Vlad Dracula's face. Lucian scoped out the cameras and lenses. We looked at bins of movies, and there was *Bram Stoker's Dracula,* starring Gary Oldman. I often touched the things I liked, triggering a memory of shopping with my mother back in West Virginia.

With Mom, shopping was all business, never fun. She hated going from store to store "just looking" and always made us write a list of what we needed and where to find each item. Mom didn't get the pleasure of shopping: seeing what was in style, having choices, exploring a new department. She shopped like a man: Get in, get what you need, and get out. Mom became caustic when my focus strayed, bringing me back into line with the equivalent of a rap to the head: "Gimme, gimme, gimmee," she'd whine, never breaking stride. When I touched the videos and jewelry in Cluj, it was a pleasure to know that Lucian would not turn to me and bark, "Gimmee, gimmee, gimmee. You want everything you see." Of course, it might have been funny spoken with a Romanian accent.

I found some earrings and a matching pendant. The price was "441,000." Lucian told me what bills I needed to pay for the jewelry, making me glad again that I had a guide.

It rained off and on. We hung out for a while, ending up at a sidewalk restaurant where we drank beers and watched people until it was time to head back to the hotel.

I dressed for dinner in slinky black pants with a matching tank top and sweater to show off my new jewelry. I put on the larger of my two crucifixes and used the chain from the smaller one for the new pendant, wearing the cross and the pendant together. After all, I couldn't be without a crucifix in Transylvania.

The previous night I'd realized that I'd actually been sleeping without a cross—not my intention on this vacation, but I'd fallen back into the habit of taking off my jewelry before bed just as I did at home. *Yikes!* I wanted to see Dracula country, not get turned into Draculette.

We ate dinner in the hotel restaurant, which was lovely but empty. This was not the first time we'd had a hotel restaurant to ourselves. The time that we ate, seven o'clock, was early for most Europeans, but on the late side for me. I hadn't had any food since my sandwich during the downpour.

I arrived in my black outfit and jewelry, but Lucian still wore the jeans and knit shirt he'd had on all day. I suddenly felt uncomfortable, and I knew why. We looked just like a couple with two different outcomes in mind.

Lucian may have missed the whole thing—it was my private perceptions that fed my anguish—but to me the dinner was quickly looking like a parody of a date, the kind I'd seen a million times in America: a bad date for which the girl might buy a two-hundred-dollar dress and the guy might not even shave. I'd seen many couples out for a night on the town looking so mismatched that it seemed one had done all of the getting ready. I always wondered which one of them was in for a disappointment.

As I sat down I was already wishing I hadn't changed my clothes, wishing I had saved my jewelry for America. My dinner with Lucian might have looked like a bad date about to happen, but of course it wasn't a date at all. I was sitting across the table from a married man. Now that I knew, it was especially important not to give him the wrong impression.

I ordered flat water to drink, and Lucian ordered plum brandy for both of us. Per Lucian, the brandy glasses would require "four times" down the hatch to polish off the now-familiar apéritif. Dinner was delicious—crisp, lightly battered fish and boiled potatoes with parsley. By the time I had finished my "something sweet," two irresistible cream-filled donuts that would have fed a family, I wasn't just suffering from too much dessert; I'd had way too much tuica.

Dressed as I was and drunk as well, if Lucian had had any thoughts of hooking up, this would have been the time. But the moment, if there even was a moment, passed. At the end of dinner we practically ran in opposite directions; or was that just me?

In the room, I thought for a few minutes that I was going to have a "commode hugger," as they used to call them in my college days. Although that didn't happen, I was feeling very uncomfortable, and throwing up in the toilet at least might have been a quick way out of that. I slept for a while but woke up around two and then again at three thirty. I got up and finished my battery-charging and picture-transferring, then started the coffee. There was a coffeepot in the hotel room. Yippee!

Later that morning I returned to the hotel restaurant and sat down for breakfast alone. For the first time in a week, I didn't see Lucian. Usually our timing was pretty close.

My stomach was still upset from the plum brandy, but who knew when I'd get another chance to eat? Was diarrhea better than starvation? At first I had only toast with butter and honey; then I had some yogurt and thought I should also ingest some protein. The buffet table was spread with platters of meat and cheese. None of it appealed to me, but I helped myself.

When I came back, a man was sitting at my table and a woman's sweater was hanging on the back of another chair. I'd read that in Europe people often share tables so I sat down, expecting to catch this stranger's eye for a hello. He didn't look at me until his wife came with her food; I might as well have been invisible. She and I exchanged tentative greetings, but the whole scene was awkward with them eating and beginning to talk to one another in French. These two were not sociable by any stretch. What was their point, then, in sitting down? This was *my* table. Did they not see the half-glass of juice, and my napkin on the chair? I decided the husband was a clod, devoid of brains and manners, and the wife was probably horrified when she saw what he had done; but by then it was too late.

After a few minutes, when Lucian still had not appeared, I went to my room to write. In the process of updating my trip journal I realized two things. The first was that I could have been wrong about the French couple. Maybe they'd given me a cool reception at the breakfast table because they'd thought *I* was the clod who'd sat down with *them!*

The second thing I realized had to do with Lucian. I'd felt vulnerable the last few days, my senses having come alive without my permission. This little sexual undercurrent of mine was about as welcome as a copperhead, and I needed to get past it. I'd be traveling with Lucian for two more weeks, sitting next to him for hour upon hour in the car, walking beside him all over Romania, and softening the dinner hour with plum brandy. I didn't think I needed to worry about his intentions, but I still wasn't sure about mine. I said a prayer of thanks for the nonevents of the previous evening and vowed to get back to my main man, Dracula.

I felt the way I do when I go gambling in America and come home reeking of cigarette smoke from the casino. The smell is all through my clothes and in my hair, branding me. As soon as I've closed the front door behind me, I strip down and make a laundry pile. Sometimes I even put the clothes in the washer that night in my hurry to undo my latest descent into sin and ruination. It was like that; I had an urge to make things right again, to show up in my traveling clothes and be regular, riding along in silence with Lucian between stops for gas and potato chips, the two of us miles apart in the front seat.

I was packed and ready to go an hour early. We were driving to Maramureş, out in the Transylvanian countryside. Lucian would show up on time as he always did to pack our suitcases in the trunk, and soon we'd be on the road. Cluj would be another memory, just like Klausenburgh.

Chapter 28

Out in the Country

We left the cosmopolitan bustle of Cluj for Maramureş, driving north. That night I would spend my first night on a Transylvanian farm. I had asked to spend a night or two in a farmhouse for the experience, hoping for the best but expecting the worst: mud, animals, an outdoor toilet, cold water, backward people, and a pervasive darkness from lack of electricity. We were booked for two nights smack in the middle of Dracula country, so in spite of the aforementioned sacrifices, I couldn't wait.

The Maramureş region borders Ukraine. It is known for its peaceful landscapes and beautiful wood carving: Wood fences and elaborately carved gates are everywhere, sometimes fronting the most ordinary homes. Wooden churches abound, some centuries old and others new.

Could it be Thursday already? I'd been gone from home nearly a week and was thinking about my mother again. I felt sure she was all right, but a call would put any doubts to rest. I tried to check for voice mail on my cell phone and got the same "no service" message I'd had since arriving in Romania: "Searching for network . . . searching . . . searching . . . no service." I guess that meant that no one could have left me a message; if I couldn't call out, they couldn't call in. I had to admit that, in a way, being unavailable was a relief.

Mom had only a land line, though she'd had a portable phone for a few years after she took advantage of a special deal from the Cincinnati Automobile Club. The phone had the AAA on speed dial, so Mom bought one as a safety device for her car. She was nothing if not conscious of all those waiting for just the right moment to clonk us on the head. The phone was about the size of a brick, the kind you see people using in old television shows on TV Land. Mom used it so infrequently that she'd always forget the steps; thus, why not save the $11 per month? When we turned it in at the Verizon office, she sat off to the side, while I waited in Verizon's version of Hell—the customer service line—with the phone in a paper sack. Eventually I got to the counter and handed it over, to the total amusement of the two women who removed it from its brown bag.

The farm that was our destination was located in Hoteni village, a place too small to rate more than a mention in the guidebooks. It took hours to get there, but at least the drive was a show of changing scenery. In the villages, we saw a microcosm of people living their lives: visiting, waiting for rides, selling produce, watching the passing parade, or leading their animals through town. Between the villages, behind them, and beyond them were miles of country. For Lucian, Maramureş was the ultimate escape. He loved the trees, the rolling hills, and the pastureland. It was beautiful and from another time; shepherds sat among the animals that grazed beside the pointed haystacks dotting the hills.

The land changed as we went north, becoming green and lush, misted from the low clouds that dripped into the valleys. There in the stretches between villages, fields offered up riots of wildflowers or sunflower gardens. We passed ferns, tangles of vines, cornfields, orchards, and a mix of trees exactly like I would see in West Virginia. In fact, sometimes the road to Maramureş looked just like the road between Falls View and Alloy. Even the telephone poles were the same, or did I imagine they were wood with those blue glass bulbs on top? Later I would see the open cinderblock poles that reminded me of the accident in Sibiu every time we passed one.

In picturing Transylvania I'd imagined thick pine forests, and now we were in one, winding upward. I wanted mist; well, here it was. Mist was above us, below us, and in front of us on the road. Sometimes it was so dark that the road and the trees and the mist blended together. Occasionally there would be a translucent spot where the light changed; I watched this while Lucian maneuvered the car around a series of S-curves and we "met ourselves coming" time after time. It was like the winding road to Chimney Corner, West Virginia, which we had to take from Glen Ferris to the 4-H park. That road had a particularly sharp curve called Devil's Elbow, but it wasn't the only one that slowed traffic down to a crawl. My mother became an expert at "straightening out the curves," which meant that many times she drove on the wrong side of the road for a piece instead of weaving around the turns. That alone should have prepared me for car travel in Romania.

As the road continued uphill, we came upon a bus making its way slowly up the mountain ahead of us. Lucian pulled over onto the first wide spot for a cigarette break to let the bus get ahead; he couldn't pass it and couldn't stand to follow the lumbering vehicle. I got out of the car to stretch my legs.

"You have to eat everything today," he said as he stood there smoking. "After here, no, but you must eat. You have to." He was advising me on the evening's activity, a home-cooked farmhouse dinner. I had read that a Romanian hostess would be offended if I didn't clean my plate, and here was Lucian confirming it. Eat or insult: Welcome to my whole life.

That morning I'd had a touch of *turista*, or its Romanian equivalent. I still had traces of stomach pain and didn't plan to eat for a long while. It wouldn't be hard to save room for the coming feast.

We crossed a mountain to get to Maramureş, stopping a few miles from the farm to see the Merry Cemetery in the rain. The cemetery, said to be the most famous tourist attraction in Maramureş, is known for its colorful and often humorous memorials. Lucian and I checked out the gaily painted, hand-carved grave markers designed to depict the departed and tell their life stories. Sometimes the marker illustrated the means of death; for example, a three-year-old girl airborne after being hit by an automobile; a young man standing beside the bike he fatally wrecked. Ironically, the wood carver's marker had joined the others. Did he complete it ahead of time, or had someone else—perhaps an apprentice—taken up the tools?

Hoteni was a village out of the past, with a winding road and a horse cart making its way up the hill as we drove by. We arrived at the farm just after the rain, carrying our things from the car across the wet grass to the guest house. It sat on a hilltop with a panoramic view of fields, valleys, and distant towns.

There were three houses on the farm: the main house where our host and hostess lived; the guest house, where Lucian and I stayed; and a third house that was under construction. The guest house was made of white stucco and stained wood. Its porches and balconies would give visitors fresh air and views of the surrounding valley. This farm was a popular stopping point for tourists, out there in nowhere-land. Lucian knew the owners, Olga and Teodor. "Welcome to my house" is what I am sure Olga said when we got there. It was a perfect greeting for Transylvania, echoing Count Dracula's famous words from the novel.

Olga greeted us in slacks and a black cotton camisole with a lace effect around the cups. She was pretty in middle age, with a sprightly quality. At the same time, she came across as physically strong, a woman used to doing work. Lucian said that she and her husband had traveled the world as dancers, and I could see it: muscles; a certain stance.

So, there I was, after many years of dreaming, about to spend the night in Dracula's Transylvania, just like Jonathan Harker. Our "castle" was a two-story guest house located across a flat yard from the main house. I had the downstairs, and Lucian's room was on the second floor. On my level were a small, modern kitchen; an equally modern bathroom; and a great room with a TV, a stone fireplace, and enough casual, comfy furniture for a large group. I could imagine friendships developing there, but when we arrived we were the only guests.

I had stayed at few farm- or guesthouses—certainly none in Romania—so I didn't know the etiquette, but it seemed I had some free time in the hours before dinner. Lucian was out doing something with the car. Olga had bidden us good-bye; I was sure she had cooking to do. She'd shown me her dining room, a showcase for handmade articles—wool rugs and vests, decorative braided breads, embroidery, and the white dress she probably wore to church. Folk customs and costumes still had a place in the culture of rural Romania. We'd peeked into the kitchen, which Olga called the "chicken" by mistake, then caught herself and laughed. Then I suddenly remembered I'd left water on to boil for tea and ran across the yard.

Sitting in the great room with my hot tea was wonderful. It was a relief from the travel and the introductions; even from the one-on-one with Lucian in the car. I liked the solitude of the farm and thought it was intentional. Let the men talk outside and let Olga prepare the meal; I would sit and drink tea and write.

It seemed that since I'd arrived in Romania, I was always getting sick or on the verge of it. I'd had every shot in the universe before I left and figured I was immune to everything. Hepatitis A and B—can't touch me! Tetanus, typhoid—forget it. Measles—no problem; I'd had a booster. Polio—no way! But here I was fighting a cold, or bug, or whatever it was that was keeping me so subdued.

I had a second big mug of tea with sugar and milk. I probably should have skipped the milk, but this was a test of my system before we dined at eight. I figured I'd know soon whether I was in shape for the coming eat-a-thon. Lucian had already told me we'd have plum brandy. He'd assured me it was not plum brandy that had upset my stomach, and I'd assured him that plum brandy caused other problems, and I wanted only a small amount tonight, not "four times," thanks.

A fly was loose in the guest house. Dracula had mastery over animals and a talent for shape-shifting; could it be *him?* Now that I was in the wilds of Transylvania, my thoughts seemed to be getting wild, too.

Chapter 29

The Camera, the Camera!

The books tell you that the best time for photography is around sunrise or sunset, when the light is changing dramatically. When other people are eating dinner, for example, *you* should be out with your camera capturing photos. I didn't have to worry about that one; by the time other people were eating dinner in Romania, I would have starved to death.

But I *was* sitting in a guest house in the Carpathian Mountains of Transylvania, looking out on scenery straight out of a Dracula movie: green mountains dotted with trees; fields; hand-woven twig fences; hillsides of flowers; clouds; and finally, the sun. I was looking out on simple sheds with high tin roofs and pear-shaped haystacks reminiscent of another time. A mist was coming down the mountain toward the farm. The sun hadn't set, but sections of the land were growing dark. It was a perfect setting for evil to be afoot. I wanted it to be so.

A golden light fell on the porch railing outside, where Olga had hung her husband's shirts to dry. It colored the fields and fences, finally finding its way to the walls and floor of the great room. Outside, four pet sheep wandered the yard, occasionally ducking their heads to eat grass. The property was bound by a handmade twig fence, beautiful in its curved rhythm and topped with an exquisite braid made from branches. The sheep, which had names, were the source of delicious cheese for the table, served at every meal.

I'd gotten used to seeing animals running loose, even large ones. The Romanians have an affinity with them. They walk along the roads leading farm animals as they would pets; they stand in fields keeping their animals company.

Animals are too animalistic for me. I'm afraid of their suddenness, their size. Once at home a deer escaped the greenbelt area near my house. It crossed a two-lane road and headed for the strip of land between my back deck and the edge of the lake inlet abutting the property. My granddaughter, Annie, and I were out on the deck. I snatched her up into my arms and hurried inside, where we watched from behind the six-foot-square living room windows. As the deer ran past, the window glass turned its pounding hooves to silence, but I could feel the vibrations. . . .

Suddenly I came out of my reverie. It was *sunset in Transylvania!* If you believe the legends, sunset is a dangerous time in Transylvania. Those that sleep the sleep of the undead will rise after the last light of day has faded and claim the woods and fields as their own. They will hunt.

Why was I sitting still? I should be capturing the actual setting sun in the land of You-Know-Who. I had to record the most famous and frightening time of day, a time of vulnerability for vampires, their victims, and all those who bought into the Dracula legend.

I got my camera from the bedroom and began photographing the afternoon sun hitting the windowsills, the unadorned sections of the porch railing, and even the great room floor, now laid with light and shadows. The August sunset is long in Transylvania, milking the last light out of the sky. I took picture after picture: sun coming through the windows, sun on the carpet, sun lying across the fields outside. Then I went out and photographed the yard and beyond, trying to capture that ultra-frightening moment when sundown approaches in the scariest place on earth. It was important to get the light just right, the way it had looked fading from the cellar window in *Horror of Dracula* just before the Count woke up for the night and Jonathan Harker looked upon the last ray of sunlight he would ever see.

Was it really that scary out on the farm? Was my heart hammering as I snapped all those photos? Did I think that Dracula would float across the darkening fields toward me? That wasn't the point. The point was to make it scary, to use my camera to depict a certain moment in time known to Dracula fans all over the world.

By the time the sun set, I'd fulfilled my goal for the afternoon; but I had a nighttime goal of capturing the Dracula moon over Transylvania. That one was still to be achieved, and I hadn't seen the moon since Bucharest.

I ask you: What is Romania, the home of Count Dracula, without a moon? Make that a *full* moon—taking center stage in a dark, forbidding sky. And who knew that a trip to Romania would have called for consideration of the lunar schedule? I hadn't thought about the moon's phases when I was planning; it had been hard enough just determining what to pack. I'd assumed it would be there—that big, yellow Dracula moon from the movies, posing in the sky, waiting for me to gaze upon it and capture it with my camera.

I didn't mind that the moon hadn't been full in Bucharest; a city moon lacks a certain bone-chilling power. But now we were in Transylvania. It was out here in the Carpathians that the moon should be at its most Dracula-like. Lucian had already agreed to help me find a nighttime landscape worthy of photographing. He'd agreed to it before we met.

Before I'd left home, I had asked the travel agent to find out if my guide would be willing to accompany me with my camera, tripod, and remote to moonlit scenes in Transylvania. After all, night was when everything happened . . . everything *evil*. If he followed tradition, he'd refuse: No driver in a Dracula movie would ever agree to such a thing. They were too frightened to venture into the Count's territory in broad daylight, let alone at night. But I'd hoped, and it looked like my wish would come true. I'd pictured it like this:

We're out in the country, the car parked on the side of a two-lane road. No one else is around. A slight wind is blowing. My guide is ahead of me, climbing a dirt path to the top of a hill where we will have a clear nighttime view of the castle. There's always a castle.

Moonlight illuminates the massive stone structure, its tranquil beauty escaping all who are asleep or less brave than I. In the distance wolves are howling, but as long as they stay in the distance,

I don't care. If conditions are perfect, a few filmy clouds will scud across the black sky the way they do in the Dracula movies—a foreboding of evil as old as time.

My guide has the camera bag, and I'm wearing my most adventurous adventure gear. My clothing is made of tough, yet light material, full of zippers and secret pockets for supplies, or maybe a few bulbs of garlic. My outfit won't wrinkle, not that anyone would notice in this place of wind and shadows.

The castle overlooks a quiet Transylvanian town with red tile roofs, straight out of the movies. I get a clear shot because there is little cloud cover tonight, and this picture of all pictures will be the cover of my book.

Perfect, if it were true.

I'd tried in every town to find Bram Stoker's moon. Stoker wrote: "There was a bright full moon, with heavy black, driving clouds . . ." and ". . . the night was dark with occasional gleams of moonlight between the dents of the heavy clouds."

A Dracula moon casts a bright light below and stirs up the animals—and not just your local dog and cat. "Then one night," a zookeeper reports in the novel, "so soon as the moon was hup [*sic*], the wolves here all began a-'owling." The full yellow moon signaled trouble in Transylvania. From the forest below it, an animal's cry or a bloodcurdling scream meant one thing: Vampires were afoot.

According to McNally and Florescu, it is common for wolves, bats, rats, rabbits, and sundry other animal life to roam the woods and overgrown castle ruins at night—creatures of the ground and air, some of which you wouldn't want to meet. In spite of all of that, I would have gone out into the wilds with Lucian; but so far the fantasy was more exciting than the reality.

When dinnertime rolled around, we ate in the main house. The food was delicious, of course. I worried about my stomach, but two glasses of plum brandy, cold appetizers, soup, and a plate of sausage and cabbage later I was full, but not to bursting. Olga served us—Teodor, Lucian, and me. She didn't sit down with us, but turned out the kitchen light and disappeared after clearing the remains of dessert, a plate of sliced cake.

At dinner I brought up the subject of vampires—in Romanian, *wampyrs*. Romanian is a Latin-based Romance language whose modern alphabet closely resembles the English alphabet; therefore, it has many words that sound familiar.

Teodor told me there was no Dracula there. Legends in Maramureș are of the Man of Night and the Daughter of the Forest, who cause changes in their victims; for example, exchanging their human limbs for those of animals. But they aren't vampires. Everyone in Romania so far had thought of Vlad the Impaler when the name "Dracula" came up.

The pervasiveness of Vlad in Transylvania didn't take away from my being there. I'd known Romania couldn't produce a black-cloaked vampire just for me. I could still look for the settings that had been depicted in my favorite movies—the castles used for inspiration, the little villages, the churches, and the people populating the countryside.

Unfortunately, the farm didn't pan out as a setting for "Transylvania by moonlight" as I had hoped. The moon remained hidden, and it was just as well; I didn't have the energy to stalk it. We still had time; I was just approaching the halfway point of my trip.

The next morning I woke up around six forty-five and looked out the bedroom window at a hard rain. When it was fully light, I made my coffee. The quiet in the guest house was complete; if I banged a cabinet door, it was like an explosion. Lucian, upstairs, presumably slept through my movements. I couldn't even picture that scene, as I hadn't gone up the stairs at all.

I went into the great room to read, but I was drawn by the view of the Transylvanian countryside. The fields lay before me in muted shades of green, and the sky was full of gray clouds, indistinct with rain.

Just beyond the tall casement windows, the beautifully stained porch railing was again draped with laundry. All of it was soaked, and not about to get any drier. Olga had a clothesline in the yard and racks that sat on the side porch, but she'd hung shirts, pants, and even tablecloths over the rail. I thought about the sunset pictures I'd taken, imposing my idea of ultrafrightening Transylvania onto a bucolic farm scene. I'd looked out the great room window thinking only of Dracula, and now I had to picture the evil undead stealing toward the house past a row of wet shirts!

Chapter 30

Prisons

It was Friday. I'd read almost half a book since arriving at the farmhouse. The weather hadn't been good for touring, and that had meant some downtime. It had been a good break for me. My body was tired and achy. I supposed some of it was from sitting in the car. We'd been jamming a lot of travel into every day, and this day would be no exception, but I hoped we wouldn't start out in bad weather.

The sun can fool you in the mountains, at least in the mountains of West Virginia. You can misread a whole day if you don't know that every day starts out overcast. Clouds lie below the mountaintops. Fog fills the valleys so that it's hard to drive; setting out too early is taking your life into your hands.

We went driving when the weather cleared, covering miles of country and passing through more villages and towns. Lucian stopped the car from time to time so that I could get pictures. At one point he parked at the foot of a hill as though he were about to unveil a surprise at the top—and that's exactly what happened. We walked up a curving blacktop road and under a tall arch to enter Bârsana Monastery, a hilltop home to fourteen Orthodox nuns. It sparkled like a fairyland. The shrines, steeples, and spires were a showcase of local carpentry. Bârsana consists of a ring of sturdy buildings, including a flower-decked, freshly whitewashed museum and dining hall; a wooden footbridge; a church and other wood buildings whose roofs, steeples, and spires seem taller than the mountains in the background; and the nuns' houses, made of wood and similar in construction to the public buildings. All were immaculately maintained. The residents presumably would spend their lives there. If a nun wanted to glimpse her future, she could turn from the picturesque, bloom-lined walking path to the adjacent hillside, where the convent had its own cemetery.

We stopped in a little village for a snack—and I mean straight off the grocer's shelf. The pork rinds I bought—something I'd never consider in America—looked delicious, as I was ready to eat the leaves off the trees. Lucian and I hadn't established a regular stopping time for lunch, or maybe he was being economical with my money. For my vote, I hated to waste time in a restaurant—even though my stomach growled in protest.

As we took our snacks to the car, we saw a hay wagon headed toward us on the road. It was piled high with golden hay and pulled by a single horse. It carried two men and a boy, all in all a perfect example of local color. I guessed the men were related—three generations. The dad, dressed in a simple white shirt, was driving the wagon. The young boy sat in back, looking modern in a baseball cap, and the sunburned grandfather rode in the middle on the hay. I held up my camera and smiled. They all waved and were glad to have their pictures taken. Now I would dare to do more of that.

Our next stop was in the town of Sighețu Marmatiei, where we walked along the streets among the locals. Larger than a village, it had a downtown with stores, colorful outdoor florist stands, and a famous landmark: Sighet Memorial Museum. The former political prison just off the town square was another sight that wasn't part of the Dracula legend, another stop I'd forgotten about; but there it was on my itinerary, and here we were.

Mountains rose abruptly at the end of the main street, a mist obscuring the tops. Men rode bicycles past the three-story yellow building that housed the memorial to victims of Communism and the Resistance. Lucian paid my admission and then waited while I toured the memorial, which I learned was founded in 1994 and which is compared to the Auschwitz Museum and the Peace Memorial at Normandy. I hadn't seen either of them.

I went in knowing nothing and came out knowing just a bit more. When it came to history, I was a skimmer: I liked the stories, but my mind resisted the smaller details—names, places, dates, battles. Even without those, I was touched by the long quest for freedom that had defined Romania's history. It had come across in a personal way through displays of rough garments and prison clothing worn by the peasants who had fought Communism. It was evident in the bare, unheated jail cells where priests and dignitaries had been housed and punished just like the poor. It reached out from the photos lining the hallways. The literature said the prison had been a place of extinction; there was no escaping it, located as it was just two kilometers from the Russian border.

I knew something about prisons, but it was not so much the institutions as the feeling of being in prison many times in my life. I knew plenty about the way we imprison ourselves with our own choices and then turn right around and try to escape. I knew it when I overate and couldn't zip my pants, or when I hit the gambling casinos and couldn't wait to wash off the evidence. I always knew it when I behaved inconsistently to my true character—buried though it was.

When you live a life of mild deceit, as I had just to survive, even your friends don't know you. So many years of Mom's verbal bites—years of feeling bad about myself—had left me feeling *not good enough*. It was a general malaise that spread to my behavior, and I became accommodating in relationships. My personality and choices always took a back seat to the other person's.

"Want to watch the game?"

"Sure!" *No.*

"Is this restaurant okay?"

"It's fine." *Whatever.*

"Do you want to see that new movie?"

"Sounds good." *Not my taste.*

I went along—it was so much easier than asserting myself—and one day I realized that I had a set of friends who didn't have a clue who I really was. Would they like me if they did? In matters of the heart, I was worse. I became a whole other person playing a role. I couldn't seem to help it.

I once lived with a hoarder. We began our life together in an empty house, but soon the garage and basement filled up with junk—ladders, boxes, broken appliances, and even the filthy drapes I'd taken down before we moved in. He couldn't throw anything away. One night I woke up to pounding, followed the sound, and found him building shelves in the basement because he'd run out of floor space. He owned low-income apartment buildings. The tenants often moved out quickly (think *fly-by-night*), leaving their possessions behind. In the evenings he would come home with old stereos, bottles of whiskey, used clothing, discarded tools, and once a set of pans he washed out with the garden hose and presented to me. I came to dread looking out the kitchen window when he drove up. Why would I, a control freak and reasonably organized person, move in with a hoarder? It defies logic, I'll tell you that.

I moved on, but I became commitment phobic, so much so that I didn't like to make social plans. As a result, I was often lonely. It can take years for these things to sink in, but when my life became unsatisfactory to me, I learned that I needed to form relationships based on who I was and what I wanted. It was a turning point.

The uplifting part of the Sighet tour was the prison artwork: sparks of the human spirit—carvings, poetry, a chess set made of cloth—created by people who should have had no hope. I finished the tour and went outside to a small garden area called the Space of Meditation and Prayer. It was a former prison yard. A wall had been erected, and more than eight thousand names were carved into it to recognize the Romanians who had died in prisons and camps as victims of Communism. The weather was misty and gray as I walked beside the wall, noting the Ions, the Radus, and the Mirceas who had paid the ultimate price for their freedom.

Dracula was a prisoner, too. A vampire's prison is its condition, spending eternity in its own body. Dracula was forced to keep certain hours, lying crypt-bound during the daylight. He tried to pass for a member of the human race when all that the monster wanted to do was roam the woods on all fours and drink blood. As a vampire Dracula had to fear the ordinary—water, garlic, sunlight—as ordinary people feared him.

Here's the irony about being undead: Would you want to live forever if you were a monster? Mortals don't have that problem; we're all going in just one direction. A woman I knew described it accurately: "I'm tied to a dying animal."

I remembered Christopher Lee portraying the loneliness of evil as Count Dracula. Were monsters lonely? Maybe, but I didn't care if they were. Anyone looking for sympathy for that position would have to knock on another door besides mine. To me, evil was evil.

Dad's mother was another family soldier gone AWOL. She'd reared Dad in Glen Ferris, but had moved to Florida when Joe and I were small. I didn't know the details of Grandma's marital history and hadn't met either of her husbands, but Dad and his brothers had two different last names. Mom, Dad, Joe, and I visited Grandma when I was fifteen. We'd been once before, so I had an impression of her and her home; but she'd moved since then from an upstairs apartment to a tidy ranch-style house in a neighborhood of similar homes, all painted in pastel colors like after-dinner mints.

Joe and I had to get to know Grandma. She was nice to us, but she was a stranger. We secretly called her "Skinny." She was of average height and on the lean side, but had a pot belly. She wore shorts and had big glasses and colored her curly hair brown. Her voice was deep like a smoker's, though I don't remember if she had the habit.

Dad hadn't seen much of his mother, and she was clearly glad to have us, so I was shocked when Mom got as drunk as I've ever seen her and stayed that way. She turned hostile, hurling insults in every direction. I felt sorry for Grandma, who was a target. So were we, but what else was new? We passed the days somehow, coming together for meals and eating in relative silence or else trying to make normal conversation, which was hard with Mom kicking Joe and me under the table.

Mom got so unruly that Dad took to sleeping on the floor at night, blocking their bedroom door to keep her inside. Joe and I—lying in twin beds in the next room—could hear the awful fallout. As small as that house was, Grandma couldn't have missed it either. One night the three of them—Dad, Mom, and Grandma—ended up arguing and scuffling in the back yard. All I could do was stand by the window and look out into the dark, wondering if the police would come and wishing for the craziness to end. I still think of that night when I hear the Bobby Lewis tune, "Tossin' and Turnin'."

The cops didn't raid us—a miracle—but we stayed at Grandma's way too long. How could Dad have let his mother see his wife at her worst and our family life as the sham that it was? If Grandma didn't ask us to leave—another miracle—why didn't Dad just get us all out of there?

To this day I hate hostage movies.

Lucian met me in front of the memorial and immediately understood that I had been affected by what I'd seen. The way his eyes slipped up to mine, I thought he was looking for it, maybe even hoping that the woman he'd been driving around to Dracula sites had gained some insight into his country. At any rate, when we looked at each other something passed between us. I couldn't explain it, but a new connection had been made, however brief. It scared me; I'd been trying to avoid such moments with him. *Here we go again,* I thought as I felt the invisible walls go up around me.

Chapter 31

The Company of Women

After touring the local attractions and the Maramureş countryside, we returned to the farm and Lucian left on some errand in the car. I got my book, fixed a cup of tea, and went into the great room to soak up the ambience. I felt like I was repeating the previous afternoon. My body still ached. I felt lazy and was glad to be alone.

I was just considering a nap in the few hours before dinner when Olga came into the guest house and went upstairs. She banged around above me for a while—a contrast to the quiet I'd been enjoying—then came down and skittered back across the yard. Had she been straightening Lucian's room? A spark of indignation flared quickly and then died. She hadn't straightened mine; I'd done it myself.

That evening, we had our last dinner in the farmhouse. I went from starved to bloated in half an hour, glad for some real food to accompany that snack of pork rinds I'd eaten earlier to tide me over.

I can't recall everything we ate and don't know the correct names, but there were fresh vegetables—those crisp cucumbers I loved and peppers that were almost white. We had something round with a soft, rumpled crust, some bread, and bean soup. Then Olga brought in the main course—chicken legs with parsley potatoes. The legs had the thighs intact, the kind that take up half the plate. While we were eating that, she served the dessert: pastries the size of my paperback copy of *Dracula,* with a quart bowl of sour cream on the side. I couldn't even finish my potatoes, let alone a pastry, but I spread one with sour cream and dug in.

When Olga saw my half-eaten pastry, she put her hands on her hips, cocked her head to one side, and gave me a scowl. Jenny Craig would have fainted by then, and *not* because I didn't clean my plate. So there you go: Olga and Jenny were the warring devil and angel of my farmhouse meals.

Teodor didn't eat with us that night, and there was no plum brandy. We had water to drink and were finished by eight thirty.

I was in the guest house reading when the car pulled up. The great room had become my official spot, as my bedroom lamp didn't cut the mustard for reading or writing. It sat low on the night table and didn't put out enough light: The bulb was encased in a rectangle about the size of a loaf of homemade bread, with open silver circles on every side. I guess you had to be there. Of course, I could have used my new headlamp to read in bed, if I'd remembered I had one.

In a little while I heard a commotion outside, but didn't stir from my reading chair. It was dark, and I didn't care enough about what was going on to get up and see. As it turned out, more tourists had arrived. A carload of women and their young male driver had driven into the yard, instantly filling it with gaiety and light and noise. Already they were beginning to set their bags in the guest house foyer. *Ah.* Their arrival was the reason for Olga's afternoon cleaning session.

The yard was now alive in the night, and my ability to ignore it was fading fast. In a moment, Lucian burst in to announce that one of the new arrivals was from Cincinnati; then, of course, I did get up. All of us were introduced on the porch—Brooke, the Cincinnatian; her aunt; the aunt's friend from England; and their guide, Razvan. Teodor had come across the yard carrying a musical instrument that was part horn, part fiddle. He and Olga sang and played for us, there in the light from the two houses.

Olga's body had not forgotten the dance. Even when she was still, it wanted to assume the pose, the way one or the other of her legs turned outward or rested on the concrete porch step as though it were the barre. At dinner Olga had not just moved in and out of the kitchen; she'd swirled

and pirouetted as if she were going on and off a stage. It wasn't a performance; it was automatic, muscle memory. Sometimes her arms would
even make a shape in front of her, the fingertips together, as though she
were holding a basket of laundry or fruit.

Brooke and her friends had made reservations at another hotel and
hadn't liked it. At the last minute, Lucian had arranged for them to take
the vacant rooms in our building. And just like that, the dynamic shifted
out at the farm: Olga and Teodor had come to life; Lucian had another
driver with whom to compare tour-guide notes; and I was being nudged
into sociability. I lingered on the porch after the music while the new
guests moved in. Lucian stood by in the grass as Razvan finished pulling
luggage from the back of a white station wagon. "Could you take a few of
these?" Razvan joked, as both of them rolled their eyes at the accumula-
tion of stuffed shopping bags crammed in with the suitcases.

The guest house filled up with female voices. What a contrast the
women were to me—the quiet, introspective writer! Their talk, sponta-
neous and unselfconscious, included Razvan and Lucian and reached out
from the get-go to me. It was tempting. I was struck by their friendliness
overall and their ease with the drivers in particular.

Days before, on the road to Targoviște, I'd wondered how other travelers interacted with their guides. Now I could see for myself. These women
didn't seem to have any of the concerns I grappled with; namely, will this
or that seem like flirting. With them, there was absolutely nothing that
could be misconstrued. It was true that there is safety in numbers.

Lucian and I were in an intimate situation every day; no matter how
I sliced it, I couldn't make light of that. Conversation might have flowed
more easily with him had we not been alone in the car, but we were. And
the tone might have been lighter if I'd been shopping instead of writing,
but I wasn't.

The new guests' bustling and chatter were welcome after my days of
silence in the guest house—though that silence had been comfortable,
I thought. I wasn't great at girl talk, but then I hadn't had any "girls" to
talk to on this trip except Olga, who was usually cooking or cleaning up.
I stayed away from the farmhouse except at mealtimes because she was
so busy. When I saw Olga outside, she was hanging clothes or gathering
something from the garden for supper. Sometimes she would put her

arm lightly around my shoulders and ask if "it is okay," meaning things in general, and then skitter off with a "See you later."

As suitcases were being carried up the stairs, I thought, *There goes my private bathroom.* With Lucian tucked away on the second floor, I hadn't had to share. That would have been too intimate anyway. Even the moist air that clings after someone else's bath carries too much information. Razvan could double up with him, but three women?

That night I deliberately slept like Dracula, on my back with my hands folded on my chest, in order not to have to shampoo my hair the next morning. I wanted a quick-in, quick-out routine, in case.

It was our last night in the guest house; in the morning Lucian and I would take to the road again, leaving the farm and the other group behind. Or so I thought.

Chapter 32

All Our Fears

"How blessed are some people," Bram Stoker wrote in *Dracula,* "whose lives have no fears, no dreads, to whom sleep is a blessing that comes nightly, and brings nothing but sweet dreams."

Something woke me up before dawn, a dream I couldn't recall. In the Maramureş countryside, the night is deep: You hear nothing but your own movements. I wasn't afraid; couldn't even call it up. There in the heart of Dracula country, in the dead of night, I was encased in a peaceful silence. It was the ultimate irony.

As a kid in Glen Ferris, I could guarantee a heart-thumping night if I merely *thought* of Transylvania. I owed that to another kid with an active imagination: that little Irish boy who grew up to write one of the scariest novels of all time. *Dracula* was the embodiment of all my fears.

In a moment, I'd swapped my bed in Maramureş for the one in my childhood room. Like many other memories that had accompanied me on my trip to Romania, this one came unbidden.

I was sweating under a yellow hobnail bedspread in the middle of summer. Lightning bugs blinked outside; our hall light laid a bright strip under my bedroom door, but it wasn't enough. Night after night I lay in my room on the second floor of our un-air-conditioned house, clutching the covers to my neck for dear life. Above all, don't expose your neck at night; if I'd learned anything from my beloved Dracula movies, it was that. Vampires wouldn't be stopped by a bedspread, but at least I could fall asleep if I held the covers up to my chin.

I slept on my back, and before sleep I always stared straight up into the dark, avoiding shadows, the night on the other side of the windows, and the closet at the foot of my bed. Eventually my body would give in, my hands would relax, and the next thing I knew it would be morning. I would have made it through another night without becoming one of the undead. This was the price I paid for loving vampire movies. Sweat equity, you might call it.

I didn't sleep with the window open; that would have been foolish. A vampire might take the open window as an invitation. And so the unrelieved heat of summer evenings pressed into my room. Oddly, a little breeze from somewhere would hit the side of my neck the instant the blanket slipped down. I would feel that coolness; then my neck would prickle until I got the spread in my grip again and wrapped myself up like a mummy.

It wasn't always Dracula coming to suck my blood; sometimes it was Aunt Lucy, the vampire who had lured the girl, Tania, into the woods: "I heard you call me, Aunt Lucy." To me it was the scariest line ever uttered in a movie.

I covered my neck at night for years—at summer camp, at other people's houses, and even in Grandmama's bedroom, which was the safest place I knew. Crickets and frogs broke the summer silence from the shallow creek by the railroad tracks. The bedroom window was open, the shade was raised, and light from the neighbors' house shone in. Grandmama was only a few feet away. She was anything but frightening, even with her long, gray hair let out of its bun and hanging straight down her back. But Grandmama would always fall asleep first, and then I was alone. Even the creepy dressmaker's dummy behind the door didn't scare me as much as the idea of Dracula. If I let myself think about vampires, my heart would pound and I would perspire, bringing back all my primal fears: "I heard you call me, Aunt Lucy. I heard you call me, Aunt Lucy."

Of course, I'd fed my fears with horror stories—the more spine-chilling, the better. Most of us like a scary story when we can approach horror from the comfort of a safer place. Sometimes I didn't have one.

At home as I lay wrapped in my bedspread, fending off the fangs of Dracula, the real monster—the one that *had* invited itself in—was downstairs watching TV. Mom had no hesitation about entering my bedroom without a knock at any hour, and I never knew what craziness she'd have on her mind. Dracula would have to get in line to scare me.

Everybody's afraid of something. The person who scared me silly, the one who hid bottles and lived a double life, was afraid of cats. They were too sneaky. She lost her balance once while carrying a hot casserole and nearly fell over backward because a cat walked behind her in a parking lot. Of course, that sent the cat scurrying. Mom was afraid of cats; maybe cats were afraid of her, too.

Dad must have had fears—my guess would be health issues—but he didn't talk about them. As for Joe, something looked in the bedroom window at him one night when we were kids. My brother saw a ghostly face floating outside in the dark. It must have been like something out of *Salem's Lot,* only Stephen King hadn't written *Salem's Lot* yet. The face was not Dracula's but belonged to Scotty Lisle, a small, pale boy who lived up the road. Joe was never sure if it had been a dream.

The scariest dream I ever had was about a wig-head, one of those white Styrofoam forms used to store wigs when they aren't being worn. I had this dream in adulthood. In the dream, I got up in the night and opened my bedroom closet. There on the floor next to a shoe rack was a white wig form, bald and silent. It stood upright on the carpet like a head growing out of the floor. This form had facial features like those of store mannequins—vague shapes without color. Hints of eyes (closed); a little tip of a nose; a wavy line and a bump for a mouth. All of a sudden its eyes flew open and its mouth was glowing like a neon sign. Two bright green lips started to wiggle like worms, opening and closing. I was astonished. "Are you alive?" I asked it.

The head replied in a slow growl like some Hell-creature: "Are *yooooou* alive?" I was seized by a fear so primal it woke me up, and I wondered if I really would be alive after my heart did its thing, practically beating out of my chest.

At six thirty in Maramureş, I was sitting on the side of my bed, already dressed. I'd done my makeup in the bathroom, as my room had no mirror. I could have made something of that—no mirror in Transylvania—

but instead I'd quietly laid claim to the one over the sink. My bed was made, my suitcase locked. We would be heading out for Gura Humorului in a few hours.

Dawn was breaking, reminding me that my sweaty nights in Glen Ferris were far behind me. It was a relief, but I guess we never stop being afraid; there's always something. I could come up with a list to rival Santa's.

I looked down and realized I was sitting with my legs together and my hands in my lap, like a nun in her cell waiting for the day to begin. In that little moment I wasn't afraid of anything, except possibly having seen too many monasteries.

Chapter 33

A Place to Go

I heard music coming through the balcony door of my hotel room in the town of Gura Humorului ("Goora hoo-MOR-loo-ey"), our home base for touring the painted monasteries of Bucovina. It was evening, but not yet dark. Lucian and I had just checked in, and I'd been putting my things away when I was lured outside.

Several stories below me, musicians had begun to play for a wedding celebration. The wedding party was emerging from a church at the foot of the curved street that ran past the hotel. As they came out, they began dancing, forming a line and then a circle in the street. Spectators cheered as the bride and groom came out and joined the dancing.

I could see half the town from my balcony. Directly behind the wedding spectators was a little wedge-shaped green park, a surprise in the busiest part of the city. The pie-shaped view continued past the residential sections, broadening where the houses left off and green hills filled the distance.

Gura Humorului has a history as a Jewish *shtetl*, a traditional pious community that remained stable and immune to outside influences for nearly one hundred years. The Jews were allowed to settle in the town beginning in 1835, and the Jewish community began to flourish in the late 1860s. Then in 1899 most of Gura Humorului burned in a terrible fire. It was rebuilt with help from Jewish communities in the United States.

When World War II broke out in 1941, Romanian dictator Ion Antonescu, who aligned himself politically with Hitler, deported the Jewish people of Gura Humorului to a concentration camp in nearby Ukraine, where many died. Survivors were permitted to return to Romania beginning in 1943, but after the war, most chose to settle in Israel. In 1988 former residents of Gura Humorului and their families based in Israel established an association to preserve the memory of the Romanian community they had built.

The happy noise of the wedding crowd sweetened the summer evening. The whole town of Gura Humorului, and especially that street, was like an invitation. My eyes followed the street past the park and church to flat-fronted houses painted yellow and white and light pink. A woman watched the dancing from her stoop; a man in a red shirt knelt on the sidewalk to play with a black puppy. And then the street curved out of sight. I wondered where it went.

It would have been fun to follow that street; to drop what I was doing, take the elevator down to the lobby, and walk outside. I could almost feel it: I'd leave the hotel behind and make my way along the crowded sidewalk among the wedding guests. I wanted to blend in, if just for a minute. I wanted to feel the pulse of the town, to be a part of it.

I recognized the urge. I'd always had it: a desire to belong, to fit in. Since my Glen Ferris days I'd often wondered what it would be like to be someone else, to live somewhere else, to step into another life. It was a version of the same urge that had brought me to Romania.

How many times had it come over me? I couldn't count them. Since childhood I'd been fascinated with families and what might go on inside other people's houses. I responded on a gut level to TV commercials showing family events, and it was a love/hate relationship: I was envious. There were all the generations—grandparents, parents, kids of all ages—gathered around the piano, smiling together on a wide front porch, or having a party in the backyard of a big, white farmhouse. There was noise, running, laughter, dogs—everything I didn't have at home. Once when I was in high school I found it.

A friend of mine was one of seven children—three boys and four girls.

The family lived in a big, white Colonial that sat back from a rural road on a knoll dotted with shade trees. The house had a shabby look—peeling paint, forgettable furniture—but something was always going on. The whole second floor had been divided into two big rooms called the boys' dorm and the girls' dorm. I'd never heard of such a thing.

Chelsea and her family lived up the river—the same area that produced my old suitor, Squirrel. "Up the river" was a place past Gauley Bridge and beyond the boundaries I usually observed in my travels. It was like another world that had opened up to me through school busing.

Chelsea's family enveloped me for a while. It was a dose of medicine, but it wasn't a cure. I still wondered what went on in other houses, behind lighted windows. I didn't cry during Hallmark commercials, but I felt a familiar tug when I saw extended families in restaurants or backyards or kitchens, celebrating some event. I still had fantasies of moving all over the country, to one place after another: cities, suburbs, a country lane; experiencing locations urban and rural, streets packed with people or a deserted bluff; a home in the desert or maybe even another part of the world. It never stopped.

Instead of walking out of the hotel, I stayed on the balcony with my camera, snapping away. I was meeting Lucian soon.

There were six weddings in Gura Humorului that night. According to Lucian, that was typical for a Saturday. The reception for one of them was held in our hotel, and he and I peeked in beforehand when everything was decorated and set out. It was fun; I liked being a spectator at weddings. I just wouldn't have wanted to be the bride.

I'd always thought of marriage as a club whose members were constantly recruiting. Only after being admitted via a wedding ceremony did a couple learn the inside scoop: that "wedded" didn't always mean "bliss"—even for them. Welcome to the club.

My second husband and I, when we saw newlyweds, used to look at each other and whisper, "Suckers!" It was a reference to the horrible odds against having a good and lasting marriage. We thought we'd beaten the odds, especially in the beginning. Our inside joke was that every other couple but us was doomed. But that was me in a different life—life in the club—before I was kicked out.

Lucian and I had agreed to meet downstairs at seven. We were supposed to join a tour group from his travel agency at seven thirty for dinner on the mezzanine, so we had thirty minutes to kill. It was good to be anchored at the hotel after the day-long drive through the mountains with only a couple stops. We stood outside on the top step and talked while traffic buzzed by.

When the subject turned to Romanian politics, I tuned out. Lucian tended to rave, so I let my thoughts drift until I realized that he was talking about our time out at the farm. "His wife, she really liked you," he was saying.

Liked me? I hadn't thought she'd liked me at all. Olga had been friendly, of course. She was a hostess; it was expected. But at times I'd wondered if running a *pensione* was a stretch for her—not the labor so much as the extroversion required for constantly interacting with guests. I certainly couldn't have done it. As evidence, I'd sequestered myself in the great room with a book at every opportunity. But it hardly mattered now; the farm was behind us.

Lucian and I had started out that morning from Maramureş at the same time as the other group. In fact, he and Razvan were intentionally traveling together, until one of the women left her sunglasses in a little museum and they'd had to go back. Then, who knows, shopping and more stops on their part would put them in Gura Humorului two hours after we arrived. By their own admission, they were not a punctual group.

On our way, Lucian and I had passed a bright blue train chugging along against a bright green hill. I'd been trying to get a decent photo of a Romanian train for days—another elusive subject—and this one would have been perfect if I'd been ready. My resulting digital picture had shown only the caboose, with the rest of the train presumably humming ahead somewhere to the right of the image area.

It was dinnertime. Lucian and I went back into the hotel, and while he connected with someone about the arrangements, I stood near the stairs. Sure enough, a group of tourists filed by, and I guessed they were the ones from the agency. They looked about as exciting as a set of white sheets—a mostly older crowd, not that I had any room to talk, all of them dressed up but lacking even the slightest attractive element. *A bunch of duds,* I thought. I didn't look forward to attempting conversation, especially if they were going to speak another language.

Lucian finally came back and we went upstairs, where long tables had been set in an "L" shape. The tour group was already seated, and they had started to eat. Only one seat remained open, so what was Lucian planning to do—stick me alone with these strangers? "Should I sit there?" I asked him. To my utter relief, he said no, and we beat a path back down the stairs.

We dined alone on the terrace. Dark fell around us as we sat at one of the umbrella tables with the wedding reception coming together in the background. We drank brandy with our dinner. Lucian had the usual tuica, but this time he'd ordered blueberry for me. Little round berries floated on top of the dark liquid. "This is better for women," he said.

"Why?"

"It's sweet." Maybe to Lucian sweet would be easier for the weaker sex to take than the plum brandy that burned your throat after you quickly sloshed the contents of the little glass toward the back of your mouth and swallowed. Or maybe he just thought *I* needed something sweet. Maybe the serious American needed a dose of sugar. It was possible.

We ate peppers and pickles, a mix of meats, including some deliciously greasy sausage, and something like a corn cake topped with a fried egg over easy. The egg had a little face on it. I ate half of everything, even the dessert, which was a scoop of delicious cherry ice cream with a serving of custard.

While we ate, the wedding party filled the ballroom behind us and the music started. Through the open doorway to the terrace I could see the dark-haired bride—recognizable by her traditional white dress, a style that would have worked as well in America as it did in Romania. Next to her, a man who was likely her father began leaping around like a puppet to the lively first number, encouraging the others to get into the spirit. Either that or he was already drunk.

My mother had been drunk during all but the main event when I married my college boyfriend. Why had I ever thought it would be otherwise? Unlike the proud dad in Romania getting loose and having a good time, she was scary, her expression murderous. Mom seemed to hate the whole wedding party. We tried to ignore her; that was our coping mechanism. I don't remember anyone even gently suggesting that she might want to go home and lie down.

When I look back on that wedding, I see the layer of craziness, and not only because Mom was drunk. Getting married was a crazy thing for me to do, even though it made sense then. It was crazy because I was twenty years old, but I didn't know squat about love or how to be a wife. We lasted nine years and had a child before my husband and I divorced, and I took on the challenge of being a single parent.

Mom had wanted me to elope; she'd dropped plenty of hints, and maybe I should have listened. For my second wedding, I did elope.

I hadn't wanted to get married again. Instead, we lived together, which of course wasn't a popular choice with the folks back in Glen Ferris. We set up housekeeping in a townhouse in Cincinnati when my son was in the second grade.

Marriage was more important to this man than it was to me. Every day he'd ask, "When am I going to get you to marry me?" Same question, over and over, and one day I said, "Okay." That was my answer: "Okay."

After the blood tests and the three-day waiting period, we were married by a justice of the peace in a neighboring state. It was a lot less complicated than my first wedding had been, but did I really wear cutoffs? I guess that one was crazy, too, in its way, but it did have a strong element of romance until he moved on.

It was a beautiful night in Gura Humorului, and I felt the same peace I'd felt in the country. I was beyond relaxed; in fact, at nine thirty I began to yawn and long for my room, where my things were still all over the place. The room looked to have been furnished in the days of Robin Hood: The sturdy, medieval-looking furniture was gray toned and masculine, accented by a rust-red carpet, spread, and drapes. It seemed both inviting and rock solid. After living at the guest house, I was glad for the anonymity of the hotel, where I could close my door and have complete privacy. We were there for two nights, so that even gave me the freedom to be messy.

My room had a French door to the balcony. It was like the doors leading to Lucy's room in *Horror of Dracula*, where she had lain on her bed and struck a seductive pose, waiting for the Count. In the movie the doors swung open as if by magic, and there *he* was on the threshold, ready to come in and bite her neck. I had no sense of vampires in Gura Humorului, though; nothing.

I crawled into bed, slept, and then woke up in total darkness, unable to find my alarm clock. I looked outside, remembering that I still hadn't seen the moon. When I turned on a light, I saw that it was 4:30 a.m. In a few hours we were going to depart for Bucovina. Instead of getting back into my cozy Robin Hood bed, I started the coffee. I was going to run out of Sweet'N Low before the end of the trip, maybe Coffee-mate as well; but my coffee supply should be fine: two of those little bags people give for stocking stuffers at Christmas.

In a while I opened the curtains to my balcony, and there was light breaking in the distance. I watched for a bit and saw the moon briefly emerge from the cloud cover. Wait. *Think*. That wasn't the moon in the sky; it was the sun, already high at seven thirty. Roosters were crowing!

I dressed and finished getting ready for a day of monasteries. Unlike a few we'd seen, these were famous. The painted monasteries of Bucovina were known the world over, so I looked forward to the day even though it wouldn't be about Dracula—or Vlad.

Chapter 34

The Girl in Pink

She was so out of place, standing alone in front of the painted monastery at Sucevița, yellow hair waving and body head to toe in bright, shocking, skin-tight pink. Even her high-heeled, pointy-toed shoes were pink.

The girl's clothes and rumpled blonde hair screamed out against the backdrop of ancient reds and browns dominating the *Ladder of Virtues,* a scene painted on the exterior of the church in the sixteenth century to depict the clash between good and evil. In stark contrast to the local peasants with their bare faces, the girl's full lips were thick with maroon lipstick, and her eyes were made up to look dark. She was probably twenty, curved like a farm girl. Her soft white belly peeked out between a bright pink camisole top and a pair of tight go-to-hell pink pants. I thought about my travel wardrobe of dark skirts and long-sleeved blouses—*dour, compared to that.*

Lucian and I had just arrived, traveling in tandem with the women from the mountains and their guide, who I knew would be along in their own time. The day was clear and bright. The seventeen-mile drive from Gura Humorului to Sucevița took us along the Borgo Pass—a road straight out of *Dracula*—into the countryside of the Bucovina region.

The road was terrible, pitted and full of horseshoe curves—and even a horse. We passed through a village where a fat, brown horse stood broadside to us in the road. It was smack in the middle, its front hooves planted in the left lane and its rear hooves in the right. Except for its mane and tail whipping in the breeze, the horse was still. Then, as we approached, it turned its head toward our car and looked straight at Lucian and me as if to say, "Yep, here I am." Lucian honked it out of position and sped on: Just another day in a Romanian village.

The road was bad, but the scenery was worth it. I had never seen so many trees; the mountains were dense with them. I had never seen evergreens grow so straight and tall; in West Virginia they grew at angles to the mountains. There, deep in the Carpathians, all of the pines pointed upward without seeming to crowd each other but sharing the air and light.

Around every bend was a vista: Streams sparkled as we zipped by, slowed down on the curves, and then zipped again. Rocks stuck out of the clear rushing water, and I half expected picture-perfect trout to jump from the streams in arcs and flip their tails. People camped in the grassy meadows, but once we got into the mountains, we went miles without seeing another village.

Finally we stopped at a restaurant/store/gas station combo. It was wonderful to pick out my crapola for the rest of the ride: cookies, paprika chips, and orange juice. While I was paying, Lucian came down from the second-story restaurant, where he'd been waiting with two cups of coffee. I'd expected him to be back in the car, wanting to get on the road. You never know, do you?

We sat upstairs near an open window, looking at those beautiful pine trees. Growing up in the mountains, you think you know mountains, but in Romania are the most beautiful hills and forests imaginable.

Sitting there with Lucian, I realized I felt relaxed. That's always big news for the hypervigilant. Maybe my time at the farm had done it— all those hours in the guest house resting and drinking tea; or it could have been the presence of the three other women, with their laughter and retail-based approach to touring. Maybe it was just the cool green of the scenery and the light breeze blowing through the pines a few feet from where we sat in the restaurant, but I could have lingered there. We didn't.

The ride was full of images to pluck at your heart. It was Sunday, and little girls walked along carrying pocketbooks. Villagers strolled to church on rutted dirt streets. The men wore suits; the women, dresses or gathered skirts. On another morning they would already be returning from the fields in simple clothing and high boots, with wet grass clippings stuck to the blades of their primitive cutting tools.

Lucian and I came upon Sucevița suddenly, as we rounded a curve. When I saw its high, thick stone walls, I didn't realize I was looking at a monastery. "What is that?" I asked Lucian. "Why are we stopping?" He looked at me with some amusement, as though the answer should be obvious. Then he pulled into a lot across the road near a string of souvenir stands.

The painted monasteries of Bucovina are located in northeastern Romania among the foothills of the Carpathians. They were named for the beautiful frescoes painted on their inner and outer walls. The churches were painted in the fifteenth and sixteenth centuries—beginning in 1487, thirty-one years after the death of Vlad the Impaler. The first frescoes were painted on the inside walls. Then, when the fortified monasteries were used to shelter villagers and soldiers during threats of war, exterior scenes from the Bible were added to educate those who could not read or wouldn't enter the churches.

Even though many of the monastery painters were unknown, their frescoes are considered masterpieces. Those decorating outside walls have held up against the weather for centuries, and the paint colors have become famous: Voroneț blue, the green-red of Sucevița, the yellow of Moldovița, the red of Humor, and the green of Arbore.

Seven painted monasteries became UNESCO (United Nations Educational, Scientific, and Cultural Organization) World Cultural Heritage Sites in 1993. A World Heritage Site is a place of either cultural or physical significance. It is considered in the interest of the entire world to preserve each site.

We crossed the street and accessed the monastery grounds through a wooden door in the wall. Sucevița is situated in a valley surrounded by low hills, fields, and evergreen trees. Picture a fairytale version of Fort Apache, a citadel with a painted church at its center. Guard towers with pointed roofs are built into the four corners. This Romanian Orthodox Church, according to its literature, is "Dedicated to the Resurrection of Lord Jesus." Monks' cells line the inside of the perimeter, and a separate bell tower stands near the entrance with its own steeple and a bell ringer who climbs a set of outer stairs to perform his ancient duty.

At the entrance you buy a ticket and then must pay an additional fee to take pictures, if they're allowed. Some monasteries display signs indicating no cameras, food, drink, or whatever they want to ban, including *indecenta*—inappropriate attire. *Indecenta* can keep a tourist out of a monastery. It is not unusual to see a stack of folded aprons on a bench near the entrance. Anyone who wants to go in but happens to be showing too much skin can grab an apron to hide exposed knees or shoulders.

When I spotted the girl in pink, my mind was full of questions. Why would anyone dress in shocking pink to visit a monastery? Where had she been when they gave out the advice on what to wear—in a nightclub? Was it her intention to be a magnet for every eye in the place?

I had to admit she was not *indecenta*. Except for the white crescent of belly above her wide belt, she was covered. And there were no rules against makeup or tousled hair. She had made unfortunate color choices, but no one was banning pink. The girl had been admitted, jarring and outrageous but breaking no rules.

She must have been waiting for someone. A service was in progress when we arrived. The painted monasteries are not just tourist attractions, but working churches for the people from the surrounding villages.

Lucian and I went in. Even though I knew photos weren't allowed inside the church, I still had my camera around my neck. If that didn't make me stand out, I had another shot at it: I was the only female without her head covered. In addition to dark, simple clothing and no cosmetics, every woman I saw wore a scarf tied in a knot under her chin. I ditched the camera in its bag and practically dove for my black silk headscarf, folded at the bottom of the bag. I wanted to blend in here—if not to be one of them, at least not to seem the crude American interested only in watching a show.

For the record, I hate scarves. I have no knack for them and would feel foolish in some dramatic drape slung over my shoulders to liven up an outfit. However, I do pay attention to wardrobe advice. The packing experts tell you to take along a "monastery scarf"—so many uses: shawl, beach cover-up, emergency blanket. Phooey. It only works for those who have the talent and can carry off the fashion statement. But that day it was a relief to fold my scarf quickly into a triangle and tie it over my head. I did so with little thought of how it would instantly smash my hair flat for the rest of the day. I was thankful for its dark color, its generous size, and the weight of it resting on my shoulders.

Lucian stood back and waved me toward the sanctuary. I quickly found myself in a crush of local people filing through the church in a path to the communion railing. The streaming pilgrims crowded the aisle, those on the way back bumping me gently as I went against the tide, trying to find a corner where I could watch the service. It was impossible; the heart of the church was too small and full of people. A nun wearing a long, black habit brushed past me as I moved back out into the aisle. Later I saw her kiss one of the painted walls.

This was a Romanian Orthodox church. I'd had a good friend who became a Roman Catholic nun after high school, forever leaving behind her life in a West Virginia coal town. Margery had told me one day at school what she was going to do, and I felt like something had been sucked out of me.

I thought Margery had too much personality to be a nun, but what did I know of nuns and their personalities? I wasn't even Catholic. Margery loved rock and roll, Dick Clark, and John F. Kennedy. She had dark hair, smooth skin, and white teeth. Her eyes danced. She laughed all the time. After graduation I never saw her again.

As I moved away from the crowd, still on its course, I thought about the women. I'd read in America that Romanian girls were very beautiful, but I'd seen that many of the women were plain. It wasn't just in church, but on the streets and in the villages as well. I had seen mothers and daughters walking together, opposites depicting before and after; youth and age.

What was the transformation process that turned a beautiful young girl into a peasant woman? When did a female put on her first peasant skirt? I'd noticed the skirts, which were often black. Gathered at the waist, they would pooch out and visibly widen the wearer's hips. The hem hit just below the knees, exposing the often bowed legs of the woman—likely a result of malnutrition.

When did the kerchiefs come out? Was there some irretrievable moment when a young woman put one on, maybe for cleaning; got used to tying her hair back; and bam, became a peasant woman? In ten or twenty or thirty years, would she be walking along the side of the road with a full bag of groceries in each hand, leaning from side to side with each step, her legs encased in leggings, boots spattered with mud, her face bare like so many others, and her hair never to be seen in public again?

In cities like Bucharest and Cluj, women often dressed for style, as did the young girls; but out here, tradition seemed to rule. I learned later that traditionally, marriage was the milestone that defined head-wear for many Romanian women. Covering the head was a significant moment in the wedding ceremony, and there were three stages: dressing the hair, gathering the hair, and covering the head. After their wedding day, married women always had their heads covered. There you go; life in the club.

I headed down the monastery steps into the fresh air. The girl in pink was standing off by herself in the churchyard like a pink flag, the painted *Ladder of Virtues* looming above her. So far she was flat-out flunking the peasant test. Was plainness in her future? Maybe I was witnessing a last gasp of fashion daring before she married.

I couldn't take my eyes off this girl. As I watched her, I caught her looking back at me. I knew I was staring, but how could I help it? She was wearing the pinkest pants she could possibly have put on, in a sea of somber clothing. She was innocence and worldliness, wrapped in eye-popping pink, at odds with the historic monastery in its simple country setting. In the mural behind her, the fight between Heaven and Hell silently raged on.

Soon a young man with a crew cut emerged from the church onto the sunlit flagstone walk and headed for the girl in pink. Was I watching the tail end of a Saturday night date? If so, the young man seemed an unlikely companion, clean cut and simply dressed in a white T-shirt and freshly pressed blue jeans. He took the hand of the girl in pink, and they walked away together.

As Lucian and I were leaving Sucevița, I needed to find a toilet. It wasn't on the grounds of the monastery but across the road and down a path, a miserable little building where a man sat in the shade selling folded lengths of toilet paper. I was making short work of the hike, taking healthy strides and swinging my arms, when I noticed my own shirt sleeve. *Pink.*

In my absorption with the place, the people, my scarf, and the girl, I had completely forgotten my own outfit. I'd worn my pink shirt, and it was not pale pink or delicate pink or peach or any other variation; it was bright, shocking pink! I was the girl in pink, too.

Chapter 35

Bucovina

After we left Sucevița we spent the afternoon touring the ancient monasteries at Moldovița, Humor, and finally Voroneț—which Lucian said was best in the afternoon because of the position of the sun.

He and I were on our own. We met Razvan and our women friends throughout the day, but it was a loose arrangement in which we'd spot the others in a churchyard or sanctuary and drift together temporarily. No one ever suggested that any of the three women ride with us or that I join them for a while.

I loved how synchronized Lucian and I were when it came to schedules. "Fifteen minutes," he had said at breakfast, and I was already waiting in the lobby when he arrived right on time.

We'd stopped in a town called Marginea, which means *margin* or border—"The opposite of middle," per Lucian. The town, located thirty kilometers from the Ukraine border, is known for its unique black pottery, and I bought some as gifts and some for myself. Never mind how the fragile souvenirs were going to survive the trip home. I could worry about that later.

On we went after the pottery stop—over mountains, past rural *pensiones*, through villages, and back out into the country. I loved the ride. Seeing more villagers dressed up and heading to church in the sunshine gave me hope, not for the trip or myself, just in general.

We passed a man selling honey by the road, his painted beehives in neat rows behind him. The colors were pastel shades of yellow, blue, and green. Lucian backed up and parked—in the road. Without saying a thing, he got out to go buy honey, leaving me exposed to traffic in the passenger seat. I felt like a sitting duck as two cars crested the hill ahead of me and a truck approached from the other direction. *Nothing like being caught in the crossfire,* I thought, like one of the damned. But the vehicles worked around the obstacle of our car and Lucian returned with the honey. Whew! I was never so glad to get moving again.

We saw long valleys, rolling pastureland, and farms where men were storing hay for their animals. Once I looked past Lucian's profile and saw a cow by the road in a perfect little setting of grass and trees, so still she seemed to be sitting for a portrait. It was the second time that day I'd been startled by a cow. After we got out of the car at Humor, a brown cow on her own had crossed the paved parking lot as if she were searching for her vehicle. She had a bell around her neck and a deliberate look as she passed among the parked cars. It was nothing; nobody even blinked.

As for the painted monasteries of Bucovina, I had enjoyed seeing them. I liked best the beautiful shapes of the buildings, combinations of angles and curves echoed in each roof and steeple. The dark roofs are like lovely hats, extending several feet beyond the sand-colored walls in every direction. Where an apse bumps out in a half-circle, the roof above it does the same. The steeples were designed the same way, creating a feeling of harmony that draws the eye up, down, and around each building. The medieval artists must have been challenged by the shapes of the buildings. Though some of the walls are flat, one or both ends of a church might be rounded. Some walls are embellished with protruding arches. Many have windows. Yet the frescoes ripple on, fitting like skin on the brick and stone.

By the end of the day I couldn't tell the monasteries apart. Which one had the golden apple? Where did we see a service, complete with singing nuns? At which entrance did Lucian have a slight altercation with one of the nuns over my admission ticket? I found it impossible to keep the information straight, even with notes, so I made a point of buying brochures to peruse once I got home.

Brochures weren't all I bought. The outside walkway to Humor was a gallery of beautiful items for sale—clothing, table linens, and rugs all pinned to clotheslines as though they'd just been hung out to dry in the August heat. The locals were taking advantage of the huge retail opportunity along the tourists' path to the painted monastery. We waited until we were on our way out before stopping.

I bought a rug I loved, and it wasn't easy. If you linger at these displays, it's all over. You must be swift and sure, as the sellers—in this case, local peasant women—will descend like vultures and suddenly you will have too many choices. The buying process is even more difficult when conducted in a foreign language, but the experience was better with Lucian at my side as four women gathered to compete for my Romanian lei. The first one joined us the minute we stopped to look; then another walked over; and before long the other two had joined the party. Once they'd ascertained that I liked the colorful wool rugs, each woman grabbed a different one off the line and held it out. One pulled out a calculator as I tried to determine whether I even had "two million," the price of the blue flowered rug I'd chosen. Not for the first time, I thought of the TV show *Who Wants to Be a Millionaire?* Once the deal was done, we headed for the car.

By five-thirty, we were back at our hotel in Gura Humorului, and for the first time since I'd been in Romania, I'd had it. According to Lucian, the other group had gone to watch a family paint eggs. Fine. They seemed tireless, determined to have every possible cultural and retail experience that Romania had to offer. All I wanted in the world was to go down to the terrace to sit and drink beer.

Lucian joined me. We were quiet, no surprise. I was relaxed, glad to be sitting outside in the warm evening. I was thinking ahead to the next couple of days. This had been a pleasant sojourn, staying in the mountains of Maramureş and Bucovina, learning about past and present life in rural Romania, but I was eager to get back on the Dracula trail. The next morning we'd be leaving Gura Humorului for places more relevant to the Count—or at least his counterpart, Vlad.

We were halfway through our beers when Lucian's phone rang. The other group was on the way. As it turned out, they hadn't left yet for the egg demonstration. Those lovely but tardy women had been scheduled to go to the egg painter's at five o'clock. They'd invited me earlier in the day, but I thought Lucian and I had surely missed them. It was now six-thirty.

Six-thirty, and we were suddenly going to the egg demo. The thought of it was painful. I was usually open to seeing something new, but that night I dreaded moving from my comfortable spot and starting out again. The tourist in me won—barely. Of course we were already late, so when Razvan pulled into the parking area just below the hotel patio, Lucian and I hopped up as if on springs to get in our car and follow him to another town. *So long, little bottle of beer. It was nice almost knowing you.*

It was dusk when we arrived at a private home. An attractive woman stood waiting in the yard for us, dressed in a traditional peasant folk outfit and holding a beautiful ring of bread with a bowl of salt in the middle. By then Razvan and Lucian had elected to wait for us; it was down to the women. We were instructed to tear off a piece of the bread, dip it in the salt, and eat it. Each of us took a turn in what was obviously a welcoming ceremony. A second woman stood by and photographed the session from that point to the end. Were we going to appear in publicity photos all over Romania? "Tourists fascinated by an ancient craft. . . ."

It *was* fascinating. We passed around eggs in various stages as examples and watched Letitia, our hostess, make delicate markings on other eggs with a horse hair dipped in warm wax. The wax would provide the pattern for each egg by sticking to its surface and preventing dye from staining those areas later in the process. Infinite combinations of geometric and floral designs were possible, as were leaves, buds, hearts, waves, and curlicues. Letitia showed us how to hold the horsehair still and move the egg under it; then she let each of us try. I was pretty good at it—surprising, as that sort of activity would usually drive me up a wall.

Letitia showed us her display cases full of painted and beaded eggs, as well as some she had for sale. They were beautiful. The colors ranged from blue on white to bright combinations of three or more pigments: blue, green, yellow, red, gold, or black.

At the end we purchased eggs, of course. It was very much like an American home party, where women gather to be shown some product—kitchenware, cosmetics, lingerie—and then the order blanks come out. I knew going in that I would buy something, but I kept it reasonable, not taking anything I didn't want to look at for the next few years in a bowl at home.

By the time we were gaily bade good-bye, it was almost dark, which put us back at the hotel at eight thirty. We would have our dinner somewhere between nine thirty and ten—too late for me. I was already grumpy.

All of this is to make a point: I couldn't travel with these women; their trip was not mine. It was fun running into English-speaking tourists for a few days, but now I wanted to get back on track—my track. I liked Lucian's and my schedule much better than theirs—and they might say the same thing about me! This is the importance of taking your own journey.

Chapter 36

The Symptoms

I almost missed the Borgo Pass having a medical crisis. After years of waiting to travel the frightening and beautiful road immortalized by Bram Stoker in 1897, I thought I might not live to the other end of it. "She passed on the pass," people would say. But I'm getting ahead of the story.

The Borgo Pass is the road in *Dracula* that leads to Dracula's castle. It winds through the forests and mountains of Transylvania, past creeks and farms, craggy rocks and pointed haystacks. In Stoker's novel, Jonathan Harker describes his coach ride through the pass to meet the Count:

> Before us lay a green sloping land full of forests and woods, with here and there steep hills, crowned with clumps of trees or with farmhouses, the blank gable end to the road. There was everywhere a bewildering mass of fruit blossom—apple, plum, pear, cherry; and as we drove by I could see the green grass under trees spangled with the fallen petals. In and out amongst these green hills of what they call here the "Mittel Land" ran the road, losing itself as it swept round the grassy curve, or was shut out by the straggling ends of pine woods, which here and there ran down the hillsides like tongues of flame. The road was rugged, but still we seemed to fly over it with a feverish haste.

Though *Dracula* is fiction, the Borgo Pass is real. Today the two-lane paved highway is still the main east-west route through the Carpathian Mountains in the part of Romania called Transylvania.

We set out from Gura Humorului at nine thirty on a Monday morning, driving straight into the view I'd photographed from my hotel balcony. Lucian and I were on our way to Bistriţa, going in the opposite direction as Jonathan Harker. We picked up the pass at Suceava in the Bucovina region.

Thousands of Dracula fans have taken this ride. According to published trip accounts, the magic and mystery of old are still afoot along the Borgo Pass. Fans say it has the atmosphere of long ago—or at least that such an atmosphere can be conjured up by a traveler. Considering that recommendation, I could barely sit back in the seat for fear I'd miss something.

Driving out of Bucovina, I understood why they call it a pass. The eastern end of the road passes between high mountains thick with dark green pine trees. There you are at the bottom, looking up at the land ascending sharply on either side of you. We had plenty of time to admire the scenery; the first miles of the pass were down to one lane, with the other lane temporarily missing. The road was marked by detour signs, potholes, and piles of dirt along the berm.

Highway crews were a common sight in Romania. It didn't help that the Danube River, which flows around the bottom of the country on its way to the Black Sea, had overflowed and sent its tributaries racing and spilling. Sometimes Lucian would try an alternate route to avoid high water, but not today. Today another road wouldn't do.

As we made our way through the mountains, I was in my glory with images from the movies:

> A horse-drawn hearse races from Dracula's castle high in the Carpathian Mountains. Dr. Abraham Van Helsing steps deftly aside as two black-tasseled steeds clatter across a wooden footbridge and take a sharp left through the Transylvanian forest, ultimately bound for a shipyard in Bulgaria. The load—a white coffin—does not shift as the horses' hooves fly over the winding dirt road.

I had replayed scene 8 on my DVD player many times. In my mind, the hearse from *Horror of Dracula* still raced around the hairpin turns of the Borgo Pass—up, down, swaying and tipping with its evil load.

About then I started having chest pains. We were riding along, Lucian absorbed in his own thoughts and concentrating on the driving and I, startled out of my Dracula fantasies to wonder why my chest hurt. *Just a little touch of hypochondria,* I said to myself, and dismissed it.

By day the Borgo Pass is beautiful, bucolic and verdant. You could snap pictures at random and put them all on a calendar. It's a fairytale setting: lush pine forests and green, rolling farmlands bound by twig and split-rail fences; clouds billowing across a blue sky.

The mountains opened up to sun-soaked valleys. We drove past fields of flowers, fruit orchards, and people petting horses or selling buckets of mushrooms by the road. There was nothing scary or sinister about the Borgo Pass so far, except that I was becoming preoccupied with my symptoms.

I remembered the two pain pills another tourist had given me for my stomach the day before. I still had one, but if I wanted to take it, first of all I'd have to ask Lucian to stop and get my suitcase out of the trunk. Then I guessed I'd have to open the suitcase along the road—certainly nothing that would raise an eyebrow in Romania. But if the pill dulled my chest pain, would I miss critical symptoms?

I felt a rising panic. I couldn't avoid thinking of the worst option: heart attack. If I were having one—and why would I be, but how could I be sure, since I'd never had one?—then I should be going to a hospital. How far were we from anything? This was a mountain road. Villages abounded; but medical facilities? I didn't think so.

Was there a quick test for a heart attack, or would I have to be admitted and looked at by someone whose qualifications I didn't know? How would the insurance work? Could I even contact anybody, or would the language barrier prove too much? And what about Sighișoara? What about Brașov and Bran? What if I had to give up the rest of my trip? What if I had to undergo surgery in this foreign country? If I were having a heart attack on the road, there would be no time to fly me home; I'd have to take my chances. What if I died? What if I was dying right now?

I thought of my family and friends back home. What would they make of such a shocking death in rural Romania? At some later point my mother—the Weather Channel fan—would be surprised that it was a heart attack and not a flood that took me. But why should she, considering Dad's history?

I kept breathing in and out to test the pain. It was in my back, too, and my upper throat and jaw. Then I felt my right arm tingle and remembered from an old Superman movie the indelible image of Clark Kent's father, Jonathan, standing there on the farm grabbing his own arm, knowing exactly what was happening to him but unable to change a thing. He fell down dead, right there.

Of course, Lucian had no clue about what was going on in my body and mind. We buzzed along the pass, and now Jonathan Harker and I shared something besides the scenery: fear.

What should I do? You can't ignore chest pains. What if I was right? What if this was it for me, the end of the road at fifty-nine? Would I even see my sixtieth birthday, only four days away? I thought of Dad, dead at fifty-one of hypertensive cardiovascular disease. What made me think I was immune?

But how ironic for me to be having the adventure of my life, seeing a new country, and finding myself in the middle of a creative time—and then having this pain. Why now? Why did I have it at all?

I kept the medical symptoms to myself for miles before saying to Lucian, "My chest hurts."

"Do you want to drink some plum brandy?" he asked, a bit too mildly for me.

"*Now?*" It was ten thirty in the morning! I felt like screaming. *Was* I screaming?

We inched our way through a herd of sheep and goats with the car windows down and I could hear their bells tinkling. By then my mind was fixed on one question: What should I do? *Don't be stupid,* I told myself as I had on a variety of other occasions. But what did it mean today?

Suddenly I was parched, my lips stuck together. Where was my bottle of water?

Lucian pulled off the road and stopped in the next village. He looked over to see if I was okay, ready to pull out onto the road again. "Don't start the car," I said. "I need you to listen to me. I'm scared. I have chest pains. I don't know what's happening to me. I don't know what to do." His fingers twitched on the key.

"You're all I've got," I said. "I need you to let me talk through this. It isn't fun to feel sick in another country when you don't speak the language and don't know anyone. What if I'm having a heart attack?"

"You are not." It was a declarative sentence, spoken with quiet authority.

"How do you know? I need information. I need you to tell me why this isn't a heart attack, because I don't know that. My chest hurts, and my arm was tingling, and those are symptoms of a heart attack. How many men get just these symptoms and say to their wives, 'I think I'll go lie down for a little while,' then die on the living room couch?"

He thought a moment. "You would not have such . . ." He waved his hands, thinking of the English word. ". . . energy."

I went on as though he hadn't spoken, my fear making me desperate. "I have to tell you these things. What if I did get sick, what if something happened? What would you do with my notes and my camera? Who would you call? How would you know where to send everything? Who is going to write my stories?" I thought of Catherine, my writing mentor. I didn't even have her address. "How will you know what to do if I get sick and don't tell you my symptoms?" I continued. "You're it; you're all I have in this country." I could practically feel him itching to put the car in gear. "Have you ever had a heart attack?" I asked.

"No."

"Have you ever known anyone who had a heart attack?"

"Yes."

"Then tell me. I need to know the difference between what I have and a heart attack. I need specific information if you have any. Tell me. Tell me!" By now I was spilling over like the Danube.

Lucian was calm. Of course he was. It was the psychologist taking over. "People who have heart attack cannot talk," he said, and it was the perfect answer because I'd done nothing *but* talk. My symptoms hadn't subsided, but I was immediately easier in my mind. For the first time since we'd left Bucovina, I thought I was not going to die.

We pulled back onto the Borgo Pass and headed for Bistriţa, passing the Hotel Castel [sic] Dracula on the way. The hotel is located at the highest point on the pass, in the approximate spot where Bram Stoker put Dracula's castle. Lucian kept saying as we went up the driveway, "You want to go *here*? It is very dangerous."

"What do you mean, dangerous?" Did Lucian think the people we saw in the parking lot were thieves? Did he not want to park the car? "You can just drive around the circle," I said. "I only want to take pictures." But we got out.

Lucian said some tourists who stayed at Hotel Castel Dracula reported having horrible dreams of being chased by something and not being able to run. "They woke up with much water," he gestured, indicating sweat. I knew about sweat—not just from my childhood days of sweltering under my bedspread, but from the scare I'd just had.

Eventually my symptoms disappeared. We reached the western end of the Borgo Pass at Bistrița, and by then I was up to having a beer. At three o'clock we arrived at the Golden Crown Hotel, the same hotel where Jonathan Harker ate his last meal before going to the castle and his untimely demise. Though he and I had shared a ride over the Borgo Pass—120 years apart—at least we weren't going to share that.

Part 3

Myth and Reality

Chapter 37

The Photo Album

Now that I was still alive, Lucian and I broke out the beer on the balcony of the Golden Crown Hotel. We sat under a long, white awning, and I contemplated the universe as someone who intended to be in it a while longer.

I couldn't understand anyone accepting death. My grandmother had started planning for hers when she was in her seventies, which turned out to be thirty years too early. Grandmama had a heart condition, but I didn't know it when I was young, and she would suddenly drop like a stone, momentarily unconscious. Just another family mystery, Folks; but maybe it explained Grandmama's eagerness to sort and label her things for future generations—that and the fact that she was on good terms with the Lord.

Grandmama was always trying to drum up interest in the family for the objects of her life. She couldn't bear the idea of her precious photos, hand-embroidered linens, dishes, or china cup-and-saucer sets being cast aside. Most of her treasures were in the dining room and had to do with cooking or serving food; she'd cooked for three generations of our family and was known for the recipes she made from scratch.

In her seventies, Grandmama began going through all of her collections, numbering the china cups and saucers brought back by relatives on vacation; taping one of our names to the bottom of each dish, pitcher, serving platter, crystal vase, and piece of furniture she wanted to hand down. She put notes on everything. Many photos carried the message, "Do not destroy" on the back.

When we visited her, Grandmama would walk me over to the china cabinet and ask me which of its contents I wanted "one day." Mom fought the whole process; she said it was too grabby and told me not to show any interest. But Grandmama knew my favorite pieces already. She and I spent hours discussing the beautiful patterns on the delicate china and the handmade wall rack where her cups were displayed. I'd admired them for years.

I wasn't interested in some of Grandmama's treasures. The photos she kept in a box in the dining room buffet bored me. Who were the subjects of those pictures? They were long gone; and how could we even guess anyway, when in the days of sepia-toned photos everybody looked alike? All the women had their hair pulled into buns; the men looked stern, their clothes dark. Blonds were rare. And did they rent out the same high-necked blouse to every woman who sat for the camera?

When Grandmama got out her box of pictures, signaling that she wanted to sift through its contents and reminisce, I dodged her like she was a live hand grenade, but others in the family made up for it. Joe liked the stories that the pictures told, many having to do with the river—for instance, a group in their Sunday best standing on the rocks of the dam with Glen Ferris in the distant background. I was glad that one of our cousins loved sitting with Grandmama and her photos, too. They'd pull a couple dining room chairs together and become lost in the past.

Grandmama began giving her things away long before she was moved into the Union Mission home in Kanawha City, her living quarters finally stripped down from a two-story house to a twin bed, a dresser, a rocker, and a TV.

One Christmas after we were grown, she gave each of her four grand-children a photo album filled with pictures. Mine had a blue velvet cover, with a hologram of roses on the front. Inside were carefully selected snapshots that told the story of the past—*my past*—much of it the part I'd missed: Grandmama and Grandpop when they were younger, sitting in the concrete boathouse by the inn on a summer afternoon with my mother between them; and cuddling on the living room couch at home. The latter photo had captured an unguarded moment: Grandmama—who usually was in perpetual motion serving others—looking serene and content as she leaned on Grandpop's shoulder. His arm was around her, his hand on her hip. It was an intimate peep at a couple I never saw kiss or touch.

There were pictures of a younger Mom with her brother; Mom playing a mean piano; Mom as a college student in saddle shoes; Mom with her baby daughter—me—under a shade tree by the river. There were a few pictures of Dad, and pictures of Joe and me growing up; shots of family gatherings over the years. But the photos that made the biggest impression on me were at the very beginning, in a section depicting my mother—known then as BoBo—as a baby and a young girl.

By then I was married and living in the East. I had a son—Mom's first grandchild. He was the best baby ever born, if I do say so—and I have, ever since the nurse first laid him down beside me in the hospital, his little eyes scrunched shut and his hands curled into tiny fists. I suppose he was worn out from fighting to get out. I slept through that part, though it hadn't been my intent. Sometimes you need to be knocked out; for example, when you feel like you're on a bucking bronco and the doctor asks you to hold still on the way to the operating room and you can't. "I'm not doing it," I yelled. "It's doing itself!" And that's the last I remember of how my beautiful nine-pound, six-ounce baby came into the world.

I'd finally been able to escape Mom's alcoholism—if not the long-term effects, at least the day to day. Mom had come to visit us a few times, but it was hard because of her drinking. I thought she'd stop temporarily, and that was because I didn't understand alcoholism. Once when she came for a week, Mom smuggled drinks in her purse, small bottles of liquor she'd gotten on the plane. She drank from her stash every day. In my frantic mind, the week was a living Bell Curve, with the tension arcing unbearably around Wednesday, when I thought I couldn't survive the remaining days until Mom went home.

Though it didn't change what Mom had been at her worst, the blue velvet photo album showed my mother in some of her best, and certainly most innocent, moments. It became one of my treasures, a safe harbor. It settled me. I took it with me everywhere I lived. Sometimes I still get it out and turn those first few pages. My mother as a baby in Grandpop's arms, him all dressed up in a dark suit, the mountainside behind him black as coal; Mom a small bundle in a baby dress on Grandmama's knee; sitting in a carriage in the sun with their frame house in Cabin Creek behind her; taking her first steps in a dirt yard; holding a cat, of all things.

Then there is little BoBo, a child of three or four, climbing a fence near the river; standing on the front fender of Grandpop's Model T; posing on the bed of a wooden hay wagon, her thick blonde hair cut in a Dutch-boy style, cheeks you could pinch, and her lips curved into a sweet smile. In another picture this beautiful little girl is dressed up in a hat, coat, and high-button shoes. My guess would be that Grandmama made the coat, a gorgeous thing with covered buttons, but I don't know. On another page is BoBo in a baggy bathing cap, climbing over rocks in a creek; falling backward into the shallow water, laughing.

This was another country, like Romania. It was a place I'd never been, a place I learned about with Grandmama as my guide. Through the pictures in the photo album, I came to know a different Mom—one who had been impossible to know in person. In that new country, I learned what Grandmama saw when she looked at my mother; what no amount of heartache could erase: the images of that guileless child; that little girl posing in pretty dresses; the lovely young woman who'd gone off to junior college to learn to be a secretary; the one who'd walked across a stage on campus in the 1930s to "audition" when studio executives conducted a nationwide search for a young woman to play the part of Scarlett O'Hara in *Gone with the Wind*.

I learned that even the monster who had dominated my teenage years was only one version of my mother, a snapshot in time. The Mom I now knew in Cincinnati was yet another version, perhaps the woman my mother was meant to be all along. I learned that nobody's life is framed in a minute. There is always more.

Grandmama lived to be 102. On her hundredth birthday, the Union Mission home threw her a party with piano playing and refreshments, bright colors and songs, family members and friends. Grandmama was interviewed on TV.

By then her memories were jumbled. She told us the same stories over and over, stories of Glen Ferris in the old days long before I was born.

She spent lots of time in a place we couldn't penetrate with conversation. It was that other country, the one that always lies just beyond our grasp.

After our pit stop in Bistrița, Lucian and I headed on over the hills toward Sighișoara ("Sig-ee-shwAR-a"). We were going south, toward the heart of Transylvania. I'd read about Sighișoara, the medieval walled city that *almost* became the location of a Dracula theme park.

Chapter 38

Dracula Park

In November 2001, the Romanian Ministry of Tourism announced plans for Dracula Park, a thirty-million-dollar tourist attraction proposed to infuse mostly foreign dollars into the country's economy. The government had sought the opinions of experts and investors regarding its plan to locate the theme park in Transylvania. Dracula Park was one of the reasons I'd decided to go to Romania when I did.

Right away upon reading the news, I'd jumped ahead to the grand opening. Of course my hero, Christopher Lee, would be there; it was unthinkable that such a major Dracula event would take place without the actor who, in my humble opinion, had played him best. I didn't even entertain the idea that he might not want to go—or might not be invited. At the park opening, estimated to be several years in the future, would be a Who's Who of Dracula experts, movie actors past and present, the world press, scholars, and, of course, Yours Truly.

A site for the park was chosen near Sighișoara, the birthplace of Vlad the Impaler. The Historic Centre of Sighișoara—the old, walled portion—had been designated a UNESCO World Heritage Site in 1999, so the announcement of the park location caused a huge international controversy. People were already anticipating the potential for the ruination of one of the most beautiful cities in Romania.

One of the opponents of the Dracula theme park, and especially its proposed location, was Dr. Elizabeth Miller, the Canadian scholar who had been named "Baroness of the House of Dracula" by the Transylvanian Society of Dracula. Miller was afraid that locating the park near Sighișoara would make worse the confusion that already existed regarding the two strains of the Dracula legend—the Count and Vlad; vampire and prince. At least some of that confusion was attributable to the theories introduced by the Professors of Horror, McNally and Florescu.

When M&F were in their heyday, charging into Dracula country figuratively and literally, Elizabeth Miller was unknown in Dracula circles—and back then the Dracula circles themselves were virtually unknown. Though she had watched the movies of Bela Lugosi and Christopher Lee with the rest of us, Elizabeth Miller had not become hooked on vampires or Dracula. That came many years later, as did international recognition of Miller as an author and Dracula expert.

One of her books is *A Dracula Handbook,* which is written in question-and-answer format to address the basics—Dracula 101. In *Handbook* she writes about the perpetuation of the vampire myth in movies and fiction. As a result of such stereotyping, Miller says, many people believe that Transylvania is a frightening and evil place—if they even know that it really exists.

The person Elizabeth Miller talks about in her book—the gullible traveler who still wants to see superstitious peasants, swirling fog, misty mountains, and Gothic castles; the one who would wear a crucifix to Transylvania—that was me. Like Julia Roberts in *Pretty Woman,* I wanted the fairy tale. In my case, the fairy tale was a crumbling castle and a full moon, flying bats and howling wolves. I wouldn't have minded Christopher Lee, either.

Miller's descriptions and explanations in *A Dracula Handbook* are cautious and objective. Though a huge Dracula fan, she plays it down in the book. I remember another Elizabeth Miller, the one who went to Romania for the first time in 1994, inspired by McNally and Florescu's book *Dracula, Prince of Many Faces: His Life and Times.* She went alone and posted her trip journal to the Internet.

It was an eager, sometimes giddy Elizabeth Miller who took that trip, and I could feel her excitement as she climbed to the Poenari fortress, collected dirt samples along the Borgo Pass, toured Vlad the Impaler's boyhood home in Sighişoara, and saw a full moon in Transylvania for the first time. I printed out her trip log and saved it. I liked that she had started late in life, as I had. She was my inspiration; I thought that if she had done it, then so could I.

I'd followed the development of Dracula Park from home in Ohio and had mixed feelings about it. If they built it, I would go, but it seemed a shame to plop an amusement park down next to a historic treasure. On the other hand, I hadn't seen Sighişoara and held no particular feelings about the city. I just hoped that the committee in charge of Dracula Park would apply good taste to the project.

What would the Romanians come up with for a Dracula theme park? Would it be all about Vlad? I thought not; the plan was to acknowledge the vampire element, too. The advance publicity mentioned recognition of selected Hollywood interpretations, so that was a good sign. I couldn't imagine what all would be in the park, but one thing seemed certain: They should have a hell of a haunted house ride.

Kings Island near Cincinnati already had a roller coaster called The Beast; that would have been a winner in Romania. In fact, for a short time in the 1980s, Kings Island had a suspended coaster called The Bat, but it was dismantled because of mechanical problems. As I write this, our theme park has a ride called The Crypt, which would have been made to order for Dracula Park. The description says, "Do you dare explore the secrets of The Crypt? You'll be flipped through a series of inversions as you navigate the dark world of the unknown."

I hoped that Lucian and I wouldn't be flipped into the dark unknown as we zipped and zinged toward Sighişoara, making few stops as the route took our little blue car over two-lane mountain roads full of curves. After all, we were in the Carpathians. After so many days in the countryside, I knew what to expect and found myself automatically bracing for the inevitable passing, swerving, and near misses that would mark our journey. It seemed like a never-ending game of chicken to me. Lucian didn't like to be stuck behind slow traffic; he liked to pass, so the instant there was an opening, we went. I was always amazed we made it, considering the odds and obstacles: Wagons, animals, bicycles, and even little children could be anywhere along the way, drawn like magnets to the roadside. If the Romanians thought they had no thrill rides, they were wrong.

We were still on the road at six, finally getting close to Sighișoara, when we came upon a truck with a heavy load of logs sitting sideways on the road. Traffic in our lane was stopped. The logs in the truck were huge, rough tree trunks—two or three feet in diameter and twenty-five or thirty feet long—hanging off the back of the truck bed the way lumber does when you pick it up at the home improvement store and have to stick a flag on it for safety. A young, barefoot boy stood next to the truck while the driver directed oncoming traffic. It was easy enough for the small Romanian cars to squeeze by. He was waving a semi over to the edge, where it could inch past the blockade. The right wheels of the semi went off the pavement, causing it to tip toward the adjacent field of high grass, where a little girl stood watching with no apparent idea she was dangerously close to being squashed. I held my breath. It all turned out well, as Romanian traffic situations tend to do.

The fate of Dracula Park was not a foregone conclusion. Back then I was still thinking it was; that the grand opening of a park that had drawn international attention would be an event to attract every Dracula fanatic in the world who could afford the price of the trip. I'd already been saving. I just needed to find out the date, or even the year, the facility would be completed.

It seemed the project was destined to be stalled. First, a feasibility study by PricewaterhouseCoopers cast doubt upon the location for the park. It was moved in 2003 from Sighișoara to the shores of Snagov Lake. In 2004 the scope of the project shifted from "park" to "complex" with the announcement that a golf course, a race track, and other facilities would be added. The expansion seemed a positive sign that the park would go forward, but it was not to be.

The next year, the project was put on hold. I knew then that the Romanian Ministry of Tourism was not a good bellwether for my plans. I needed to go to Transylvania with or without the park as a destination. By then Elizabeth Miller, Raymond McNally, and Radu Florescu were bigger than life to me. I'd been planning my trip with all of them as my virtual companions. I read their books and searched the web for every shred of information I could find. Sometimes I came upon a treasure, such as Elizabeth Miller's photo gallery from a convention in California called "Dracula '97."

It was a combination scholarly conference and fan venue that had culminated in a costume contest and masked ball. Photo highlights were posted on Miller's website. When I saw them, I ached to be a part of it, even though it was long over. The best photo was a shot of Miller flanked by none other than McNally, Florescu, and "Vlad the Impaler," who looked pretty good for someone who died in 1476. Other photos showed author Chelsea Quinn Yarbro, who'd answered my question about her book dedication; Elvira, Mistress of the Dark; horror movie actresses Ingrid Pitt and Veronica Carlson; and even Bela Lugosi, Jr.

All of those Dracula heroes had traveled in a special world, one I envied, a world that seemed as far away as the moon. All of them had played their parts in stories of horror, vampires, and Romanian history; but it was largely the work of McNally, Florescu, and Miller that explained the Dracula legends to the public, making it possible for people all over the world to tour the famous Dracula sites in Europe. Well, they might not know it, but they were all with me on my trip to Romania.

Chapter 39

Creatures of the Night

Both of us were tired and out of sorts by the time Lucian drove up the cobblestone road, passed under an arch in the thick wall surrounding the ancient citadel of Sighişoara, and pulled in next to our hotel. I sensed his grumpiness, and he surely sensed mine.

The hotel was lovely from the front, three stories painted mint green with colorful flower boxes below the windows and multiple flags flying above the entrance. We entered the lobby through a long, arched hallway lined with chairs. I couldn't wait to get to my room. While Lucian checked us in, I stood to the side looking around the lobby, which was done in a half-timber theme—or was it a theme? Maybe that was just the style when the hotel was built. It was centuries old; off to my left I could see a set of wooden stairs, each step worn down in the middle. The walls were partly white and partly some kind of exposed stone. Was it fake or real? At that moment I couldn't have cared less.

My guide seemed to be taking his sweet time. Just as I was thinking he should stop gabbing with the desk clerk and get the show on the road, my camera bag crashed onto the bare bricks of the lobby floor. No one was even near it. The bag had been stacked on top of my upended suitcase.

Oh, my God. I felt sick. Every record of my trip was in that bag, a growing collection of words and photos. I scooped up the bag and ripped the zippers open to check my equipment as I offered up a quick prayer: *"Please, please . . ."* My AlphaSmart and my camera—the two most important tools I carried with me—were working. As the adrenaline rush subsided, my previous state of fatigue and impatience filled the void.

Lucian and I went our separate ways upon climbing the worn wooden steps to our rooms. I'd arrived in Sighişoara hungry, but we didn't make plans to eat.

My room was on the third level. I set my things down inside, fussed with my clothes and electronics for a while, then sat down to write. As I wrote, I relaxed. Having my equipment in one piece was a relief; having an hour to myself was therapeutic.

Lucian knocked on the door while I was writing. He rarely came to my room; usually we set times to meet and inevitably arrived at the meeting place within minutes of each other. This time he'd come to get me for dinner. We ate out on the back patio of the hotel, which Lucian called a garden. He ordered polenta and sour cream for both of us, with beer to drink. I wasn't sure if the two mounds of polenta and half a plate of sour cream were the first course or the whole meal, so I followed my rule of caution: Eat only half. Jenny Craig might have turned up her nose at a bowl of mush made from cornmeal, but once Lucian told me we were looking at our supper, I finished it.

Sitting in the "garden" at sunset in Sighişoara made me think of bats. "I haven't seen one bat," I said to Lucian. "How can a trip to Transylvania be complete without a bat?"

"They come out at night," he said. "You won't see them now." Of course they came out at night, like vampires. But that hour was coming soon.

The fact that they are nocturnal beings has given bats an air of mystery and a long association with the supernatural and the unknown. That reputation was sealed in 1897 with the publication of *Dracula,* which linked bats inextricably with vampires.

As every fan of the Count knows, a bat is another form a vampire can take. In *Dracula,* Jonathan Harker witnessed the Count crawling down the outer wall of Castle Dracula "*face-down* with his cloak spreading around him like great wings." A large bat appeared at Lucy's bedroom window in Whitby, England, after the Count had taken up residence there. Lucy's friend, Mina, who'd been watching Lucy to keep her from "sleepwalking," wrote in her journal:

> Between me and the moonlight flitted a great bat, coming and going in great whirling circles. Once or twice it came quite close, but was, I suppose, frightened at seeing me, and flitted away across the harbour towards the abbey. When I came back from the window Lucy had lain down again, and was sleeping peacefully. She did not stir again all night.

There are more than one thousand species of the flying mammals, including three species of vampire bat, whose sole food source is blood. Vampire bats, like their namesakes, hunt only when it is fully dark, locating a host and then using their razor-sharp teeth to create a small incision from which they can lap up—not suck—the victim's blood. Their saliva contains a substance called *draculin*. Named after Count Dracula, it prevents the prey's blood from clotting. Every vampire bat also has a heat sensor in its nose that helps it find a spot just beneath the skin where warm blood is flowing. They feed mostly on animals, but have been known to bite people.

Bats abound in vampire literature, but liberties may have been taken to create the perfect alter-ego for Dracula. Although some species can have wingspans up to five feet like the bat that fluttered outside Lucy's window or the ones that hovered under a full moon in the Dracula movies, vampire bats are tiny—less than three inches long. They fly low to the ground, often landing to hop or walk on all fours. And, according to the experts, no vampire bats live in Transylvania! Their habitats are in Central and South America, spreading south from Mexico to Brazil, Chile, and Argentina. In other words, I wasn't going to spot a huge vampire bat flapping its big, black wings in the sky while I sat there with Lucian on the patio of our hotel—even if we were in the heart of Dracula country. There was no such animal.

I remembered the house where I'd lived in with my hoarder boyfriend, how the back yard was deep and graded so that from the porch, we had to look up at the big trees that grew midway to our property line. Flocks of winged creatures would head for the bare branches of those trees in the evenings, flapping black silhouettes against the bright blue of twilight. I thought they were birds.

"They're bats," he said, and I watched them with fascination, glad for the distance between us and the trees.

He had a "garden" in that yard up past the bat trees, *garden* being a euphemism for "pile of weeds." It was a circular plot of chewed-up land where he dumped the grass clippings when he deigned to mow, stashed bushes after he'd overbought, or plunked one of his five-dollar plants after it bit the dust. Fertilizer, you know.

Now I went upstairs with two thirds of a beer still on the table; just not interested in drinking, especially after beginning our meal with a swig of strong plum brandy. Lucian believed plum brandy killed disease, which was probably why he ordered it—just in case I wasn't done with my ongoing litany of symptoms. In polishing off my share of the tuica I tried to drink from the little flowered teapot of a thing they'd served instead of a glass. True to form, I overestimated the tipping angle and spilled the brandy on my skirt. Luckily I'd packed a travel laundry kit. If it weren't for being able to do my wash in hotel sinks at night, I'd be a sight.

When we'd finished dinner it was too late to explore the old town, and the shops were already closed. I had no inclination to move from the hotel anyway. I was content to putter around my room arranging my bags, washing the plum brandy out of my skirt, and recharging my electronics. That was my big evening. Lucian was planning to meet friends. By the time he did, I'd be asleep.

Chapter 40

The Bath

The silence in Sighişoara is absolute at four in the morning. My point of reference was a narrow twin bed in our hotel, located down a stone-paved street from Vlad Dracula's birthplace.

The little window overlooking the street was dark, its black curtain pulled across the glass. At that hour the souvenir stands in the square were still covered and the shops, still closed. No tourists drove their cars over the bumpy stones leading into the walled city or roamed the streets looking for souvenirs of Dracula. I couldn't even go to breakfast; it was too early.

Sighişoara has been described as the most beautifully preserved walled city in Europe. We were staying in the historic section of what was once known as Schassburg, a fortified Saxon settlement built in Transylvania between the twelfth and seventeenth centuries.

My bed with its cross-beamed head and foot could have been around to serve a medieval knight. It had that look. The mattress was as hard as a slab of rock, which might have been why I was awake. The other furniture matched the bed in design, all of it rustic.

A bell sounded somewhere at six o'clock. I sat up to write a while, and by seven I was in the shower. The room had a particularly long and narrow bathtub—in fact, the longest bathtub I had ever seen. *Christopher*

Lee would like this one, I thought, and immediately I could see him easing his six-foot four-inch frame into it.

Lee brought power and dignity to the screen, and I was sure he would look just as dignified in the bathtub. At the same time, I was envisioning the scene through a filter. Mom would have said, "If you see anything you don't recognize, shoot it," but I had no desire in this case to see sharp detail.

I liked the idea of this bath, set in historic Sighişoara. Lee would have no trouble climbing in, although many people would. The side of the tub was several inches above the tops of my knees. There was a handle on the wall, the kind placed for an old person to grip. Even at eighty-three, Christopher Lee would not need it; he was anything but wobbly. Besides, it was too low.

I could see him luxuriating in the warm water, making little ripples as he adjusted his back to the high, slanted back of the bathtub. The top, where his head would rest, was molded for fit. If I'd had a tape measure, I might be able to tell you for sure that his feet would not reach the spigot end of the tub; but a tape measure is one of the few gadgets I didn't take to Romania. At the least, Lee could wiggle his toes under the flowing water—the spigot must have been a foot long—but he would likely have to bend his knees.

If he stood up to shower off, he'd need to move the shower head upward on its pipe. Luckily I didn't have to, as I couldn't figure out the mechanics of it and dreaded spraying the whole bathroom; but I did have to duck to wash my hair. At the end of his bath, the towels would be soft and white, hanging just above the rear of the tub. They would be skimpy for Lee's size, but that could be taken care of in advance with the hotel.

Even though the room surely wouldn't be as luxurious as Lee was used to, a soak in the bathtub would be an ideal fit, and I had no trouble picturing it. I had seen that body before.

In 1975, Hammer Films released its "last" horror picture, *To the Devil a Daughter,* in which Lee played a defrocked priest opposite sixteen-year-old Nastassja Kinski, whose character was Catherine, a young nun chosen to bear a demon baby. The movie was released with this tagline: "Warning! This Motion Picture Contains The Most Shocking Scenes This Side Of Hell!"

To the Devil a Daughter included scenes of painful births, bloody devil-babies, and—the most shocking of all—"The Devil's Orgy," identified on the DVD as chapter 14. In it, Catherine envisions her participation in a robed ritual of devil-worship and sex. The orgy takes place outside at night. The participants stream into view, one carrying the sleeping Catherine. She is placed on her back on a low bench. Another female, dressed in white, lies down in the foreground and spreads her arms and legs into a set of straps.

The orgy sequence is jumbled and hard to follow, but the general idea shines through. Christopher Lee as the priest is going to engage in a sex act, one of many that will play out during the evening. While Kinski's character is occupied, Lee approaches the other female, opens his white robe—baring his chest—and drops the garment off his shoulders. We next see the priest from behind, standing over the spread-eagled woman, and this is the big surprise: There is the tall frame with its muscled back and narrow hips, *naked*. The priest gets down on one knee and stretches his nude body out over hers.

In America I had mentioned the scene to my son. "I bought another Christopher Lee movie," I said. "It's called *To the Devil a Daughter*. And guess what?"

He was silent.

"Na-ked." I mimicked the inflection of the Church Lady, a character from *Saturday Night Live*. "Can you believe it? Christopher Lee without a stitch."

Now, I wasn't naïve. I'd seen a few men in the nude and imagined many—including my guide—that way. But I didn't expect to see Christopher Lee naked; it seemed too far-fetched, too unlikely; and watching it, too invasive—all in all, too freaky to contemplate.

By the time I envisioned the bathing scene in Sighişoara—thirty years after Lee made *To the Devil a Daughter*—I felt no embarrassment at imagining the long, lean body turning pink in the water, because I knew that the body I pictured was not Christopher Lee's at all but that of his body double, Eddie Powell.

Powell was the one who performed the nude scene in *To the Devil a Daughter*. He was Lee's stunt double for many years, beginning with *The Mummy* in 1959. I wondered what Powell's story was. Lee had not made much mention of him during interviews; thus, it was hard to know what their relationship was—if it was ever more than actor and stunt double.

The skinny on Powell was just that: skinny—a few stories, a seemingly finite amount of information: That when Powell was approached to become Lee's double, he didn't know who the actor was; that Powell almost drowned during filming of the Count's icy death scene in *Dracula: Prince of Darkness* because of a set malfunction. Powell continued to work in films through the mid-1990s, doing mostly stunt work, and died in 2000 at age seventy-three.

Eddie Powell was a ringer for Christopher Lee, not only bodily but also above the neck. I gasped when I found two head shots of him on the Internet. This man could have been Chris Lee's brother, his twin. Powell's long face, the shape of his head, the slant of his eyebrows, his sunken cheeks, and his patrician nose all resembled the features of Christopher Lee. His ears, like Lee's, were close to his head; and the two men shared the same high forehead and receding hairline, the question-mark shape at the back of the skull, and even the tilt of their heads with the chin slightly raised.

Naturally, the two were dressed in identical costumes for work. Watching the old Hammer movies, you would have to be paying close attention to tell the difference between Eddie Powell and Christopher Lee. No wonder I had not known it was Powell dodging bullets on the ice in *Dracula: Prince of Darkness*! But I didn't know Powell existed back then, any more than I knew when I first saw the movie that he was the nude in *To the Devil a Daughter*.

I wanted to know more about Powell. One day I saw in a posting on the Internet that an interview with him had been hidden on the DVD of *To the Devil a Daughter*. I followed the directions, and there it was. I couldn't get close enough to the TV as Powell answered questions that addressed the story of his reluctant involvement in chapter 14: "The Devil's Orgy."

The stunt double recalled that when he had first been asked to do the nude scene, he had refused. The ante kept going up until finally he agreed. Powell was told his role would be to carry a nude woman to an altar and place her on it. "Chris has got a bad back," he explained, so Lee could not do the carrying himself.

On the day of the shooting, everything was rushed; Powell figured that no one had wanted to give him time to ask any questions. The set was cleared for the scene. "I'll walk you through it," the director assured him. Powell had requested a g-string for the filming. He got one, but if you didn't know, you wouldn't spot it in the movie.

When the cameras started to roll, Powell was to work with the actress who was spread-eagled on her back. He was told to shed his clothing and kneel between her legs. Still thinking he had to pick her up, Powell was flabbergasted when the instruction came to sweep her robe aside and simulate sex. It was a smiling Eddie Powell who told the interviewer he had done chapter 14 in one take: "I'm good at that sort of action."

And that is how Eddie Powell, the real nude priest in *To the Devil a Daughter,* popped up more than thirty years later in my bathtub in Sighișoara—once again standing in for the star.

Not long ago, I read a story in which the author actually did see one of her heroes naked. After years of worshipping him through his writing, she met him on a nude beach and they held a conversation. If I saw Christopher Lee naked on a beach—which is about as likely as seeing him fly past my window on bat wings—I'd run; I'm sure of it. Lord, I'd run so fast I'd start a sandstorm.

I'd wanted to see Lee in Transylvania; maybe that was the reason for the bath scene. I believe you should see your heroes in your lifetime, but let's not be too literal. I'll take Lee with his clothes *on.*

By the way, that wasn't really me taking a shower earlier in the story. In case you're inclined to picture it, that was my body double.

Chapter 41

Vlad's Town

I had breakfast alone in the hotel dining room. The restaurant was intimate, a bit like eating in one's own dining room—or, in my case, the dining room of a friend who cooked. Soft light from wall sconces shone on cloth-covered tables and a buffet spread with breakfast fare. Across the room, large windows draped with bright curtains framed the emerging day. I moved among the round tables to a corner near a window. I deliberately took the best people-watching seat, only the joke was on me; there was no one to watch.

I wondered where Lucian was. We usually ran into each other at breakfast, but maybe he'd stayed out late. It didn't matter; I knew when I'd see him. We'd agreed to meet in the lobby at nine thirty, ready to explore the citadel on foot.

I loved Sighişoara—even just saying the name—and looked forward to seeing its attractions. The town reminded me of a scene from *Dracula Has Risen from the Grave,* with its sea of old, red-roofed buildings clustered along narrow, curved streets below the spires of churches. In Hammer's 1968 movie, a monsignor riding through the countryside spots a "village in the valley" complete with a clock tower. Though I suspect that scene was a matte painting and not a real place, the commonality of the clock tower linked the movie to Sighişoara in my mind. I also thought

Christopher Lee had visited the city in the early 1970s when he traveled to Romania to play Vlad in the documentary *In Search of Dracula,* based on McNally and Florescu's book.

By the time Lucian and I left the hotel together, the morning was sunny and warm. At that hour there were few other tourists. Businesses were just coming to life in the heart of the citadel. We passed a little store with an "I (heart) Dracula" bumper sticker displayed in the window, but the door was padlocked. Maybe it would open later.

Sighișoara has a total population of 32,000. The fortified section was built on the top of a hill to protect the citizens from invasions. Lucian had estimated four hours to see it. The area looked compact and easily walkable to me, so it must be packed with history. As we headed for the most famous landmark in Sighișoara, my tour was starting to resemble what we'd done before in other towns—except for one thing. This time Lucian didn't cut me loose.

The clock tower, at five stories high, rises above the other buildings in the citadel and reigns over the lower town as well. It is a solid-looking stone building with walls seven feet thick. The elaborate roof has four corner turrets and a central spire that's nearly as tall as the building itself. A small, golden sphere sits on the very top of the spire and functions as a weathervane.

The tower originally controlled the main gate through the outer wall. It became the clock tower after its defining feature was added in the seventeenth century. The clock sits near the top, with one dial visible from the lower town and the other facing the citadel. Figurines carved from wood move with the clock's mechanism.

Inside, a multilevel history museum houses clocks, pottery, old painted furniture, tributes to famous citizens, and even a model of the walled citadel encased in glass. Lucian and I browsed at a pace that gave me a sense of the exhibits without the mind-boggling details I preferred to skip.

The old wood floors of the museum squeaked so loudly that more than once I turned to see if someone above us had fallen through. The doorways were low. As we approached one, a passing tourist said in accented English, "Watch your head." I thought the people of Vlad's time must have been very short, but Lucian said the doors had been constructed that way to make entry difficult for one's enemies, no doubt the Turks.

At the top we went outside onto a balcony and walked around its perimeter. The view from any side is magnificent, a straight dose of atmosphere. Little metal plaques attached to the top of the leaning rail indicate the compass direction and mileage to other cities.

From the balcony the lower town looks like a typical shopping district and spreads out to residential and industrial areas, with mountains and pastureland beyond. A river winds through the lower part of the town. The German influence is still present in the architecture, flat-fronted buildings of assorted colors whose red-tile roofs have the distinctive small windows, called "eyes," above the roofline.

Vlad the Impaler's birth house was directly below us on the citadel side. I had a birds-eye view of the three-story yellow building that now housed a restaurant with a little outdoor café. The employees were preparing to open, setting out tables and chairs on the cobblestone street and standing a large, wooden sign outside the entrance. The sign bore the surprising image of a vampire Dracula. For once it wasn't Vlad, but that time it should have been. He was the one who'd lived there.

We descended the clock tower and stopped in the adjacent torture room and weapons museum before going on to Vlad's house. The museum featured a whole Dracula family tree in printed documents and drawings. Instruments of torture from earlier centuries were the main attraction, among them hanging ropes, handcuffs, footcuffs, a "yoke for neck and hands," and a "Spanish boot" designed to crush a victim's leg. *Ouch!* The collections represented weapons used in Sighişoara in earlier times, some to extract information and confessions during the violent conflicts of the Middle Ages. These weapons were the difference between watching Count Dracula close in on his victims on the big screen—where many times the gory details were left to my imagination—and standing among instruments of torture that were not the products of fiction but were used on real people. I don't recall any particular weapons attributed to Vlad, but what else do you need when you run skewers through people?

The Impaler's former home was only a few steps from the museum. The sign I'd seen from the clock tower was a nod to tourists for sure, a full body image of the Count about five feet tall, painted in red, black, and white. His hands stretched upward to invite us into the restaurant.

I could almost hear Bela Lugosi saying, "Velcome to my house," in his Hungarian accent, as I posed so that Lucian could take my picture next to my fanged friend.

Signs affixed to the outside invited patrons into a three-star restaurant called Casa Vlad Dracul, with a bar called Alchemy. When Lucian and I went inside, I thought of Dr. Elizabeth Miller's account of her visit. She'd become excited about standing at the very window where Vlad may have looked out onto the street as a boy, so I had to do the same thing, drawing aside a lace curtain in the upstairs restaurant. I looked out onto the curved street that ran from the clock tower to the square. It might have been busier in Vlad's day, but that morning I gazed upon a lone tourist with a camera to his eye and a few stone buildings in the background. Maybe little Vladdie, as Miller called him, had liked to watch the street life in the early fifteenth century; or maybe he stood behind the glass longing to play outside. Maybe he waited every day at the window for his father, who was then the military governor of Transylvania.

Leaving Vlad's birthplace behind, Lucian took me past the mayor's office, which was housed in a lovely old building. City hall had a gated drive, bright flowers, a fountain out front—and, next door, a statue of Vlad on a pedestal. The whole country had him on a pedestal, if you ask me.

We doubled back to the main square and poked through the shops along its border before leaving the citadel to head up to the highest point in old Sighișoara: Biserica Din Deal, the Church on the Hill. To get there we climbed the Scholars' Stairs, 180 steps through a wooden tunnel built in the seventeenth century to protect churchgoers and school children in winter. I knew exactly how those children felt, climbing the steps in the cold.

Our high school was at the top of Gauley Hill, a densely populated area accessed by two steep and narrow roads. The school buses would go up one road in the mornings and down the other in the afternoons. In inclement weather—which seemed to mean anything from a raindrop on—the roads could be slippery, posing a risk for the buses and everyone on them. So we walked.

A long set of concrete steps with a metal railing led from the bottom of the hill to the top—much like the way to the Poenari Citadel, but without the woods. They, too, became slippery in the rain or snow, so I dreaded the moment when we'd feel the bus slowing down, hear the brakes grinding to a halt at the bottom of the hill, and know to gather our things in our arms because we were getting off the bus to take the steps. Usually I was dressed for riding a school bus, which meant that I was often caught with bare legs and inadequate shoes for the climb. More than once I slipped and fell or at least dropped my books, which would land open and then slide down the hill leaving wet homework papers in their wake.

By the time I was climbing those steps, I had a new best friend. Billie had moved away after junior high. It happened quickly; her dad took a job transfer to another state, and they were gone. For me, a bit of the magic of Glen Ferris went with them. Billie had been daring and adventurous. I was the shy and sensible sidekick, the one who pushed her glasses up on her nose while storming the fort. My life was better with Billie in it. She knew all about Mom and seemed to take her changing personality in stride. Billie and I had fun. Together we were a force.

People move in and out of our lives, but I didn't know that then. Billie was my first loss—except for Mom, of course, who was still there. I would always hate being left behind; much better to be the one moving on.

I rode the high school bus with a girl named Natalie who lived in the upper end of Glen Ferris. She was pretty and popular, but not sophisticated the way her name might suggest. Nat's family lived in a white two-bedroom bungalow in a row of similar homes on the side of a hill. The hillside location—even considering the killer view of the river—was unremarkable because half of Glen Ferris could be described the same way. Nat's house was smaller than ours, with everything on one floor. I could have thrown a stick from the front door through the living and dining rooms and hit the kitchen table where Nat and I liked to gobble down homemade French fries cooked in a cast-iron skillet and doused with black pepper.

Nat had two sisters, so one bedroom was for the parents and the other was for the three girls. The girls' room held a set of bunk beds against one wall and pushed up against another wall, a twin bed with a single nightstand. The furniture arrangement left a walking path three or four feet wide to the beds, the window, and the tiny closet.

I remember withered corsages hanging on the walls beside heart-shaped lids from Valentine candy. These girls had boyfriends, got ready for dates in the same room; retrieved their crushed clothing from the same crowded closet. They took their baths in a little bathroom whose location near the middle of the house exposed the sounds of their bodies sliding through water, their girlish rituals before the mirror.

Everyone's privacy was compromised in Nat's house. I remember lying on the top bunk one morning before light even penetrated the house. One of the sisters had gone to spend the night with a friend, thus freeing a bed for me to spend the night with Natalie. The house was early morning quiet; Nat's dad had gone to work. As far as I knew, everyone else was still asleep. Suddenly Nat's mother passed gas in the other bedroom. It exploded out of her, the noise amplified by the close quarters. I started giggling and couldn't stop. The bed shook under me. I suppose if Nat's mom had one wish, it would have been that we'd all slept through her gigantic fart, but how could we? She probably never knew that from that day forward we called her "Hot Butt."

Lucian and I made our way back down the Scholars' Stairs. As we ended our tour of the citadel, one thing was certain: Vlad the Impaler's presence was still strong in Sighişoara more than five hundred years after he was gone. I was glad that morning for Lucian's presence; it was more fun touring with him than alone or with strangers. In the tunnel I heard a dog barking, its barks regular and rhythmic like the ones in the old Christmas hit, "Jingle Bells" by the Barking Dogs. Memories: They were everywhere.

Chapter 42

Killing Time in Sighişoara

Lucian and I interrupted our day in Sighişoara with a short drive to the neighboring fortress town of Biertan. We were returning on a rural road, nothing much to see, and I was slumped in the corner of the passenger seat letting my mind go where it would.

Suddenly Lucian spotted a train, a coveted photo subject I seemed to miss every time by having my camera neatly put away. The compulsive personality strikes again. This time I grabbed the camera just as the train fell below our line of sight, and Lucian accelerated. *Now we chase trains.* Past the cornfields we flew, me with my right elbow and my Nikon hanging out the window. It was exciting, but the train outran us.

When we got back to Sighişoara, Lucian said he was going to talk to the "chief of the hotel." I knew his errand was related to the aftermath of our car accident in the Gypsy enclave. It had preoccupied him since Sibiu, nearly a week now.

I waited a while in the square where he could find me. We always connected at least to make a schedule, but there was no sign of him. As time ticked by, it seemed I was on my own; and, in spite of being a capable adult, I was at a loss. What was I supposed to do, wait? Entertain myself? I felt a little stab of panic, the kind that doesn't make any sense but takes over your body just the same.

Lucian had gone to the hotel. How long could that take? He hadn't given me a clue, but I wondered if he'd finished his business and gone to his room. There was no way I was going to look for him there. I didn't even know where his room was.

Maybe he'd just gone out again. Lucian had friends all over Romania; sometimes he'd get together with them and go off for a few hours, but usually it was at night and he let me know beforehand. We hadn't talked about any such plans for today. It wasn't like him to disappear, and my old abandonment issues kicked in. They'd been there all the time, of course.

Once a boyfriend left my bed in the middle of the night and drove home without telling me. I woke up in the dark to a set of flat, indifferent sheets where he should have been. "Fred?" I called out, thinking he was in the bathroom. There was no answer; the house was telling me what I didn't want to hear. I got up, thinking he must be downstairs in the kitchen; or, worse, maybe he'd moved to the couch for the night. "Fred?" Nothing came back but the echo of my townhouse in the wee hours.

I went through the living room and opened the door to the garage, where I'd let him park overnight. Empty. He was gone. Something must have come up, but what could it have been? I went through the house looking for a note. From him it wouldn't have been much, most likely a scrap of paper torn from something of mine—a grocery list, a magazine—with two or three words on it. "Couldn't sleep," he might write, or "Call you tomorrow," with *tomorrow* misspelled—probably with two *m*'s. But there was no note. It was as though he hadn't been in the house at all. In a second I was consumed with outrage, pain, and the inevitable questions as familiar as childhood. What had I done? What did I lack, that he had thought leaving that way was all right? What did it say about our whole relationship? What did it say about me?

Now I walked to the patio area in back of the hotel, hoping to see Lucian. The garden restaurant was full of men who looked like conventioneers. They talked in clumps, some standing and others seated at tables. Lucian wasn't there, so I went out walking.

People were still milling around the shopping square, but not energetically, and many of the shops were closed. I decided to stop for a drink and watch people. Maybe I'd spot Lucian, who was still at the center of all my thoughts. *Where was he?* What if he went looking for me in the hotel and I wasn't there? I staked out a bench that could be seen from the hotel and from where I could view its entrance.

I watched people for a while and tried to keep my mind off Lucian, but I was in a dither. I hated having my whole brain focused on his absence. How had my feelings about him evolved into this?

In Bucharest I hadn't even liked him—or a nicer way to say it would be that I didn't quite appreciate him yet. By Curtea de Argeş, we'd found a companionable pattern of traveling together, and by then I'd become curious about his private life. In Sibiu, there were the healing incidents and then the surprise of my libido flaring up at the Brukenthal Museum. In Cluj, I'd embarrassed myself by dressing for dinner as though it were a date. In Maramureş, walking along the streets of Sighetu Marmatiei, I'd simply appreciated having Lucian as a guide.

He usually kept a good balance between leaving me alone and being alert to my needs as a traveler. He respected my need to write by letting me initiate most of our conversations. When I was quiet and preoccupied, he could have called his wife more often or simply spaced out to relieve the boredom and silence of the road. But he'd kept my needs ahead of his own. That very morning, I'd been glad—and relieved—to have him walking the citadel with me. And just hours ago, out of the blue, he'd chased a train so I could get a decent picture.

Now it seemed I'd become dependent on Lucian. That afternoon in Sighişoara was the only time we'd been apart for even a few hours without a plan. Since he'd gone missing my whole equilibrium was off, and I hated it.

Then I saw him.

I'd been watching the dwindling foot traffic, absorbed in my thoughts, when I spotted Lucian crossing the square. A wave of relief hit me, but then I noticed he wasn't alone. He was with a group, and they were heading down the hill. They were talking and laughing, and he didn't see me. Were these merely friends going on their merry way to downtown, or was the outing more of the police business Lucian had been taking care of earlier? Either way, apparently I had some time to kill.

Now I felt the red carpet of boredom rolling out just for me. I'd exhausted the exploration possibilities there in the citadel and had nothing to write. Take heed: However beautiful, there isn't much to do in a walled town on a hill in Transylvania in the twenty-first century after you've done the tour. My energy level sank. At least I knew where Lucian was, but seeing him leave had struck me like a blow. I walked to the hotel and went to my room, feeling strangely left out.

Chapter 43

Devil House

It was a gorgeous day in Sighişoara, and I was on my own with little to do. Lucian had left the building—our hotel—and I was back inside. Soon I found myself hanging out the casement window of my room like a washwoman, studying the streets below. Apparently this Transylvanian fortress town was like Mexico, where everything shut down for a siesta. Under the summer sun, the medieval walled section of Sighişoara was as quiet as a grave.

The hotel was located right off the little commercial square—in the middle of the action when there was any—and my room was on the front, a perfect vantage point. So now, instead of being out in the Romanian sunshine, I was looking out across Scolii Street.

The street was short, and I could see it all—at one end, the walk to the Scholars' Stairs; at the other, the Stag House, a local landmark. The hotel and bar was known for the real stag's head that had been affixed to the corner of the building four centuries earlier. The skull had been enhanced with a mural of the animal's body.

A line of old German row houses stood across from the hotel, each one a different color—white next to yellow, then red, green, and gold—with steeply pitched roofs, arched doorways, and casement windows. Some had apartments on the upper floors, with lace curtains at the windows. I could see vague shapes of furniture inside—a light couch or perhaps an unmade bed; a covered chair.

Scaffolds had been erected outside two of the houses, and it was easy to see why: The walls were splotchy from missing paint. Most of the buildings needed work. Somehow that was charming, given the mix of colorful exterior paint, window boxes dripping flowers, and even a yellow flag hanging from an upstairs window.

The house directly across from me could have been painted from the same bucket as Vlad's birth house. It was yellow-orange, with "Anno 1902" carved into the peaked façade. I would call the color by its correct name, *ocher* (also *ochre*), if I'd never worked for the *Bluefield Daily Telegraph* in West Virginia. Once in my days as a young reporter there, I submitted an article describing colors in an art show. The proofreaders changed *ocher* to *orchid,* thinking I couldn't spell.

The façade of the yellow house was decorated with fancy shapes—posts, a circle, and a face. The posts rose from triangular shapes that looked to me like rams' heads. I knew that rams and goats had been worshipped by some civilizations. Christopher Lee starred in a movie called *The Devil Rides Out* (1968) that featured a satanic goat. The Goat of Mendes—depicted in the movie as a man with a goat's head—was a god of Ancient Egypt summoned during a Black Mass.

The circle on the house was in the middle, then above it the face. *The face.* It was pagan, male, and reminiscent of clowns, jesters, and movies in which just such a face can scare the crap out of you. In *Poltergeist,* a child's clown doll turned evil, slithered out from the dark under the bed, and tried to kill him.

Historically, jesters served a king's court. Often mentally handicapped, they provided simple entertainment such as juggling and could speak their minds boldly without punishment. In the harsh world of medieval Europe, people who might not be able to survive any other way thus found a social niche. Jesters weren't considered evil beings, so maybe the face on the house was some kind of faun or demon.

The face had prominent cheekbones. Its mouth was open in a grimace, as if it had seen something terrible—or *was* something terrible. It had hollow eyes; a wide, flat nose; and a beard. Two small horns protruded from its forehead, and a shape ran off each side of its head, curling downward. However the carving was intended, to me it was the Devil, and the house across the way was the Devil House.

The cornices and balcony below the peak were adorned with scary faces. One had leonine features: heavy brow, broad nose, whiskers, and a background shape spread out like a lion's mane. Its tongue, stretching down from a frozen scream, looked like the one in the logo for the Rolling Stones. Two grimacing demons were mounted on the corners of the house, eyeing the street. Each had something tied around its neck that looked like a necklace of garlic flowers.

If you considered Vlad Dracula to be a devil, that made two in this town. The other one was staring at me across the summer air above Scolii Street; and of the two, I might take Vlad.

I was facing off against . . . well, a face, and recalling the vile deeds of Vlad the Impaler, but the truth was that I could tell both of those devils a few stories. I'd done time in a devil house too—just part of a grab bag of Glen Ferris memories.

By 1975 I was divorced and the custodial parent of a five-year-old. Life was tough. In addition to struggling socially and financially where I lived, I was the first known member of the family to get a divorce. Mom and Grandmama did their best to keep my messy life a secret in Glen Ferris, and through their shame they turned against me when I needed their support the most. I stayed away for a long time.

My mind flitted to Lucian's disappearance, prompting a visit to the minibar in my room after which the Devil watched me stress-eat a whole can of paprika peanuts. As I brought the first delicious handful to my mouth, our eyes met. His were black holes.

Yes, I know: Jenny Craig would advise eight nuts as a snack. In addition to exceeding the food limit, that fat foray cost 75,000 lei—a devilish amount, probably twice as much as the nuts would cost in a store. At that point, price was irrelevant; I was starving. The Romanians have a saying: "Have breakfast alone, share lunch with a friend, and give dinner to your enemies." I would have contemplated that further, but a bee came along and drove me inside.

Lucian eventually returned from his outing and we ate dinner in the garden. He didn't offer a word about how he'd spent the afternoon—and I didn't ask.

I didn't ask because I didn't care where Lucian had been or what he'd done. The question I wanted to ask was bigger, louder, a screamer: *WHY?* It went back to the deepest roots of my life, when that old devil, Abandonment, got me in its clutches and taught me to take it personally—whatever the evidence—when someone left.

Lucian wasn't Mom, and I wasn't thirteen; but I felt a surge of rage, pain, powerlessness, and need bubble up inside me as I sat across the table from my guide. It was an overreaction; I knew that. So I did what I always did: I swallowed it.

With more simmering between us than plates of polenta, my chances of posing a casual question to Lucian over dinner were nil. My chances of calmly asserting myself on the topic of schedule synchronization were remote. These were truths I knew from experience. At times I felt like I might explode from the force of my feelings, just shoot up into the sky and break into a thousand pieces.

This was my secret. I had a monster, too.

I didn't want it or ask for it, but a monster slept inside me. It didn't look anything like Dracula; maybe Puff the Magic Dragon, only mean. I came to recognize it as my own pain and rage, curled up in the dark since childhood. Certain things would wake it up, and when I felt it stir, I thought the best I could do was to tiptoe past it.

My last image of Sighişoara was a big, white Romanian Orthodox church on the outskirts of town. Maybe it would serve to neutralize my inner monster along with the carved Devils that continued to gaze upon my little window long after Lucian and I were gone.

Chapter 44

"If You Love Miss Lucy . . ."

I felt a pang as Lucian and I passed the large, white church on the edge of Sighişoara—not because I had any attachment to *it*, but because I'd felt the presence of Christopher Lee in the town and didn't want to leave him behind. On the other hand, I was glad to leave the Devil behind.

I'd all but lost touch with Mom when I'd heard she'd stopped drinking after an intervention. It was news in the abstract—distant, unreal—and after such a long time, hard to believe. But it was welcome.

Mom had nearly set the house on fire—probably the brown chair again—and the news had traveled. I guess Mom's drinking wasn't much of a secret in the valley after so many years, in spite of the energy we'd all spent trying to hide it.

One of Mom's friends had come to the house and sat her down for a dose of straight talk, something like, "If you don't stop drinking, you're going to set the house on fire one day and kill yourself." Apparently the intervention had worked, and that was all I knew.

Intervention played a key role in *Horror of Dracula.* Sitting in the movies at age thirteen, I didn't know what an intervention was, but I was spellbound as Dr. Van Helsing stepped in to save Lucy Holmwood from the evil curse of Dracula. The only one to realize her true affliction, he pleaded to convince Lucy's family they were battling for her soul: "If you love Miss Lucy, be guided by me, I beg you." I loved that quote and all it meant, but I'd given up on Mom's soul years before. Now it seemed that "Van Helsing" had come at last, in the guise of Viola Weaver.

So my mother was sober. I wondered if it would last. Was she going to AA? Meetings had been established in two nearby towns, Montgomery and Gauley Bridge, in the1960s. I hoped Mom had found them, but I might never know. Her drinking remained an unexplored dark corner in our lives. I was busy with my own life far from Glen Ferris: glad to hear the news about the intervention, but unaffected until Mom became a person of leisure. Then I was at a crossroads.

Mom retired at sixty-five from her secretarial job, and her free time could have swallowed her whole. She wasn't the type to volunteer, take courses, or seek part-time work. She kept up her Garden Club membership and played bridge, but she still had loads of time. Eventually it worked its way into my life, because she wanted to visit.

By then it was the late 1980s. Time had flown, and my son was a teenager. I'd remarried and divorced again, but this time my family didn't desert me. The first time around, I'd divorced someone they liked. The second time, someone they barely knew had divorced *me,* and that was different. Things began to turn around.

I'd been working on myself after discovering Adult Children of Alcoholics. I don't remember how I found ACoA, but it was a lucky match. That was where I began to learn how the past had stamped itself on me and what I could do about it.

It was in ACoA that I began to study the works of recovery pioneers like Melodie Beattie, John Bradshaw, and Charles Whitfield, and where I first heard the term *codependent.* Dr. Whitfield called it a "disease of lost selfhood," a condition that stifles the Child Within. When a passive, dependent personality—say, a child—is fixated on a stronger personality—say, an alcoholic parent—that child learns to neglect his or her own needs. We repress our feelings, develop destructive behaviors, and become increasingly tolerant of emotional pain. Ultimately we can lose our identities and fail to take responsibility for our own lives.

Mom's drinking had affected our whole family negatively. Even though the damage had occurred many years before, I recognized in my adult self the telltale signs of codependency—traits I'd been exhibiting most of my life. The list is long—neediness, perfectionism, control issues, low self-esteem, frozen feelings, people pleasing, and fear of abandonment are just a few. The enlightening part of ACoA was that I could put a name to what had shaped my personality.

I worked the twelve steps of ACoA for several years, attempting to understand and change my behavior. The process is called recovery because it's long and does not promise a cure. However, we can heal.

I needed to heal. All my life I'd felt a pervasive sadness, a heaviness I couldn't shake, like carrying a backpack full of rocks. People would pass me and say, "Smile! It can't be that bad." I desperately wanted to feel better.

The promise of healing was there in ACoA, but the reality eluded me. I wanted to know, not to struggle. I was looking for an identifiable moment, an event. I wanted a whole new feeling to wash over me like one of those giant waves at Myrtle Beach and make me different inside—better, kinder, bolder, more emotional, less—less *me*. I wanted a miracle. Nothing like that happened, and eventually I drifted away from the program.

I did make new friends in ACoA, friends who understood me, and for the first time in my life I felt relief from the awful vigilance of living a lie. How was that going to work with Mom coming back into my life?

I wanted a mother—I always had—but not the monster from my past. I'd never be ready for her again. Could I have a normal mother a few times a year? If so, I wanted it. Did I have the fortitude to find out? In hindsight, the answer seems obvious. After all, I was accustomed to disappointment, but a sucker for hope. It was a gambler's mentality.

I decided to give Mom a chance, and I guess she did the same for me. We took baby steps, seeing each other for a few days at a time. So far, so good; but I wasn't blinded. I kept an eye out for the devil I knew.

I turned my attention to the present. Lucian and I were nearing Brașov—and the next big Dracula thing.

Chapter 45

The Good and Bad of Braşov

We'd set out for Braşov on a hazy morning. As we wound through woods and villages, up the hills and down again, I felt a familiar tug: Braşov County could easily pass for a section of West Virginia. The drive made me think again of my mother expertly ascending Gauley Mountain. On that mountain, there are places where the road crumbles away, places where you can look over the guard rail and down between the trees to see the Gauley River in miniature far below.

The road from Sighişoara to Braşov was good—no potholes, construction sites, slides, or mud—a miracle. I took in the scenery and tried not to focus on the winding road, the other cars whizzing past, the white center lines with their built-in ridges to keep drivers on their own side, and Lucian taking the curves like he wanted to qualify for a Grand Prix.

We hadn't gone far when Lucian came to a quick stop for an old man crossing the road. He was walking so slowly that he was just this side of standing still; the only important thing that separated him from a snail was the absence of a silver trail. When Lucian hit the brakes, the old man didn't even turn to look. Even the threat of being mowed down didn't put any spring in his steps. That was Romania: Drivers had to defer to any person, animal, or object in the road.

We arrived in Braşov just before eleven in the morning. Lucian told me it was the first town founded in Transylvania. Braşov is also the home of Mt. Tâmpa, a Dracula site tied to Vlad the Impaler and known in his day as Timpa Hill. Why did the Romanians keep changing their vowels? Wasn't it enough that many of the place names had been changed completely over time to reflect the shifting population? In the old Dracula movies, Brașov was called Keinenberg, even though its actual German name was Kronstadt. That might explain why I didn't find a trace of Keinenberg in Romania.

Today Brașov is a happy place, but it has taken a few hundred years to get there. According to the earliest documentation, it was founded in the thirteenth century and the next four centuries were spent building walls to fortify it against—guess who—the Turkish armies. Only parts of those ancient walls remain, but the city is surrounded by mountains. It was in those mountains that Vlad the Impaler reportedly committed one of his infamous atrocities. In 1459, during his second reign as Prince of Wallachia, Vlad determined that the Saxon merchants of Brașov were not showing him the loyalty he required. He ordered his troops to round up the merchants as well as other residents and take them to the top of Timpa Hill, where they would watch their city burn while being impaled on stakes driven into the hillside. That grisly event was the one depicted in the woodcut image I'd seen ten days earlier in the Chindia Tower.

The Brașov we saw was lovely and modern, but vestiges of violence and misfortune lingered. When we arrived, Lucian parked near the Black Church, the best-known landmark in the city and the largest Gothic church in Romania. The church survived a horrible fire in 1689 that blackened its walls—thus the name. Though it has nothing to do with Dracula, the Black Church is something to see if you go to Brașov. In fact, it's impossible not to see it rising above the other buildings as though it could lift off at any minute on its own and go clear to Heaven.

From the church, it was a short walk to the heart of the old town. Dracula seemed far in the past as we crossed a bright plaza said to be the place where the legendary Pied Piper brought the children of Hamelin.

The tale emerged in the Middle Ages. As with the story of Dracula, many versions of *The Pied Piper* have been told. Perhaps the best known is that captured in Robert Browning's 1888 poem: When a plague of rats threatened the town of Hamelin, Germany, a piper dressed in pied (multicolored) clothing came forward and convinced the town council that he could lure the rodents away by playing a tune on his pipe. Boasting that he could charm "All creatures living beneath the sun / That creep or swim or fly or run," the piper even claimed he'd worked his magic on a "monstrous brood of vampire bats."

A fee was set. As promised, the piper led all the rats away—to a river, where they drowned; however, the citizens refused to "pay the piper" the agreed-upon fee, and he retaliated by turning his magic on their children.

He led the children of Hamelin away with a haunting tune and promises of a magic land. When they reached a certain hill in Germany, a "wondrous portal" opened in the mountainside. The children entered the cave, and when the last one was in, the door quickly closed. They were never seen by their families again.

The Pied Piper has been called a metaphor for Death, a pedophile, and a devil. Like Dracula, he was a combination of evil and irresistible charm. His story is a tale in which the sins of the parents are visited upon the children.

Historians have speculated about the children's fate. Some have suggested that the story of the Pied Piper has a basis in truth, and that the children's exodus from Hamelin relates to the actual colonization of Eastern Europe—including Transylvania—in the thirteenth century. The boys and girls of Hamelin could have been taken out of Germany underground and sold into an eastern colony as slaves. That would support the local legend that the children emerged near the site of Braşov's Council Square, where Lucian and I now strolled.

Today the plaza is surrounded by restaurants and retail businesses. Red and white Coca-Cola umbrellas lined the edge of it that day, shading wrought-iron tables rich with flowers. We walked past a circular fountain and made a stop for coffee at one of the sidewalk cafés. By the time we were done, the haze had burned off and the plaza had come to life. Boys on bicycles chased one another around the fountain. Women hurried by with shopping bags. Yellow flowers burst from cement containers, wooden benches sat with their warm slats back to back, and pigeons landed to peck at the pavement in the sunshine and then take flight again.

I was glad to have Lucian back. Now that we'd returned to a normal routine, my feelings of abandonment had faded and I felt my inner balance restored. I'd managed to tamp down my rage of the previous evening, and now I had to admit to another weakness: Relief was a piper's tune to me. Whatever the slight—large or small, real or imagined—I just wanted to move past it. It was always the way.

We headed for a street off the plaza that was closed to traffic. Crowds and street bands made a festive atmosphere as we drifted along the rows of pastel buildings. In the distance, mountains rose above the business district. Somewhere a cable car went up the steep incline of Mt. Tâmpa, but Lucian and I stuck to our shopping.

Walking that sunny street in Brașov was a bit like the time I took a bus tour of Hollywood on a business trip to California. The bus went right past 5555 Melrose, home of the gated arch that marks the entrance to Paramount Pictures. I looked up between the buildings, past the Paramount arch, to the giant, white letters of the famous "HOLLYWOOD" sign on the side of the mountain.

By the craziest of coincidences, you can look up from Council Square in Brașov, Romania—over the tops of the red-roofed stores, banks, and pharmacies—and see a big white sign on the mountain. Constructed in the same block lettering as its California counterpart, it spells "BRASOV."

Partway down the street we saw an official Columbia store selling the famous outdoor adventure wear. My first reaction was surprise: a Columbia store in the middle of Romania? The obvious draw was the ski resorts—Predeal, Sinaia, Poiana Brașov—that dotted the Carpathians.

I loved to read stories of outdoor adventure and survival, especially tales of Mt. Everest and the Alaskan wilderness, extreme settings where people had to fight the elements and often became trapped in impossible situations. Those stories were like the Dracula movies—best from a distance. I wouldn't have tried to climb Mt. Everest, even if someone had written me a check and bumped me to the top of the waiting list, but I liked to dress like someone who would. Lucian and I had that in common. He was an outdoor person, more so than I was. Not only did he dress the part, he told me he'd camped in the mountains of Romania in summer and winter. He'd skied the Carpathians and knew the resorts. As a magazine photographer, he'd traveled the country to take pictures.

We swooped into the Columbia store like two homing pigeons. Lucian bought a pair of walking shoes, and I got a shirt.

I didn't see Timpa Hill—Mt. Tâmpa—up close, but it didn't seem important. Vlad was still the manufactured Dracula to me. His misdeeds had taken a back seat that day. I had seen Braşov with its fountain and pigeons, street bands playing in the sunshine, a Hollywood-style sign, and a real Columbia store. It was enough.

Chapter 46

The Move

As with Lucian in Sighișoara and Brașov, I was glad to have Mom back in my life. As she and I got to know each other, it seemed that the monster from my past had been replaced by a new and better version of my mother, one I liked so far. Maybe I was gradually lulled into complacency; maybe that was the reason I didn't anticipate the next turn of events—the Big Bomb.

Mom had been to see me several times after her retirement. A fearless driver then, she didn't mind making the trip alone. She was always sober during those visits, and I began to discover in her a smart, funny, independent, mobile person who was interested in doing things. We went shopping, and she actually tried on clothes. She gave me no grief about what I bought. We went out to eat, trying different restaurants, and once we even went downtown to a TV studio and sat in the audience of a popular talk show.

By then my son was off at school, and I was living alone. Instead of feeling lonely, I found that being by myself suited me: There was no one else to serve or please. Being on my own eliminated the guessing I'd always had to do in relationships. Even being a parent had proved a mystery, and I'd made mistakes. We'd been broke at times, we'd moved around, and there was that stepfather thing about which my son had had no choice; but I hadn't been a drunk and I'd always told my son I loved him more than the sun and the moon and the stars.

Mom's Big Bomb was that she wanted to move to—as she put it—"Cincinnatuh." I won't say the idea hadn't entered my mind—but it hadn't stuck. I'd had years of practice trying to figure Mom out and stay ahead of her moods. I knew when to walk away and when to run. I was the champion, but that time I was surprised.

The news held an ironic twist for me: After a lifetime of abandonment issues, I found myself panicking because she *wasn't* abandoning me! This was the other side of neediness.

My initial reaction to Mom's news was cold fear. Even though she was talking about getting her own apartment, it was still a big step—for both of us. Who knew what she'd be like on a full-time basis? I hadn't lived in the same town as my mother since I was sixteen. I could be seeing her best behavior now; I probably was.

Would I be Mom's only friend in her new hometown? Sure I would—at least for a while. We didn't see Joe, and she didn't know anyone else. What would she expect from me? When she came to visit, I gladly devoted a couple of days to being with her—but that couldn't continue if she lived nearby. It was unrealistic. I worked all day; did she realize that?

I could see my freedom slipping away. I'd made a life in Cincinnati, but could Mom do the same? She was leaving home for a city of strangers. Did she understand the extent to which she'd be starting over? It could take years to learn the city and make friends; to find doctors, support systems, and things to do. Life in a small town was slow, especially for a retiree. Choices were limited. Did she see that there was no comparison between Glen Ferris and Greater Cincinnati?

I worried that Mom would be out in society and someone would offer her a drink. Of course they would. Would she take it? Did Mom realize she *couldn't* drink? I had no idea if she had the necessary insight into her disease. Even though I'd relaxed a bit around her, I was still afraid she'd turn. Do you ever get over that? Years later the monster reaches out from some dark, haunted place, and there you are again, caught in its terrible grip.

Did Mom worry about her sobriety, as I did? We should have talked about it more, but I couldn't. It was like opening Dracula's coffin—too scary. I did want to give this thing a chance, but at that point my relationship with Mom was a house of cards. I knew it, and I didn't want to knock it down.

As Mom's plans became known in Glen Ferris, people were shocked that she was planning to move when Grandmama still lived down the road—alone—and wasn't going anywhere. "How can she leave her mother?" they asked. What they didn't realize was that, aside from the way Mom had abandoned us all for the bottle, she had never left her mother.

The comments intensified after fate took a sad turn. One morning several weeks before Mom was to move, Grandmama fell going down the stairs in her house. She not only hit her head against a heavy vase at the bottom of the steps, she ended up in the hospital with a broken hip. Mom and I made the drive to Charleston every day to see her. It rained hard that first week. I can still picture Mom in her beige raincoat and hat, sitting on the passenger side of the car, staring out the window, awash in guilt.

Here was a woman who'd lived most of her seventy-two years in Glen Ferris, about to move to a city where her children would be nearby and where all kinds of opportunities could open up for her. My grandmother never would have wanted to stop Mom from going, but there it was. The agony of Mom's conflict played out in that car every day: Should she carry out her plans or be a good daughter, please the neighbors, and stay in Glen Ferris with Grandmama?

Fate decided. My grandmother was unable to return to her beloved house in Glen Ferris. She moved to the Union Mission home, and Mom went ahead with her own move. Now all traces of our family were gone from the little town on the Kanawha River that held our history.

When Mom had announced her intention to relocate, I hadn't wanted us to be close neighbors. I figured that, with its population of two million people, Cincinnati would be an ideal place to keep her at a distance. I welcomed her to a neighborhood that was a thirty-minute drive from mine.

Mom had expressed the desire to live in a walkable area where she could easily get to a drugstore or market. It was a nice idea; the trouble was, she couldn't walk very far. Mom had arthritis in her hips, and even crossing a room would put a grimace on her face.

I found a lovely apartment that had an underground garage, a large balcony, and even someone on the premises to help Mom carry groceries. The apartment had architectural features similar to those in her Glen Ferris house. It was perfect, or would have been if Mom hadn't gone into shock when the time came to actually move.

The first clue should have hit me weeks before in Glen Ferris. Mom had thrown away or donated many of her possessions, regardless of their value, in an attempt to pack efficiently. With her skewed perspective, she was convinced there would be no room for all of her things on the moving truck. She was sleeping on a bare mattress because she'd stripped her bed three weeks ahead of time and packed her sheets. Mom had never moved like this and simply didn't know what to do. She had a crisis, and no one saw it.

On moving day, two friends and I arrived at the Cincinnati apartment early to wait for the movers and welcome Mom. I wondered who would be the first to pull up out front. The furniture came, was unloaded and placed, but still no Mom. Where was she? She'd made that drive before; what could have happened? The truth was, anything could have happened. That was before the days of cell phones in every pocket and purse. We had no way of getting in touch with Mom short of calling the police or setting out ourselves to drive in the opposite direction.

The movers left. My friends left. Finally I left, too, returning home with a sick feeling inside. There she was, pacing on my front porch, her tan raincoat flapping. She looked wild, panicked. "I'm going to ruin you," she said. "I'm going to embarrass you. You'll hate me. You're going to wish I'd stayed in West Virginia." Mom wasn't making threats; she was scared, and raving like a lunatic.

"What are you talking about?"

"I'm broke. I won't be able to pay my rent. I'll end up in jail and disgrace you." She kept repeating the same messages with slightly different words. My mother was sober, but she was a mess. She'd made the drive from Glen Ferris at eighty-five miles per hour with little memory of it. She'd wet her pants. She had six hundred dollars in her purse and much more in the bank back home, but she arrived in Cincinnati convinced that she was broke.

After seeing her new home with her things in place, Mom was anything but settled. She wandered around her apartment in a daze, not even picking up after herself. I went to see her every day, and what I saw was that she was barely functional. She couldn't focus on or perform the simplest tasks, like locking and unlocking her door. Mom would stick the key into the keyhole, barely wiggle it, and then look helplessly at me. "I can't do it," she'd say, and I'd have to take over, showing her again and again how to work the lock. There was no obstacle I could identify except her defeatist attitude.

Mom became obsessed with her purse, constantly digging in it. She carried it with the shoulder strap around her neck and the purse hanging at her chest. In restaurants she'd keep the strap around her neck but set the purse part off to the side on the table, where she could eat and still see it. Often she'd clutch it as though someone were about to snatch it from her. Why she guarded it so closely when she thought it contained nothing of value was just another mystery. Eventually we met with bankers who tried to assure Mom that she had a healthy account she could transfer, but she wasn't convinced. She couldn't take in the information.

Mom wasn't the only one in a wild panic; so was I. Why was she acting this way? *She* was the one who'd wanted to move to Cincinnati. She'd looked forward to living here. I'd accepted it. We'd even seemed to be on an equal footing for once, possibly on our way to being friends. I'd knocked myself out to make the move easy for her, and still she couldn't cope.

I was disappointed in Mom during those first weeks. Worse, her utter helplessness woke up the monster in me—big time. I could feel my rage rising up like the undead, and what was I supposed to do with it? I couldn't unleash it on her when she was weak and lost. I wanted to, so when *it* threatened to escape, *I* ran away—straight to my car and up the road for home.

Even through my anger and disappointment, I knew my mother needed help. I found a social worker to help Mom adjust to her new life and scheduled a meeting in Mom's apartment. That first home visit seemed to be a trigger. Mom pulled herself together, got dressed in nice slacks and a matching blouse, and even baked a casserole for lunch. From there, everything went smoothly. In a few weeks she was settling in for real and beginning to venture out. The most important thing was that, in all the stress of the move, she hadn't reverted to drinking.

When her lease was up, Mom moved again—closer to me. She joined a senior center and found new friends. She played bridge every week. She joined the library and sometimes went to church. I saw Mom often, and she didn't miss a holiday at my house. Few others knew about her past. My friends loved her. They thought she was nice and funny, and they always asked me, "How's your mom?" There's a saying, "Wherever you go, there you are," but it wasn't true of Mom. She'd changed her whole life. Was the saying true of me?

Sometimes, when an alcoholic gets sober, other family members find that they're still stuck in old patterns or saddled with old feelings. The event they thought would end their troubles doesn't, because it doesn't change them. I still didn't feel right. I was still waiting for that big wave.

Chapter 47

A Tale of Two Castles: Bran

As Lucian and I neared the village of Bran, I could see Bran Castle in the distance. I expected something sinister; after all, in the movies the local villagers would not acknowledge the existence of the castle or even speak the name of its inhabitant. They avoided the "shadow of the castle" at all costs. I looked through the car window to see what might be in the shadow of Bran Castle and was disappointed that nothing fit the description. The castle is too high and isolated for its shadow to touch the village in the frightening way suggested in the movies. But perhaps I was being too literal as we approached the most famous Dracula attraction on earth.

Known the world over as Dracula's Castle, the striking structure rising above a small Transylvanian village could be expected from its reputation to radiate mystery and evil. The truth is, the same castle that has been called ominous, dark, gloomy, and grotesque has also been accurately described as a peaceful refuge, picturesque and joyful, straight from a fairy tale. Bran Castle has also been called a fake.

The castle was built in 1377 as a fortress against the Turks. Today it is structurally intact, with towers and turrets, a maze of rooms, a courtyard, and even secret passageways. So far, so good as the world headquarters of the Count, or even Vlad the Impaler. But before it became a museum and tourist hot-spot with its own website, Bran was a royal residence, the summer home of a queen. Long before that, it was a fortress in war. It endured years of abandonment and neglect in between, its masters—both real and imagined—running the gamut from evil to beloved.

More than 400,000 visitors a year are drawn to Bran, many of them following the footsteps of Dracula. The popularity of the castle has turned the surrounding village into a tourist center and provided many of its residents with work. Though McNally and Florescu claimed in 1972 that Bran was *erroneously* termed Dracula's Castle, the bottom line is the bottom line. The castle is a must-see for anyone interested in Dracula—whether that interest springs from the novel, the movies, or the history of Prince Vlad.

As we drove in, the area below the castle was crowded, unlike the quiet simplicity of the Poenari Citadel. Parking is a commercial venture at Bran, and finding a space in Dracula's parking lot was like staking out a spot at a busy mall; but the parking area was compact when compared to the acres of asphalt back home. In fact, the whole village seemed compressed. Souvenir stands butted up against one another, and many of the shops were built as simple stalls with a common roof. All of what we saw was contained in an area about the size of a city block, with the castle dominant.

The outside walls of Bran Castle are whitewashed, with orange tile roofs topping its wings and towers. Even with the woods of Transylvania forming a backdrop, I had a hard time reconciling the soaring structure with an image of the evil undead—or even the evil dead, which would be Vlad. The castle seems a much better fit for its real residents—Romania's Queen Marie and her children, who owned it between 1920 and 1948. I was not there based on any interest in Queen Marie, but I had to admit that from the outside the castle still looked like a royal residence, not a vampire's lair.

As we climbed the stone-paved walkway to take our tour with the throngs, it was easy to imagine Queen Marie eighty years earlier, strolling the tranquil grounds below us. A lovely lake is situated among trees and flowers in the grassy castle yard at the base of the hill. Someone has placed benches near the water.

But Queen Marie had nothing to do with Dracula, the reason most of us were there. I wanted to focus on him—or *them*, if I considered both Vlad and the Count—as I approached the castle entrance.

On the vampire side of things, some people believe that Bram Stoker used Bran as the model for his fictional Count's castle. Elizabeth Miller disagrees. She writes in *A Dracula Handbook* that Stoker could not have heard of Bran Castle when he was writing *Dracula*.

Another popular belief about Bran Castle, connecting it to a different Dracula, is that the horrid Vlad the Impaler lived there in the fifteenth century. Experts agree on this one: The castle was constructed before Vlad was born, and he did eventually spend time there as a guest or even a prisoner. It was never his residence the way it was Queen Marie's.

There she was again.

Once when my mother was about eighty-five, we took her to see *The Nutcracker* for the first time. Growing up in West Virginia, she didn't have the kind of life that included attending the ballet. Neither did I.

We were dressed up; it was the Christmas season. My son and daughter-in-law had gotten the tickets. Mom sat beside me, and all through the performance I stole glances at her to see if she seemed to be enjoying the ballet. We could hear a pin drop in the audience and you never know what a person who's eighty-five, hard of hearing, and occasionally outspoken is going to do. I was glad to see that her attention was focused on the stage.

All was well until *The Nutcracker* progressed to the concluding scenes in which the lead male and the lead female dancer were showcased. They would dance together, and then one or the other would solo. About the second or third time the male dancer took the stage, my mother called out into the darkness, "Is he back *again?*" That was the way I felt about Queen Marie.

How did the queen fit into the Dracula story? She didn't, exactly; while Bram Stoker was writing *Dracula*, Marie was just settling into married life—at seventeen—with King Ferdinand, her third cousin. The marriage was disappointing to her; in fact, the popular queen was miserable.

Ferdinand was German, ten years older than his English-born wife, and said to be unattractive. Marie later confided her feelings for her husband—"distaste, which grew to revulsion"—in a letter to a friend. Her true love had been a prince who had proposed marriage, but her mother had disapproved of the union.

Queen Marie was one of the kindest rulers in Romania's turbulent history. Her reputation was that she would go out into the streets and mingle with the peasants, often giving them gifts such as warm hats for winter. In her travels, Marie had noticed what she called a "pugnacious little fortress" in the village of Bran.

Soon the queen was looking longingly at Bran Castle, which appeared as lonely and forlorn as she was. Described in her memoirs as being "as bare and empty as a forsaken heart," Bran became Queen Marie's dream castle, a source of joy and hope. It must have seemed like a miracle when in 1920 the nearby city of Braşov presented the castle to her. As the new owner, Marie was determined to transform the neglected fortress into a place of beauty. She filled the rooms with furniture and light and flowers, bringing life to the castle as it did the same for her.

By the time Queen Marie moved in, twenty-three years had passed since the publication of *Dracula* and fifteen years since its author's death. Did she know about the book? Did anyone speculate back then that her lovely, pugnacious little fortress was the model for Dracula's castle?

Bran Castle remained the property of the royal family until the Communists forced them to leave the country in 1948. It then became the property of the state until it was returned to Queen Marie's grandson, Dominic Habsburg, in 2006. He later returned the castle to the Romanian government. In doing so, he stated that he did not want Bran Castle associated with Dracula, and plans were in place for the castle to close to visitors by 2009. Fortunately, it became a museum instead and remained open to the public. Many items from Queen Marie's reign were added to the display—including her heart!

I wasn't looking for a queen, or even Vlad or the Count, when I stood at the foot of the long, steep staircase leading to the entrance of Bran Castle. I was looking for Christopher Lee—or at least I was looking for the spirit of him: to stand where he had stood, to walk where he had walked, to turn and face the view he had seen when the cameras were rolling to film *In Search of Dracula*. Think about a crush you've had and how you behaved. The tiniest souvenir would have been a treasure: a discarded candy wrapper, a handwriting sample, a lock of hair to take home and press in your diary. Or maybe you felt a yearning, a need to be where that person had been, to share—if asynchronously—an experience or physical space that would bind you together. It was the same for me: I was trying to be in a moment I'd had no part of, which is the best we can do with history.

Lee was filming around Bran Castle in the early 1970s. In his auto-biography, *Tall, Dark, and Gruesome,* he described how startling his appearance was to soldiers who were conducting maneuvers nearby: They crossed themselves as though he were his most famous character. Lee played both the Count and Vlad the Impaler in the documentary. In *A Dracula Handbook,* Elizabeth Miller noted that having Lee play the part of Vlad Dracula further cemented the connection among all the Draculas—including him.

How I would love to have been there, watching Lee practice his moves as Vlad, striding among the tall pines in a black wig or taking the castle stairs two at a time the way he did in the movies. As it was, I didn't know exactly where he'd been when he visited Bran. I'd watched *In Search of Dracula* right before my trip, but the castle scenes meshed together in my mind.

So there I was, finally standing on the front porch of Bran Castle. In the Dracula movies, the castles always had a wide paved area in front of the door where the Count's distinctive black coach would pull up and let the passengers out. I didn't know the name of this wide area—which is also where fights happened and occasionally one of the mortal enemies wound up falling over a wall or through a gap into the distant river valley below. In one movie, Dracula himself took that dive, with a burning sword in his back.

There are web pages that list the parts of a castle, but I found none that included a description of that area in front of the door. Why? I finally realized it was because what I'd seen in the movies was a stage, created just for the story of Dracula! I didn't understand that the real castle wouldn't be that way. Castles are fortresses; the builders didn't want any-one to have easy access. The entrance to Bran wouldn't accommodate a carriage, even Dracula's. It's a set of steep steps leading up to a little stoop large enough for half a dozen people.

As we passed through a pair of huge, arched doors made of thick brown boards, I saw immediately that the castle was no match for Ber-nard Robinson's vast sets in the movies. Robinson was the set designer at Hammer Films during the company's horror heyday, from the late 1950s until his death in 1970. He created the interiors for Hammer's versions of Dracula's castle: usually an entry hall; a great room with a dining table placed next to a huge fireplace; a staircase; balconies, hallways, and bedrooms; a study; and of course the crypt.

There is nothing scary about Bran Castle. On a sunny August afternoon it was hard to imagine Dracula in any form inhabiting the castle. The whitewashed rooms tend to be small; you know it the minute you enter the first one. And there is too much light; a vampire would have hung heavy drapes over every window. I also could not picture Christopher Lee in those spaces; as Count Dracula, he would have longed for elbow room. There would have been no leaping from balconies as his character had done in *Horror of Dracula,* no echoing of black boots on tile during a frantic chase, no giant study window with curtains for the hero to rip down.

Some of the rooms are furnished, with the mixture of styles making it easy to imagine the pieces belonging to both Count Dracula and Queen Marie. Dracula would have chosen the trestle tables with heavy carved side chairs and the canopied beds of dark wood like those in the movies. In contrast, rooms still bearing a touch of Queen Marie held such treasures as Persian-style rugs, delicate daybeds, upholstered armchairs, and a piano.

We went down to the courtyard and I asked Lucian to take my picture by the well at its center, figuring it might be a place where Lee had filmed. I could feel a kinship to him there. Who knew, maybe our feet were planted for a moment in the same spot. Little did I know until later that it was the castle entrance, at the top of that long flight of steps, where our footprints had mingled—if footprints can do that thirty-three years apart.

Between the tours of rooms and gardens and even a secret staircase, we stood on a balcony decorated with half-timbers and surrounded by curving red-tiled roofs. Below us a two-lane road led out past the border that divides the provinces of Transylvania—home of Bran Castle—and Wallachia—home of the Poenari Citadel. Two castles with very different histories stand a few miles apart in Romania, and Bran is the closest you'll ever come to Dracula's Castle. Elizabeth Miller says the only real one is in the novel, of course. Of course.

Chapter 48

Catching the Train

After Bran we set out for Sinaia, which was in the mountains. We were coming into Romania's ski country: Poiana Brașov, Predeal, Azuga, and Bușteni lay like beads strung along the road from Brașov to Bucharest. Sinaia was the farthest south, the closest to Bucharest, but it didn't seem at all that we were near the city where we'd started. Each new place was a whole world to explore, and in that respect each seemed a million miles from the others.

Had Christopher Lee been to Poiana Brașov? I thought so, even though I couldn't picture him skiing. In his autobiography he'd written, "When we alighted at Pojana, above Brașov . . . ," but Lucian and I weren't planning to stop there.

After we left Bran we crossed a large, flat plain. I looked out the car windshield and saw in the distance a very large structure crowning a hill. It hung onto the mountain like a light-colored hat pushed too far forward, as though it could topple off the front at any time. "What is that?" I asked Lucian.

"I don't know. It wasn't there yesterday." He said it so straight-faced that it took me a second to realize he'd made a joke! I smiled. I hadn't seen that side of Lucian, and he certainly hadn't seen a joking side of me.

We ended up at the place on the mountain, which turned out to be

Râșnov, a thirteenth-century fortress that was still a populated town. Like many other Romanian locations, it had a violent history, having been destroyed more than once by invaders.

Inside one of the buildings, a wall display paid tribute to Vlad the Impaler. Two pictures hung there, the first being "old faithful," the portrait of Vlad that had more mileage on it than "the shot heard 'round the world." The other likeness had Vlad facing in the opposite direction. He was wearing a traditional crown, and that time he managed to look quite handsome. A dozen documents, most of them hand-scripted, were posted next to the images, and all of it put under glass.

Outside one of the village shops was a large painting on a stand. It depicted a vampire baring his fangs as he prepared to do what vampires do best. In the background, bats flew past a full moon. The other subject was a woman wearing a low-cut dress, but instead of a face there was an opening in the painting. I gave Lucian the camera, stuck my head through the hole, and changed my expression to a horrific scream as though I were the victim. The photo wasn't free, but I gladly paid. Afterward we walked to the top of a hill where we could see all the way back to Bran; and then we were off again, passing forests and villages as we rode toward Sinaia.

As usual, I had my camera within reach in the car. I'd taken a hundred pictures a day, but I still hadn't gotten two I particularly wanted: The full moon at night and a train in the daytime. I knew why I wanted a photo of the moon, but what was it about trains?

The train was invented in England in 1825. Bram Stoker put Jonathan Harker on one in *Dracula*. Taking the train to Transylvania, Harker stopped for the night in Klausenburg—now Cluj-Napoca; went on to Bistritz; and from there hired a coach to take him to Dracula's castle.

I'd loved the Romanian trains on sight because they were bright blue. They were old and close-up would no doubt appear in poor condition; but in the summer, chugging along with the Transylvanian countryside as a backdrop, they called to me. I could see the passengers' arms sticking out the open windows, the bare elbows of men and boys riding home from work. It had been a long time since I'd felt the pull and rhythm of a train.

Trains had been part of my life in West Virginia, just like the river that flowed beyond our front yard. The railroad tracks carried coal trains back and forth through Glen Ferris and on to the next towns east and west.

The railroad ran behind the garages in our area of town, and the garages were behind the houses, so the track was removed from view. Even so, the trains were noisy enough to command attention. They seemed majestic to me, and I often stopped what I was doing to watch one go by. The tracks ran right past Grandmama's yard. As kids we crossed them, walked up and down them, and even played on them. We learned to put pennies on the rail so the train would smash them flat. We walked along the rails trying to balance, our arms straight out and shifting up and down. We had contests to see who could stay on the longest.

On the other side of the tracks behind Grandmama's house, running parallel to the railroad, was a little creek full of frogs. We'd take sticks and move the frog eggs around on top of the water. Later on, those eggs would become tadpoles; but lying there on the water, each one clear with a black dot in the middle, they looked like little jelly eyes watching the trains come and go.

Sometimes in the movies a child loses a limb—or his life—by fooling around where the trains run. Accidents like that didn't happen in Glen Ferris. We were always aware of the trains; we looked for them. When we saw or heard or felt one coming, we knew to get out of the way.

I had an affinity for trains. Maybe it was the tarry smell or the soft brown wood of the railroad ties. It might have been the big spikes holding the tracks together, rusty and driven in so hard we couldn't dislodge them, as many times as we tried. Was it the trains coming through in the night, the sudden whistles, the rhythmic clacking of train on rails, growing soft as the heavy cars passed the Mooneys' house, then the bowling alley and the plant, and finally went out the lower end of town? It was all of those things.

Billie and I hopped a train once. The trains went slowly sometimes, shifting back and forth to pick up cars. Catching one was easy. We stood on the other side of the tracks beside the creek, so we wouldn't be seen from town, and when the train came through we each grabbed a handle and pulled ourselves up onto one of the little ladders on the outside of a boxcar. We didn't go far before we hopped off again—just far enough to say what we'd done and have it be the truth.

On the way to Sinaia, I had another shot at a train photo and missed it. We were between towns then. The setting sun signaled the end of another day. I was tired, and I put my camera away. I'd given up—but Lucian hadn't.

Lucian knew the countryside. He knew the way the train tracks crisscrossed the land, how they followed a curving path past fields and orchards, veering away from the road and back again. In his typical silent fashion he took up the chase, and after the train passed us, we passed it. I sat up straight in the seat.

Before long we came to the resort town of Bușteni. We were barely into town when Lucian took a sudden left turn down a gravel road, sliding to a stop beside a set of railroad tracks. I heard a whistle and looked to our left. The same train was coming! I quickly got my camera back out.

I jumped out of the car and got a perfect shot. It was dusk, and the train had its headlights on. The curve of the tracks exposed the first three cars as the train came toward us: The engine was white, the next car was red, and the third one was blue. As he had a few days before on the road to Biertan, Lucian had chased a train for me. This time, we'd caught it.

Chapter 49

The T-Shirt

I stood barefoot on the bed in my hotel room in Sinaia, looking down through the lens of my camera at the T-shirt of all T-shirts. I'd laid it on the bed face up and was now zooming in on the central design to avoid the sleeves. Had I smoothed out all the wrinkles? After all, this was a portrait I was taking.

The T-shirt was black with a bright yellow moon, flying bats, and Dracula's face from the movies—symbols of everything I wanted to find in Transylvania. The countenance of the Count was Christopher Lee's, complete with wild eyes and bloody fangs. The front of the T-shirt said, "DRACULA . . . COMING STRAIGHT FROM THE HEART OF TRANSILVANIA"—with the key words printed (and one misspelled) in blood red. Yep. I'd found Christopher Lee in Transylvania—on a T-shirt.

I'd found my prized shirt in a souvenir stand at the foot of Bran Castle. Bran has more souvenir stands than Austin has bats. The souvenirs themselves tend to repeat; Vlad T-shirts were sold all over the place. Although I'd warmed up to Vlad as my trip went on, I wasn't ready to wear him home on a shirt.

One stand had the T-shirt I was hoping for. I even found my size. I quickly scooped up my ultimate souvenir of Transylvania and determined to guard it with my life.

It wasn't the highest quality T-shirt ever made; Glen Ferris Mom probably would have shrunk it in the wash. Back when I was learning that clothes could do more than cover me up, I had a new knit shirt I loved. It was gray with orange accents, soft and supple and sophisticated with its cowl neck and drawstring bottom. Bringing home that shirt was a victory. It marked one of the rare times I hadn't been talked out of something because Mom thought I wanted everything I saw or Grandmama could make one just like it for a fraction of the price.

I've rarely paced myself with new clothes; I want to wear them right away and then again as soon as they come out of the wash. Our washer and dryer in Glen Ferris sat in a dim corner of the basement under a pair of dirt-caked windows. The light above them was a bare, low-wattage bulb with a pull string. Add in the old, black furnace and that might explain why I didn't involve myself much with the laundry. I was excited when Mom came upstairs with the clean clothes—until I saw my new shirt.

It looked slightly bigger than the upper part of a doll's outfit. I was crushed. I kept that shirt for a long time, folded in my dresser, even though I could never wear it again. One day I would not be a victim of Mom's domestic shortcomings—or worse. I sometimes wished my life away with such thoughts.

The T-shirt laid out below me in Sinaia closed a chapter. In the last thirteen days I'd seen what Romania offered the Dracula fan. Bran was the last of the real Dracula sites on my itinerary. Even so, my trip wasn't over. We still had to go to the Black Sea. It was mostly for R&R, and to say I'd seen it. The days so far had been busy and full; I was ready for a rest.

Finding the Christopher Lee shirt was a little dream, the way finding the man himself in Romania had been a big dream. In fact, all of my Dracula dreams had come together in the only place they could have—Bran. It was a convergence of Christopher Lee, Stoker's vampire, and Vlad—each "Dracula" in his own way.

Before I found the T-shirt, I'd wondered if such a shirt even existed, and—if it did—how. Lee would never approve such a use of that image—the one he'd been watching in his rear-view mirror for thirty years. But whoever made that T-shirt probably hadn't asked.

I didn't plan to wear the shirt because I didn't want anything to happen to it. I couldn't easily get another one. So now I had a shirt I'd never wear and a Dracula doll I'd never opened. What was I trying to do, start a museum? Maybe I was becoming one of those people who dedicate entire rooms of their homes to their collections—baseball bobble-heads, Christmas ornaments, Elvis memorabilia . . . or Dracula.

I snapped a picture of the T-shirt on my bed. Then I took two more. Before I got down, I thought about the famous MasterCard slogan. Let's see . . . Christopher Lee T-shirt: 250,000 lei. Finding it at the foot of Bran Castle in Transylvania: priceless.

Chapter 50

Three for the Road

I spent most of my sixtieth birthday riding in the blue car I'd begun to think of as my second home. After two weeks of touring, I was looking forward to some R&R, and I knew that Lucian felt the same way. Our destination was Mamaia, a resort on the Black Sea, but first we were making a stop in Bucharest—to pick up Lucian's wife!

He'd told me his wife worked for a women's advocacy organization and was traveling for business. Yesterday he'd found out she was heading to the sea coast, to the same resort town where we would be. It was one heck of a coincidence. I could tell he was happy, and I was more than agreeable.

I was eager to meet this woman, and curious. What did I know about her? Just that she was younger than Lucian, that she worked, and that she might have been one of his patients. I hadn't even heard him speak her name; what was it? I knew she must want to meet me, and surely she wanted to see Lucian after all the days they'd spent apart, living on phone conversations.

Gabriela was already waiting at the curb when we arrived at their apartment in the city. Lucian got out of the car to load her bags, and I hopped out, too. I had to go to the bathroom, so after the warm greetings they let me inside. It wasn't the plan, clearly, but there I was, making my way through unlit rooms toward the bright blue toilet seat that shone like a beacon amid the dim clutter of renovation. I felt like a spy, even though I couldn't tell much about the apartment with the lights out and the windows covered. I did know that it had belonged to Lucian's parents, and that he hadn't exaggerated about needing to fix it up; the place was a mess. As I did my business I wondered how he and Gabriela got cleaned up with their bathtub repurposed to hold construction debris. I thought little about the symbolism of being partially naked in their house; just finished my mission and went back outside.

Gabriela was beautiful, and quite nice to the woman who had just spent the past two weeks alone on the road with her husband. I was relieved I had nothing to hide—and wouldn't now—because the three of us became more emotionally intimate than Lucian and I ever had, if *intimate* is the word. It was inevitable, sitting in the small car—where now the back seat was put to use. Gabriela gave up her usual place next to Lucian, insisting that I stay up front so that I could see everything.

The dynamic changed the moment we were settled and on our way. Suddenly there was buoyancy to the conversation, as though the car might not contain it all. Lucian and I had kept our exchanges down to necessities; now we had chatter, unselfconscious and entertaining. Gabriela's English was very good—better than his—and even when all of us were quiet, her personality spilled into the little car, filling it up. I felt like I had an ally; not that Lucian hadn't been catering to me from the beginning, but this was different. I didn't realize until then how much I'd missed female companionship, how I'd liked the oasis of the three women in Maramureş, and how I liked this.

Gabriela was forty-six. She had gorgeous wavy red hair down to her shoulders that blew in the wind as we rode. I once worked with a woman who had hair like that, and skin that was milky and perfect—not a freckle on her face. She was much younger and more self-aware than Gabriela. She was beautiful, too, and calculating—the kind of woman men can't see through for beans, the kind who would toss flowers and jewelry aside from boredom, unlike those of us with a different kind of dating history. Once she got bitchy with me on the job. Later she offered a tearful apology that might have worked if she hadn't already bragged that she could cry on cue.

Gabriela had a lovely personality. I could tell that she was open and compassionate by the way she talked about the devastation in New Orleans from Hurricane Katrina. It was the first I'd heard the news. I hadn't watched TV since before Sighișoara. In the last few days, making my last Dracula stops in Romania, I'd forgotten about the rest of the world.

Once we'd made our way out of Bucharest, we started south on a new four-lane highway. Traffic was light, the day was warm, and the sky was blue. It was big, too, the way it is in Texas—sky reaching down to the ground in every direction, unlike the view in the mountains. Electric lines and towers were etched against the horizon. Lucian had said the land would flatten out after we left Bucharest, and it had. Yellow fields and marshlands spread out from the road, dotted with flowers and grasses. Industrial areas, refineries, cities and small villages, bridges and locks entered the mix as we got closer to the sea.

Villagers selling fruits and vegetables stood along the road with cars and semis speeding by. By then I didn't even blink, didn't stop for a second to be amazed—or horrified—at the potential for accidents. The roadside was so full of people that it was like a parade, and I was the one going by.

I thought about American kids who join gangs and take their own early deaths as a given, hardly batting an eye at the thought of getting shot. The Romanians weren't fatalistic like that; it was the opposite. They seemed to think they were immortal. Maybe they were right; maybe they were all vampires and knew darn well a mere speeding car couldn't do them any damage.

In the car—between hair-raising episodes of Romanian dodgem cars—I got sleepy. When the sun hit the window my hand loosened its death grip on the door handle and I relaxed, slipping into little dreams and becoming alert again when we approached our destination.

Mamaia was said to be the best resort area on the coast. In contemplating what it would be like, I remembered the lake resort in Sibiu and tried not to get my hopes up; but when we arrived I could say with extreme relief that I couldn't have asked for more.

Our hotel was like a place from a dream. I felt like one of those people in the cruise line commercials, the ones who say they're treated like royalty.

I had a balcony off my third-floor room overlooking a park with a fountain and trees. To one side of the hotel, tourists could wander past ice cream stands and restaurants lining a paved walking path just off the beach. My room wasn't on the beach side; I could see water, but the way Gabriela explained it, the land we drove in on is like a long tongue between the lake, which I could see from my room, and the Black Sea.

Even before unpacking, I pulled my desk chair out onto the balcony. It looked like we were going to get some rain: My favorite kind of wind was blowing, the kind that is just this side of chilly, when you keep thinking about that sweatshirt but don't quite want to get up to go get it.

Two children pedaled "dune buggies" on the blacktop below. A horse and carriage stood at one of the roads through the park, and a surrey without a fringe on top passed by below me. A breeze moved the trees across the way. Of all the choices—beach, pool, walkway—my balcony was the best place I could be. I liked that it was isolated from the balconies on either side; a guest would have to climb out on the rail to see the neighbors. Here I could watch the world go by without attracting attention, and I settled in to write. In a little while I'd have to get moved in and wash a few things, but I couldn't bear it yet.

Lucian and Gabriela had the room next door, and I made a point of giving them time together. They invited me out to take a walk just after we arrived, but I begged off, saying I'd see them at dinner.

Chapter 51

Birthdays

I went exploring just before dinnertime. Outside the lobby, between the hotel and the sand, was a giant pool with sky-blue water, surrounded by white deck furniture. It was empty at that hour. Beyond it, all I saw was the sea, stretching to the horizon where ships were passing in the distance.

The hotel dining room was elegant: as large as a ballroom, with a marble floor, high white walls, mirrored posts, and tables topped with clean white cloths. The color scheme was delicate and of the sea, with toile figures on the chairs and a starched napkin ready at every place. Lucian, Gabriela, and I took a table by the wall of windows so that we could look out until it got dark.

"Let's order a bottle of wine for my birthday," I said, and Gabriela jumped up and excused herself. A few minutes later she returned with a little paper gift bag, the kind you can buy in card stores in America. "I don't know how religious you are," she began, and offered the bag to me. It held a lovely icon of the Virgin Mary and Baby Jesus. I didn't have one; that was for sure. She and Lucian must have made a special shopping trip just for me. I knew instantly that I'd hang the picture at home, a reminder of Lucian and Gabriela and my sixtieth birthday in Romania, by the sea.

Sixty was a significant age—a milestone like thirty and twenty-one and sixteen. I had no particular memories of turning thirty and remembered my twenty-first birthday only because my new husband was younger, and I teased him about still being a minor. But my memory of turning sixteen was vivid.

It had started many months before my birthday, when I'd decided I wanted a portable typewriter for my gift. I was already interested in writing, and a typewriter would be the perfect present on the perfect day.

To me, sixteen was a magical age. When I turned sixteen, I would be starting my senior year of high school. I could get a driver's license. I would be graduating the following spring and going away to college in the fall. And I was always catching up.

I'd started school early. When the last of my friends went to first grade, I was still officially too young. We had no kindergarten in Glen Ferris, so I was home with no playmates. Mom recognized that I'd always be a year behind my friends, in elementary school when they moved on to high school; still in high school when they went away to college. She went to Glen Ferris School and enrolled me in first grade when I was five.

I loved school and did well. The downside was that from then on I'd always be the youngest person in my class—the last to drive, the last to do everything important.

I wasn't just looking forward to my sixteenth birthday; to me it was a turning point. I was convinced that my life would get immeasurably better starting that day. I looked ahead on the calendar to see if it would occur on a Saturday. *Yes!* Everything was falling into place. If I received the gift I'd asked for, I would spend my birthday starting my first book on my new typewriter.

It was an extravagant present for our family—in 1961, $49.95 plus tax, equivalent to the cost of a low-end laptop today—and I wasn't sure my parents would buy it for me. Dad complained a lot about money, the general idea being that we were all doing our best to spend more than he made. If a present had a practical application, I stood a better chance of getting it, so I prepared a defense. I took typing classes.

Typing I and II were my only high school business courses. I needed them for two reasons—one you already know. The other reason—the one I gave my parents—was college. I would need a typewriter when I was up in the wee hours writing all those term papers teachers tell you about to scare you.

It was a wonder I didn't flunk typing—if that's even possible. I sat in the last row, farthest from the teacher, next to a cute boy. Normally I was a studious student, but in typing class I was distracted by Jeff's lanky frame, silky skin, and especially his shyness. Every now and then he would smile and show his perfect, white teeth. He didn't date, which was just the ticket for me: unavailable. I was always conscious of Jeff sitting beside me, like the day I looked up and saw the teacher holding a stopwatch while the rest of the class began typing furiously. I'd missed the instructions for a timed writing test.

My friend Sharon was in the class before mine. She liked to type funny notes and leave them for me under the typewriter. For instance, she might pretend she was the typewriter, wondering why people were always pounding on her. She had a way, and when I read Sharon's hilarious notes, I had to reply. It probably helped my typing speed, because I still had to finish my lessons, too.

I learned to type well because I was motivated. Besides the classes, I staged a campaign for a typewriter. I knew exactly what model I wanted and where it was sold. I'd practically drawn my parents a map to the store in Charleston that stocked the Royal Futura 800 with its own carrying case. When I thought about owning it I could feel my fingers on the thick plastic keys and hear the sound of the letters smacking the paper. I could almost smell the ink from the new black ribbon as I pictured myself creating stories.

My birthday finally came. I woke up and remembered, as excited as I'd been on any Christmas. I got dressed and bounced down the stairs—that is, until I had my first glimpse of Mom sitting in the living room. It was like Jonathan Harker in *Horror of Dracula* coming upon the beast in its lair.

My mother was full of whiskey. She was in the brown chair, the one that had seen so many cigarette burns it looked like a game of "connect the dots," or maybe a constellation of distant stars. Joe and Dad were somewhere else that morning. The house was as silent as a grave—mine.

My hopes for a smile and a cheery greeting died violently when I looked into my mother's face. Her eyes were puffy, the skin on her cheeks saggy and pale. Her lips were out of sync, and she had the look of someone itching for a fight. All of Mom's bad energy was radiating across the room at me. It was worse than the Dracula movies.

No birthday cake awaited me on the dining room table. No cards or candles or crepe paper had been set out. On the floor next to Mom's chair was the typewriter in its case. I knew because it wasn't even wrapped.

She called me one of her favorite names: *Your Royal Highness.* The essence was that she hoped I was satisfied, meaning the opposite. The exact words are gone by now, the ones she spat at her self-centered daughter who had the nerve to want something special; words that spelled out just how expensive the typewriter had been, what a sacrifice; words that screamed how ridiculous it was that she had to go to Charleston to buy a certain item in a certain store for a certain spoiled brat. It was bad enough the first time, but I knew that Mom would go on and on, repeating herself. There was no way to make it better, so I ran.

I ran straight to Nat's house on the hill in the upper end of town, a long way to run. I ran up the porch steps, which were tall and steep like Grandmama's. I suppose I knocked, but what I remember is running inside, past the family and into the bedroom, where I climbed onto the top bunk; Nat followed me. Then I let it rip. The humiliation of my birthday; all my pain and sadness and shame; my stoicism about what went on in my family—all of it spilled over as I lay in that little room and sobbed and wailed and in the end hid nothing at all. I'd laughed in that bed, and now I cried in it. Once again the bunk beds shook. I sobbed out the whole story, not caring that Nat's family heard it or that they now knew my mother was sitting at home drunk and that my sixteenth birthday was one of the worst days of my life.

The occasion had been a turning point—just not the way I'd thought. My present had been handed over in a drunken fury. My mother's whiskey-soaked torrent had nearly crushed me: It symbolized all the resentment Mom had toward me and could no longer hold. That's when I learned that some things do cost too much.

I went home at the last possible minute that day. I can't recall who was there or what they said or did, but my typewriter was miraculously intact, still in the same spot by the brown chair.

In our house, an expensive gift often became a family gift; for example, when "I" received a stereo for Christmas, I was the only one in our family who had one. Instead of keeping it in my room, I was expected to play it in the living room where it could be shared. Well, after the day I'd had, I picked that typewriter up and took it straight upstairs to my bedroom. If I was supposed to use it at the family desk, it would have to be on another day.

I managed to start writing on my birthday in spite of everything. I had the typewriter, so why abandon all of my dreams?

I still saw sixteen as a magical age, but I could add a new reason. It was the last year I would ever live in that house. Nat's quiet understanding had given me hope. The typewriter gave me hope; the plan of going away to college gave me hope. I could see the end.

In Mamaia, Lucian and Gabriela and I finished a delicious dinner and then walked a mile along the lighted pathway that paralleled the beach. I got a dish of ice cream, and then we turned around and came back. By then it was ten thirty. Soon I'd be in bed, turning out the light.

It had become my habit to take stock of my life twice a year, on New Year's Day and my birthday. I hadn't gone through my usual birthday ritual in Romania, but my customary practice was to sit at my computer and write whatever came to mind—anything from thoughts on my weight and current hairstyle to my financial status and relationships. As I typed I always learned something.

Before I fell asleep that night, my thoughts turned back to Mom. Thank God she'd become sober. Thank God for the forty-four years now separating me from the nightmare of my sixteenth birthday.

By 1999 Mom had been in Cincinnati nine years. On my birthday that year, I wrote this: "My mother told me yesterday that I'm her best friend, and I replied, 'And you're mine.'" Had I ever actually said that to anyone else? If I had, it was a very long time ago.

Chapter 52

A Day at the Beach

I heard nothing until my little alarm clock went off at six o'clock, mark-
ing another day of vacation in Mamaia. I got up and made my coffee. On
the TV, New Orleans: 27,000 refugees were being housed in the Houston
Astrodome, possibly for weeks. The world was getting battered—I suppose it always is somewhere. This time the devastation was at home.

I'd kept my real life at bay for more than two weeks, but now I was
beginning to process different information, preparing to be back in
America where I'd collect my accumulated mail, wash my clothes in a
machine instead of a hotel sink, organize my writing files, and look at the
pictures I'd taken in Romania. And soon I'd be tapping my "*Da*-ta-da-da-
da"—our signal—on Mom's front door. She'd get up from the end of the
couch, already grinning, and I'd hear her light footsteps just before she
peeped out and saw me. Mom always laughed with delight as she opened
her door to me. Who would have predicted that? Now the thought of it
warmed me when I felt the first pull of home.

I moved the desk chair out onto the balcony again. The scene below
me was different that morning; no one was walking or riding. Only the
sea gulls called and moved about in a cloudless sky. In that moment I
understood the removed life of the rich. This might be a typical day for
them, at one of their homes or resorts, waking up and having nothing

but a beautiful day ahead. Of course they had everyday worries like the rest of us, but what were those worries? Surely the worries of the rich were different from mine, different from the tasks and obligations I was slowly beginning to acknowledge again. I wasn't willing to think very much about my return to work, still days away. I preferred to think of the place where I was, and the people in the room next door.

As my days shifted away from Dracula, I let myself relax in the sun and try to build up a tan, pathetically late in the season. It was heavenly, lying by the pool on a yellow-and-white-striped cushion with the wind and the sun on me. I let my mind drift to nowhere or read my book. Sometimes Gabriela and I would go down to the place where the water met the sandy beach and set ourselves up in chairs that never had to be moved because the tide didn't go in and out.

Every day I was glad I'd focused my energies on Dracula and Christopher Lee instead of Lucian. In the mornings, he left us alone to sunbathe. It was exquisite—so relaxing—but how would it have played out if I'd had anything to hide? I was beyond relieved that I didn't have to find out. I hadn't been perfect in my life, my relationships, but that kind of deliberate duplicity wasn't my thing.

Now I could enjoy my time with Gabriela. She and I were ladies of leisure, beach buddies, while Lucian went about whatever business kept him in civilian clothing while we whiled away our mornings in bathing suits.

I wondered what Lucian would look like in swimming trunks—and I guessed they wouldn't be trunks. I figured Lucian, being a well-built, sexy European guy, was more the Speedo type. Sleek. Gabriela wouldn't have minded a bit, but I would have squirmed if in fact he'd come strolling across the sand in a little fitted male bikini. But Lucian never joined us except to tell us where he was going and what time he'd meet us back at the hotel.

In the afternoons, we all piled into the car and toured. The first day it was the ruins of the ancient seaside city of Histria. The wind was up as we tripped through tall grass, past acres of low stone walls and handmade brick columns and arches. The sea was choppy and gray, turning dark blue out toward the horizon, and clouds whooshed above. I was glad I'd worn long sleeves.

We wound our way farther along the coast, stopping in the port city of Constanța. Gabriela took me through a museum while Lucian sat on the steps outside and smoked. Next, he drove us to a bar in a rundown section. I was surprised to see it about half full of well-dressed young people, most of them smoking. We'd seen see a billboard for "Winston" with no sign of cigarettes on it, no people lighting up. Those images were not allowed, Lucian said. So the poster showed a romantic couple cuddling on the beach. It was a close-up of their smiling faces, especially hers.

As we were driving back at twilight, Lucian saw a bat fly past the windshield of the car. We were on a deserted road between Constanța and Mamaia, and I was looking somewhere else. He called out, and I turned to see a small black blur that I would have missed had it not been for him. At least now I can say that I saw a bat in Romania, though I couldn't identify it in a lineup.

The next morning Lucian and I ran into each other in the dining room, but we ate separately. There was no sign of Gabriela. Just before he walked out the door, I saw him take a whole plate of cake from the breakfast buffet. *Ah.* In a moment my thoughts had invaded their bedroom. I pictured Gabriela stretching like a cat, moving slowly over the warm sheets, her smile relaxed. Too much trouble to get ready and go downstairs, so she begs off and sends Lucian. Such was their intimacy, or at least how I imagined it.

Lucian drove us south in the afternoon. We were headed toward Varna, the Bulgarian port city in *Dracula* from which the ship *Demeter* sailed for London with its deadly cargo of coffin, dirt, and the Count. One by one, the crew died mysterious deaths, usually at night. When the *Demeter* reached its English port in Whitby Harbor, "an immense dog leapt up on deck from below . . . and running forward, jumped from the bow on the sand." The dog ran up the hill toward the abbey where Lucy had encountered the Count. Was it *him?*

We couldn't cross the border into Bulgaria, but we went as far as we could, to a beach community named Vama. It is the point farthest south on the Romanian sea cost. Vama is an artists' colony where hippies live in tents and sell jewelry. It also has a nude beach, and from a distance we saw adults and children walking along the water naked. Eddie Powell, the stunt double, might have liked it; Christopher Lee probably wouldn't.

Although there was nothing fancy about Vama, we had fun. Things were winding down for Labor Day. It was the last beach day for some of the people there; for example, the owner of the little open-air restaurant where we ate. A radio was on; Roy Orbison was playing in the background, then someone who sounded like Neil Diamond, though I couldn't be sure over the din in the restaurant. I had on my new Columbia shirt. We ate "Romanian hamburgers," which are buns with sliced chicken, French fries, onions, tomatoes, pickles, and mayonnaise—very messy, at least for me.

We drove through the seaside resort towns of Neptun, Jupiter, and Venus and stopped in Olimp, where Lucian saw a friend of his. The four of us had ice cream sundaes at an outside table with a birds-eye view of the pool and sandy beach. Wind ruffled our hair. The sun shone down on colorful tents and umbrellas that defined pockets of people on the sand. When we left, Lucian spotted a Batman toy in a store display. "Look," he said, smiling, "another bat."

Chapter 53

La Revedere

In the final scene of *Horror of Dracula,* Van Helsing has chased the Count through the night, ending at Dracula's Transylvanian castle. Their battle moves inside, to a study. As they scuffle, Van Helsing spies a slit of daylight coming through the heavy curtains. He springs up, runs across a tabletop, and leaps up onto the curtains, pulling them down. Immediately the sun's direct rays begin to turn Count Dracula into dust. Van Helsing then jumps back onto the table, grabs two huge candlesticks, and holds them together in the shape of a cross, making sure the vampire cannot get away. In moments, all that are left on the floor of the room are a few motes of dust and Dracula's ring.

On our last morning in Mamaia I brought my desk chair out to the balcony for the last time and wrote my farewell to Romania. I had loved it, loved it all for its surprises and lack of perfection and its similarity to the home I'd known as a child. I'd loved the footprints of Dracula—the castles, the monasteries, the Argeş River, and the pine-covered mountains of Transylvania. I'd loved the villages and peaceful countryside as well as the tourist sites and souvenirs. I'd loved seeing the places where I could imagine Christopher Lee, or Elizabeth Miller, or McNally and Florescu in earlier times. I'd even developed a little warm spot for Vlad.

As for my movie-induced dreams of Dracula, I knew now that the movie images of my youth were a world apart from the reality of Romania. Film studios are magic places; that's their business. Actors play parts and then move on.

The real locations on the Dracula trail had delivered one surprise after another, the biggest being the memories they stirred as scenic reminders of home—the home I'd left when I was sixteen. As Lucian and I had driven through the historic provinces—Wallachia, Transylvania, Maramureș, Bucovina, and Dobrogea by the sea—those memories had taken me on an unexpected inner journey. But why wouldn't Romania—Dracula's land—remind me of home? I'd lived with monsters, dreamed of rescue, and looked for heroes.

I'd survived a monster—and it wasn't the Count. My mother's drinking had put a stake in my heart. There's a movie called *Scars of Dracula*. We all have our scars, and the same childhood that had given me the wonderful woods and river and railroad tracks of Glen Ferris had also been the Petri dish for my worst nightmares.

I'd kept secrets—lots of them—so I knew that protecting other people's secrets, especially, is a terrible burden. Sometimes that terror bursts back out of us in strange ways. Psychologists say that whatever we repress comes back in another form. It's the basis of many horror stories.

I'd seen my scary side. It was yet another monster, one that slept fitfully inside me. My monster had taught me that no one is perfect; no one has absolute control. All of us have that darkness inside us as well as light.

Mom had nightmares after she was older. Some mornings she'd wake up with the vestiges of horrific dreams, all similar: "You and Joe were small," she'd tell me, "helpless, somewhere in the house. I woke up late, and I couldn't find you. I didn't know what to fix for breakfast; there was nothing in the house." As each dream faded, it left a wave of sadness behind that Mom would have to overcome upon waking for real. Who says there are no ghosts to haunt us?

The past hung over me sometimes; I wondered if Mom and I needed to take another step to clear the air. We had unfinished business—so many buried feelings and family secrets. I felt the weight of them, especially as Mom aged. Would breaking the long silence be the right thing to do? I knew it would have to be me; she wasn't going to do it. But so far I couldn't think of one good reason to dredge up the past with my mother. Who would benefit? My answer was always the same: No one.

What started with Dracula had taken me down many roads. With Romania as the catalyst, the wayward nature of memory had bumped me back through my life—the good and bad of a small-town childhood marked with monsters. I'd found my "slit of daylight" in the curtains, too, years later when my mother finally came back to herself and to me.

When a vampire is destroyed—at least in the movies—it can return to its former self. This is true death, when the beast can finally be at rest. Once the stake is driven into its heart, once its screams die down, its evil countenance vanishes. In its place is a face full of sweetness and innocence and peace.

In her later years, Mom's beverage had again become predictable. *Water*—plain, no ice—was her drink of choice. Even at celebrations she stuck to her plan: not even an iced tea. Once when I had her over for dinner, I slipped a lemon slice into her water glass to dress it up. Upon discovering the lemon, she said three little words: "Don't surprise me."

The morning was already warm when I ventured out onto the terrace of our hotel. The wind was down, and if it hadn't been for two bumblebees circling my plate, I'd be writing about how I ate my final seaside breakfast outside.

I ran into Lucian in the dining room, and in a while we took our coffee back out and sat together in the sun. We'd soon be driving back to Bucharest, where I had a room for the night. I wouldn't get much sleep; Lucian was picking me up at four in the morning to go to the airport.

"Has the trip been what you expected?" I asked him across the table.

"I do not take every job from the travel agency," he said. "I look at the papers to see if I want to guide. I saw your papers and thought your trip would be interesting."

"And was it?"

He nodded. I smiled.

By the time I'd finished packing, the sun was hitting the fountain in the park under another cloudless sky. A light breeze was blowing, and I could clearly see the town across the lake. Nothing about it reminded me of a vampire.

Lucian and I said our good-byes at the airport the next morning. He pulled the car to the curb and got out to help me with my bags, setting them down at my feet. I slipped him his tip, an envelope full of Romanian lei, and our business was done. Then, and only then, did Lucian put his hands on my shoulders and pull me to him in a warm hug. I felt his soft, gray beard against my face for the first time. He planted a kiss on my cheek before he got back in the car and drove away.

Chapter 54

Healing

I'd been healed twice in Romania, more if I counted my recuperative time at the farm and the easing of my "heart attack" symptoms on the Borgo Pass. I could thank Lucian for most of it.

That giant, healing wave I'd imagined as the adult child of an alcoholic eventually rolled over me, too. Like the ones in the ocean game I'd played with my brother, it came when I wasn't looking.

I'd envisioned one big, isolated moment, but my wave occurred over time, starting in Romania and ending on this side of the Atlantic in Cincinnati, Ohio, many months later when I was writing this book. It built slowly, and I didn't see it until it crested. We don't always, unless something makes us look. That wave was like Romania picking me up and setting me down again in a slightly different spot.

When you travel to a foreign place, all the advice says to open your mind and let in whatever the trip brings. I'd done that and experienced both the expected and the unexpected.

I read this in a novel: *Time and place have a mind of their own.* With my mind laid open, long-buried memories became unexpected companions on my trip. As Lucian and I traveled the roads of Romania, I found myself picking through the dark country of my childhood, my later life as a wife and mother, and the years when I'd transitioned into living alone, with Mom as my loyal but unlikely friend.

Romania stayed with me after I came home, too, the way vacations do when you let *them* take *you*. Or perhaps it was the just feeling I'd had there. Even though my mind was busy, I'd relaxed and laid down my everyday burdens for a while.

Memories that had begun as random, swirling bits with no apparent pattern came to rest after I started writing this book. I'd intended it to be just a travel essay, but the other story—the one about Mom and me—emerged after I'd connected my early life to *Dracula*, West Virginia to Transylvania, and the strange mix of love and fear that bound me to both.

Dr. Charles Whitfield says that telling our story frees us to heal. When we expose our dark secrets to the light, we begin to see connections that allow us to reframe our life events, behaviors, and emotions into a more insightful and healthier whole.

He also says that happiness and peace are not states we must earn or attain, but our natural right. All my life I'd looked for happiness and what the twelve-step programs call serenity. I didn't know I was supposed to have them all along; that we *all* are.

The "Aha" experience is a term for discovery, something that happens to give us new insight. To the child of an alcoholic, such an experience results from getting in touch with ourselves. That becomes possible when we find a safe place and discover meaning in our life story. It has to do with the Child Within, the one I could never find.

Suddenly I understood.

Peace and happiness had not come easily in my life, but it wasn't because I didn't deserve them, as I'd thought. It wasn't because my laugh was too loud one summer night, or because I wasn't pretty, or said the wrong things, or wanted too much in a store. It was because the happiness I should have had was taken away. My mother did that to my brother and me when she succumbed to alcoholism and failed to love and nurture us as parents are supposed to do. The outrage of that loss had lurked inside me for many years as the monster I'd struggled to suppress.

Once I knew the source of my monstrous rage, I wanted rid of it. If happiness was my right, I needed to claim it. It was time to heal that little girl from the past, the one who was so needy and sad. We can nurture ourselves, which is another miracle of recovery. It's a shame that we have to, but a blessing that we can.

I guess that's why I finally forgave my mother. It wasn't because I ever forgot what she'd done, or thought it didn't matter. It was a conscious choice I made because I finally learned what forgiveness is: It's a gift we give ourselves, one that lets us move beyond our grudges and nurture the Child Within. Forgiveness frees us to find the happiness we deserve.

It's said that travel transforms us. Travel also helps us to see ourselves—where and what we came from, where we're going, and who we are. I'd found a metaphor for my life in the Dracula legend. Many of my worst moments and deepest secrets had been brought to light along the roads of Romania.

I believe we *need* to hide things sometimes, even parts of ourselves, to feel safe. Families are complicated. Some are terrible. Sometimes we need an escape until we find that safe place. Maybe you'll find yours, as I did, somewhere between the movies and your wildest dreams.

Epilogue

My brother came back to us in 2006. That story is his to tell, and we're developing it together under the working title *Mr. Joe.*

Why do people write memoirs? I guess we have a need to tell our children what was important to us. As we age, we begin to hate change and cling to the past. I feel that now, as Joe and I sit in the twin cloth chairs on his little porch, looking out over a sand volleyball court—usually empty—and say whatever comes to mind. Sometimes nothing comes to mind, and the quiet is comfortable. At other times we delve into our family life and try to unravel the mysteries that so few of us are left to solve.

Our mother passed away in 2008. She had developed Alzheimer's and had moved to the Alois Alzheimer Center, a wonderful residential facility in Cincinnati. Though she occasionally displayed the bluntness that is a characteristic of the disease, Mom was most often sweet and agreeable. She was always glad to see us. Sometimes she would say with pride to the other residents, "This is my son. This is my daughter." Once in a while, though, she would look at me and ask, in that pleasant tone we reserve for strangers, "Are you staying here, too?"

Some of Mom's things now decorate my home: the needlepoint pillows and footstool she made; the plates that hung in our dining room back in Glen Ferris and later in Mom's Cincinnati apartment; the glass rose she gave me, yellow for friendship. No bad memories reside in these objects; instead, they comfort me and give me a sense of home. I feel safe, and there's something else.

"I think I'm getting a heart," I said to Joe on a recent fall afternoon.

I wasn't talking about being cleared for a transplant, but my own heart coming to life.

"I think so, too," he said. We were sitting on his porch. The bushes on the far side of the volleyball court were blazing red.

Once in a movie, Dracula was frozen in an icy stream in the mountains of Transylvania. A priest inadvertently freed the Count when he fell going down the mountain and cut his head on a rock. The priest's blood trickled onto the surface of the stream, ran through a crack in the melting ice, and reached the vampire's lips, bringing the preserved body of Count Dracula to life.

"You know me," I said. "I don't reach out to anyone." It was true, but lately I'd felt a thawing, too, and my feelings had been buried a long time.

My new emotions surprised me. Suddenly I was craving sitcoms— which I'd always found stupid and predictable—and laughing out loud. I'd even made friends with a dog! I was learning to take compliments better, too. Instead of rejecting them automatically, I tried to stop myself long enough to consider each one. And then I said, "Thank you."

I'd felt new levels of sadness, and not just for myself as I once had. It was a tectonic shift. "The other day I was walking," I told Joe, "and I came up behind an older woman. She was making her way slowly, slowly, with her daughter beside her. I had to stop short or bump right into her. Her hair was gray with a bit of leftover brown, about collar length and flat in back, the way Mom's got before she went to the beauty shop. She was about Mom's height, too, all skin and bones, dressed in a white sweater and brown slacks. Her waist even tipped the way Mom's did with her arthritis, one hip higher than the other. My heart broke. Of course, I realized she wasn't Mom—couldn't be—but for a second it *was* Mom again."

Sometimes I forget Mom is gone. Joe says he does, too. I'll half turn to say something to her or reach for the phone before I realize she's not there, won't ever be there again.

Joe has been "talking" to our mother for a while. He believes she can see us, and when he faces a challenge or has trouble making a decision, he'll ask Mom to give him a sign. Lately he's been finding shiny new pennies in unlikely places in his apartment. Pennies from Heaven, they're called.

Joe talks a lot about the Universe, too. I think the Universe is a lot like the Higher Power I heard about years ago in ACoA: "God as we understand God." I understood it all right, but I didn't get it—if you see the difference.

Joe says we can ask the Universe for help with anything if we thank it in advance. I guess there's a rule or two. In the past I would have pooh-poohed the whole idea, but lately I find I like it. When I have to solve problems, I find myself looking up toward the sky and saying the magic words: "Thanks and praises."

Book Club Discussion Questions

- Jane's motivation for her trip was to find out whether a place she'd seen in the movies was real. In *Imagined London,* Anna Quindlen journeys to England in search of settings from her favorite childhood stories. Have you ever wanted to see a TV, book, or movie setting? If so, what drew you to it? How else have you been influenced by books or movies? Have you ever had a life-changing experience as a result? What was it?

- Life doesn't always hand us what we expect or deserve. How did Jane's early years bear that out? How did her childhood experiences color her expectations for the trip? How did they affect her ideas of marriage and family? How have your ideas of marriage and family changed through the years? Do you still believe in the "white picket fence"? Why or why not?

- Jane uses Dracula as a metaphor for her mother's alcoholism. What are some of the ways that was accomplished in the book? What metaphor could be assigned to your life story? Explain.

- The relationship with one's mother is said to be the most complicated of all. How does your experience support or refute that theory? What makes a good mother? Is the definition in the eyes of the beholder, or is it universal? Thinking about your own mother, what are you grateful for and what would you have changed?

- The book's epigraph is, "We escape one thing with another." Why do you think Jane chose it? How does the statement fit her life as described in the book? When have you used a means of escape—be it food or drink, shopping, sports, entertainment, or something else—and what were you running from? Did a temporary escape solve your problem? What did?

- Jane's relationship with her guide is a theme in the book. How did her past influence her behavior with Lucian? Would you take a trip to a foreign country alone? Would you hire a guide of the opposite sex? If so, what kind of relationship would you expect to develop between the two of you?

- Jane's interest in Dracula brought her joy as a girl and has remained strong throughout her life. Can you identify with an adult still excited about a childhood passion? How can such a fascination be beneficial to a child? To a grownup? Name a hobby or passion that has helped you to retain your curiosity and keep the "child" alive in you. Has your hobby evolved over time? How did you first discover it, and why has it held your interest?

- In chapter 37, "The Photo Album," Jane learned about a part of her mother's life she'd missed. How did the album change Jane's view of the past? Genealogy is a passion for many people. How can we benefit from knowing what our parents were like as children and what our grandparents were like as parents? Have you ever been surprised or shocked by something in your family's history? How did you find out? How did your discovery affect you? How did it impact others?

- Childhood innocence is precious, but sometimes it is ripped from us. What traits lost in childhood do you think Jane recovered by the end of the book? Can you pinpoint a time when you thought your innocence, faith, or joy was lost? How did you feel, and what did you do about it?

- Jane panicked when her mother decided to move to Cincinnati. Do you think their relationship would have had a chance to improve if Mom had stayed in West Virginia? Do you think Jane would have been able to find peace with the past? Have you ever faced a challenge when you or someone else relocated? Who was it, and what happened?

- Something magical and surprising happened to Jane in Romania when she began having memories of her childhood home. Those memories helped her to connect with the girl she had been, see her mother in a new light, and put her childhood into focus. Did a travel experience ever provide you with time for reflection? Did you ever have an "Aha" moment far from home? Where were you? What was the significance of your revelation, and how did it change your life after the trip?

- Near the end of the book, Jane writes, "I'd lived with monsters, dreamed of rescue, and looked for heroes." Do you think Jane was ever a hero in this story? Was her mother? How? Give examples of monsters, rescue, or heroes from your own life. What did they do to earn a place in your life story?

- In seeking closure with her mother, Jane decided to accept the gift of their present relationship instead of forcing a confrontation about the past. Do you agree with Jane's decision? Were you surprised by it? What would you have done? In your opinion, must we confront the past, or can we let it be and move on? Give an example from your own life.

- We discover at the end of the book that Jane's mother has passed away and her brother feels their mom's presence. Do you believe, as Joe does, that those who have passed on can communicate with us? Do you believe in "Pennies from Heaven"? Have you ever sought or received a sign from someone deceased whose presence you still feel? How did your experience impact your belief system?

About the Author

Jane Congdon's thirty-year publishing career encompassed textbook and software production, content development, and acquisitions. Before retiring from Cengage Learning, she traveled the country attending professional conferences and speaking to groups of educators. A graduate of Concord University in Athens, West Virginia, she is a member of West Virginia Writers and a veteran of writing workshops including the Split Rock Arts Program at the University of Minnesota and the October Writing Festival at Ghost Ranch in New Mexico. A Dracula fan forever, she is also a member of the Transylvanian Society of Dracula.

Jane lives in Cincinnati, Ohio, with a few choice (artificial) bats and vampires. To contact: www.janecongdon.com.

Other Books by
Bettie Youngs Book Publishers

The Maybelline Story
And the Spirited Family Dynasty Behind It

Sharrie Williams

A woman's most powerful possession is a man's imagination.
—Maybelline ad, 1934

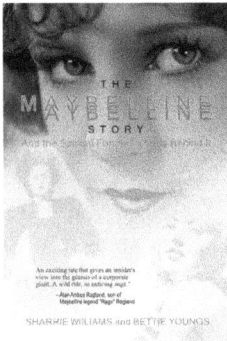

In 1915, when a kitchen-stove fire singed his sister Mabel's lashes and brows, Tom Lyle Williams watched in fascination as she performed what she called "a secret of the harem"—mixing petroleum jelly with coal dust and ash from a burnt cork and applying it to her lashes and brows. Mabel's simple beauty trick ignited Tom Lyle's imagination, and he started what would become a billion-dollar business, one that remains a viable American icon after nearly a century. He named it Maybelline in her honor.

Throughout the twentieth century, the Maybelline company inflated, collapsed, endured, and thrived in tandem with the nation's upheavals. Williams—to avoid unwanted scrutiny of his private life—cloistered himself behind the gates of his Rudolph Valentino Villa and ran his empire from a distance. Now, after nearly a century of silence, this true story celebrates the life of an American entrepreneur, a man whose vision rocketed him to success along with the woman held in his orbit: Evelyn Boecher—who became his lifelong fascination and muse. Captivated by her "roaring charisma," he affectionately called her the "real Miss Maybelline" and based many of his advertising campaigns on the woman she represented: commandingly beautiful, hard-boiled, and daring. Evelyn masterminded a life of vanity, but would fall prey to fortune hunters and a mysterious murder that even today remains unsolved.

A fascinating and inspiring story, a tale both epic and intimate, alive with the clash, the hustle, the music, and dance of American enterprise.

A richly told juicy story of a forty-year, white-hot love triangle that fans the flames of a major worldwide conglomerate.
—Neil Shulman, associate producer, *Doc Hollywood*

ISBN: 978-0-9843081-1-8 • $18.95

In bookstores everywhere, online, or from the publisher:
www.BettieYoungsBooks.com

Out of the Transylvania Night

Aura Imbarus

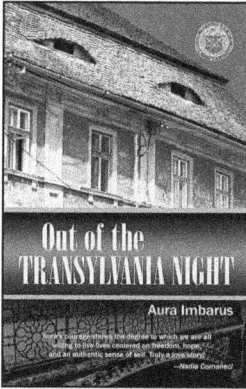

An epic tale of identity, love, and the indomitable human spirit.

Communist dictator Nicolae Ceausescu had turned Romania into a land of zombies as surely as if Count Dracula had sucked its lifeblood. Yet Aura Imbarus dares to be herself: a rebel among the gray-clad, fearful masses. Christmas shopping in 1989, Aura draws sniper fire as Romania descends into the violence of a revolution that topples one of the most draconian regimes in the Soviet bloc. With a bit of Hungarian mysticism in her blood, astonishingly accurate visions lead Aura into danger—as well as to the love of her life. They marry and flee a homeland still in chaos. With only two pieces of luggage and a powerful dream, they settle in Los Angeles where freedom and sudden wealth challenge their love as powerfully as Communist tyranny.

Aura loses her psychic vision, heirloom jewels are stolen, a fortune is lost, followed by divorce. But their early years as lovers in a war-torn country and their rich family heritage is the glue that reunites them. They pay a high price for their materialistic dreams, but gain insight and a love that is far richer. *Out of the Transylvania Night* is a deftly woven narrative about finding greater meaning and fulfillment in both free and closed societies.

Aura's courage shows the degree to which we are all willing to live lives centered on freedom, hope, and an authentic sense of self. Truly a love story!

—Nadia Comaneci, Olympic gold medalist

If you grew up hearing names like Tito, Mao, and Ceausescu but really didn't understand their significance, read this book!

—Mark Skidmore, Paramount Pictures

This book is sure to find its place in memorial literature of the world.
—Beatrice Ungar, editor-in-chief, Hermannstädter Zeitung

ISBN: 978-0-9843081-2-5 • $14.95

In bookstores everywhere, online, or from the publisher:
www.BettieYoungsBooks.com

On Toby's Terms

Charmaine Hammond

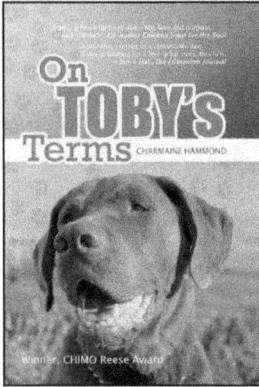

When Charmaine and her husband adopted Toby, a five-year-old Chesapeake Bay retriever, they figured he might need some adjusting time, but they certainly didn't count on what he'd do in the meantime. Soon after he entered their lives and home, Toby proved to be a holy terror who routinely opened and emptied the hall closet, turned on water taps, pulled and ate things from the bookshelves, sat for hours on end in the sink, and spent his days rampaging through the house. Oddest of all was his penchant for locking himself in the bathroom, and then pushing the lid of the toilet off the tank, smashing it to pieces. After a particularly disastrous encounter with the knife-block in the kitchen—and when the couple discovered Toby's bloody paw prints on the phone—they decided Toby needed professional help.

Little did they know what they would discover about this dog.

On Toby's Terms is an endearing story of a beguiling creature who teaches his owners that, despite their trying to teach him how to be the dog they want, he is the one to lay out the terms of being the dog he needs to be. This insight would change their lives forever.

Simply a beautiful book about life, love, and purpose.
  —**Jack Canfield, Coauthor** *Chicken Soup for the Soul* **series**

In a perfect world, every dog would have a home and every home would have a dog—like Toby!
  —**Nina Siemaszko, actress,** *The West Wing*

This is a captivating, heartwarming story and we are very excited about bringing it to film.
  —**Steve Hudis, Producer, IMPACT Motion Pictures**

ISBN: 978-0-9843081-4-9 • $14.95

In bookstores everywhere, online, or from the publisher:
www.BettieYoungsBooks.com

Diary of a Beverly Hills Matchmaker

Marla Martenson

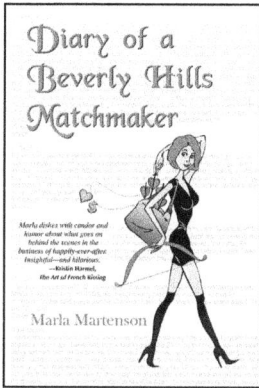

The inside scoop from the Cupid of Beverly Hills, who has brought together countless couples who have gone on to live happily ever after. But for every success story there are ridiculously funny dating disasters with high-maintenance, out-of-touch, impossible to please, dim-witted clients!

Marla takes her readers for a hilarious romp through her days as an L.A. matchmaker and her daily struggles to keep her self-esteem from imploding in a town where looks are everything and money talks. From juggling the demands her out-of-touch clients, to trying her best to meet the capricious demands of an insensitive boss, to the ups and downs of her own marriage to a Latin husband who doesn't think that she is "domestic" enough, Marla writes with charm and self-effacement about the universal struggles all women face in their lives.

Readers will laugh, cringe, and cry as they journey with her through outrageous stories about the indignities of dating in Los Angeles, dealing with overblown egos, vicariously hobnobbing with celebrities, and navigating the wannabe-land of Beverly Hills. In a city where perfection is almost a prerequisite, even Marla can't help but run for the BOTOX every once in a while.

Marla's quick wit will have you rolling on the floor.
—Megan Castran, international YouTube Queen

Sharper than a Louboutin stiletto, Martenson's book delivers!
—Nadine Haobsh, *Beauty Confidential*

Martenson's irresistible wit is not to be missed.
—Kyra David, author, *Lust, Loathing, and a Little Lip Gloss*

ISBN: 978-0-9843081-0-1 • $14.95

In bookstores everywhere, online, or from the publisher:
www.BettieYoungsBooks.com

Living with Multiple Personalities

Christine Ducommun

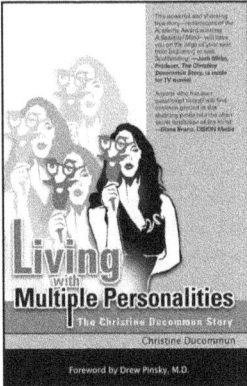

Christine Ducommun eloquently shares her story of her descent into madness, struggling to regain her sanity as four personalities vie for control of her mind and protect her from the demons of her childhood. A story of identity, courage, healing, and hope.

Christine Ducommun was a happily married wife and mother of two, when—after returning to live in the house of her childhood—she began to experience night terrors, a series of bizarre flashbacks, and "noises in her head." Eventually diagnosed with dissociative identity disorder (DID), Christine's story details an extraordinary twelve year ordeal of coming to grips with the reemergence of competing personalities her mind had created to help her cling to life during her early years.

Therapy helps to reveal the personalities, but Christine has much work to do to grasp their individual strengths and weaknesses and understand how each helped her cope and survive her childhood as well as the latent influences they've had in her adult life. Fully reawakened and present, the personalities struggle for control of Christine's mind and her life tailspins into unimaginable chaos, leaving her to believe she may very well be losing the battle for her sanity. Christine's only hope to regain her sanity was to integrate each one's emotional maturity while jettisoning the rest, until at last their chatter in her head could cease.

Anyone who has ever questioned themselves—whether for a day, a week, or longer—will find themselves in this stunning probe into the often secret landscape of the mind.

A powerful and shocking true story. Spellbinding!
—**Josh Miller, Producer,**
The Christine Ducommun Story,
(a made for TV movie)

ISBN: 978-0-9843-0815-6 • $14.95

In bookstores everywhere, online, or from the publisher:
www.BettieYoungsBooks.com

Blackbird Singing in the Dead of Night
What to Do When God Won't Answer

Gregory L. Hunt

"Blackbird singing in the dead of night,
take these broken wings and learn to fly..." —The Beatles

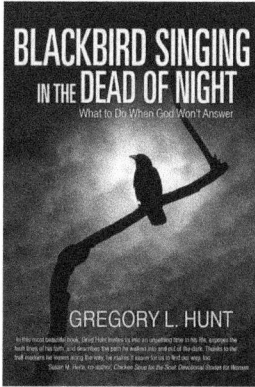

Pastor Greg Hunt had devoted nearly thirty years to congregational ministry, helping people experience God and find their way in life. Then came his own crisis of faith and calling. While turning to God for guidance, he finds nothing. Neither his education—a Ph.D. in theology—nor his religious involvements—senior pastor of a multi-staff congregation, and a civic and denominational leader—could prepare him for the disorienting impact of the experience.

Days turned into months. Months became seasons. Seasons added up to a year, then two. He began to wonder if his faith had been an illusion. Was God even real? In the midst of his struggle, he tries a desperate experiment in devotion: Could he have a personal encounter with God through the red letters of Jesus, as recorded in the Gospel of Matthew?

The result is startling—and changes his life entirely.

Sometimes raw, always honest, and ultimately hopeful, *Blackbird Singing in the Dead of Night* speaks to the spiritual longings of the human heart. —**Julie Pennington-Russell, senior pastor, First Baptist Church, Decatur, GA**

In this most beautiful memoir, Greg Hunt invites us into an unsettling time in his life, exposes the fault lines of his faith, and describes the path he walked into and out of the dark. Thanks to the trail markers he leaves along the way, he makes it easier for us to find our way, too.

—Susan M. Heim, co-author,
Chicken Soup for the Soul, Devotional Stories for Women

ISBN: 978-1-936332-07-6 • $14.95

In bookstores everywhere or from the publisher:
www.BettieYoungsBooks.com

Amazing Adventures of a Nobody

Leon Logothetis

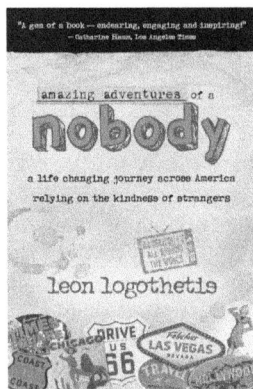

In a time of economic anxiety, global terror and shaken confidence, Englishman Leon Logothetis, star of the hit series *Amazing Adventures of a Nobody* (National Geographic Channels International, Fox Reality), shows us what is good about mankind: the simple calling people have to connect to others.

Tired of his disconnected life and uninspiring job, Leon Logothetis leaves it all behind—job, money, home, even his cell phone—and hits the road with nothing but the clothes on his back and five dollars in his pocket. His journey from Times Square to the Hollywood sign relying on the kindness of strangers and the serendipity of the open road, inspire a dramatic and life-changing transformation.

Along the way, Leon offers up the intriguing and charming tales gathered along his one-of-a-kind journey: riding in trains, buses, big rigs and classic cars; sleeping on streets and couches and firehouses; meeting pimps and preachers, astronauts and single moms, celebrities and homeless families, veterans and communists.

Each day of his journey, we catch sight of the invisible spiritual underpinning of society in these stories of companionship—and sheer adventure—that prove that the kind, good soul of mankind has not been lost.

A gem of a book: endearing, engaging and inspiring!
—**Catharine Hamm**, *Los Angeles Times,* **travel editor**

Masterful storytelling! Leon begins his journey as a merry prankster and ends a grinning philosopher. Really funny—and insightful, too.
—**Karen Salmansohn, AOL Career Coach, and Oprah.com Relationship Columnist**

ISBN: 978-0-9843081-3-2 • $14.95

In bookstores everywhere, online, or from the publisher:
www.BettieYoungsBooks.com

Bettie Youngs Books

We specialize in MEMOIRS
. . . books that celebrate
fascinating people and
remarkable journeys

VISIT OUR WEBSITE AT
www.BettieYoungsBooks.com

www.ingramcontent.com/pod-product-compliance
Lightning Source LLC
Chambersburg PA
CBHW031233090426
42742CB00007B/177